Designing Places
for People and
the Environment

ORO Editions
Publishers of Architecture, Art, and Design
Gordon Goff: Publisher

www.oroeditions.com
info@oroeditions.com

Published by ORO Editions

Graphic Design: Pablo Mandel / CircularStudio.com
This book has been set in Lyon Text (main copy), Bau (headlines), and Dala Moa (main book title)

Copy editor: Ryan Buresh
Production Assistance: Alexandria Nazar

10 9 8 7 6 5 4 3 2 1

First Edition

Library of Congress data available upon request. World Rights: Available

ISBN: 978-1-941806-43-2

Color Separations and Printing: ORO Group Ltd.
Printed in China.

International Distribution: www.oroeditions.com/distribution

# Designing Places for People and the Environment

## KALVIN PLATT

Lessons from 55 years as an Urban Planner
and Shaping the Global Landscape Architectural
Practice of the SWA Group

# TABLE OF CONTENTS

6 Preface: Was the Tree There Before the City?

8 Introduction

13 Acknowledgments

14 CHAPTER 1
Learning About Cities, Architecture, Construction and Planning
1931–1959

32 CHAPTER 2
Finding the Right Partners and Places in Life and Work
-Choosing Landscape Architecture
1959–1967

60 CHAPTER 3
Planning, Designing and Building Cities, Communities and Places
1967–1974

92 CHAPTER 4
Sasaki, Walker Associates Becomes The SWA Group,
and I Become a Leader
1974

128 CHAPTER 5
Growing Nationally the Group Practice Matures,
New Offices and Teaching in the East
1980s

176 CHAPTER 6
A Global Practice
1990s

212 CHAPTER 7
A Transition to New Leadership
1996 to present

228 CHAPTER 8
Shaping the SWA Group: Lessons from 55 Years of Practice

272 CHAPTER 9
Making Landscape Architecture and SWA Group
More Visible to the Public

280 CHAPTER 10
Epilogue: Thoughts on Landscape Architecture, SWA Group
and Designing Places for People in the 21st Century

299 About Kalvin Platt
300 List of Illustrations and Case Study Index

## PREFACE

# Was the Tree There Before the City?

When I was a small child in New York City, I was familiar with trees that were planted and grew out of holes in the sidewalks where I played and walked. I sometimes saw men fixing sidewalks, then carefully planting trees in the holes they had made for them. My parents took me many times to the Bronx Zoo and Botanical Gardens where there were many trees, but they were planted in manmade patterns or grouped in carefully planned gardens with sidewalks and buildings around them that allowed you to visit the many wonderful places.

One day, when walking with my uncle along my street in the Bronx, West Farms Road, we came upon a huge old tree that took up a lot of space on the sidewalk and even spread into the street. I thought the men had made a mistake when they planted the tree. My uncle told me that the sidewalks and streets had been paved around it to save the beautiful old tree, which was part of a farm that was here before the city—and that is how our street got its name. I was astounded that the big city could be built around a single old tree. I had assumed that trees always came after the city was built, but now I knew that trees could come *before* the city!

I liked that old tree and how good it made the people in the city feel when they were around it, and from then on I really paid attention to the city around me, noticing where things came from, those natural and those man made, and how people used its different parts. I think this is why I became interested in building places for people in cities and communities and spent almost 55 years working on building cities around the big beautiful trees, rivers, beaches, prairies, lakes and mountains I found around the world.

**Opposite Page** Cocoplum Community, Coral Gables, Florida.

# INTRODUCTION

This book is about a personal journey and begins by telling the story of my experience in New York learning from the streets and blackboard jungles of the Bronx, to bicycling the privileged avenues of Manhattan and attending the elite Stuyvesant High School, to experiencing suburban life in Florida in the beautiful planned garden city of Coral Gables, to attending architecture school, to enlisting in the Navy Civil Engineers in historic Charleston, to an internship with a brilliant architect, and finally studying city planning at the Harvard Graduate School of Design.

My work as an architect and city planner is demonstrated in the first four case studies in the book. I had many satisfying results but still felt something was lacking in fully addressing how these places were to be finally built as better places for people. I found the answer to that gap in Landscape Architecture and in a particular firm, Sasaki, Walker Associates that had put together the necessary ingredients and processes to make that happen

Hideo Sasaki and Peter Walker had started a firm while teaching at Harvard University, the original home of Landscape Architecture and City Planning education in America. They reinvigorated the profession from the doldrums of the depression and World War II and put it back into the center of the vibrant building of America after the war. They focused on a broader perspective bringing natural and environmental systems into the design and building of the landscape in urban places. Working closely with like minded architects they recognized the importance of the site planning and urban design of "the spaces in between" the buildings in creating a true sense of place for people to enjoy as they went about their lives.

Realizing this was the place to do my life's work, I joined Sasaki, Walker Associates to not just plan but to also design and build in cities, master planned suburbs that were true communities, and the variety of places for living, learning, working, shopping and carrying on all the social, educational, cultural and recreational activities required for a good life. I try to show how we did all this in case studies of my work and some illustrations of iconic work of the entire firm. The work demonstrates that, in the second half of the 20th century, cities and places were built by a dynamic combination of public and private entities that became our clients as we planned, designed and built "everything outside the buildings," the urban landscape including streets, parks, waterfronts and public and significant private spaces that were used by the public. We were able to do this by working closely with the architects, citizens, public and private clients, economists and engineers.

Then with some brief histories and more case studies of my work I follow the remarkable transition as Sasaki, Walker Associates becomes the SWA GROUP. I lead the firm for its first 23 years as we grew and learned to manage up and down cycles as an employee owned group practice. Over time we became a successful national and then global landscape architectural, planning and urban design firm, and then with new leadership we continued to enhance our capabilities in overseeing the building of sustainable places for people in cities around the world.

In the section of the book "Shaping the SWA GROUP," I look back on my role as the first President of the SWA GROUP and explain our thoughts as we formed the basic structure of the new firm. I recognized that our heritage was the exemplary quality of our work and that needed to be the bottom line of our business structure, period. We then took the ideas of employee ownership and a real group practice seriously, so we would need to go beyond solvency to taking the best care of our people who were in fact our owners and our major assets. I led, but WE created an unique entity that carries on 40 years later as a successful enterprise with the highest employee benefit structure in the industry and known as a "world leader in landscape architecture". In explaining how we set that up I pay tribute to those of us that made it happen.

In the last section of the book I take a personal look at SWA GROUP in the 21st century from my perspective of 55 years of professional practice, the past five where I have not been active on projects—as a Consulting Principal and member of the Board providing oversight and careful observation of the firm's exciting activities. My focus here is on the enormous challenge the 21st century provides where by 2050 it is projected that the current 50% of the planet's population in urban areas will rise to 67%, some 2.75 billion more people in cities and urban places, facing increasing environmental degradation. I reflect on how I think the landscape architecture profession and particularly the SWA GROUP has stepped up to this challenge by continuing to improve its planning and designing of the essential elements of the total landscape creating better cities, communities and places for people, where they can live sustainably in dignity, health and happiness.

**Pages 10-11** Long Beach, California Shoreline.

Barrett Avenue

Nevin Avenue

Macdonald Avenue

Bissell Avenue

Eighth Street widened

Sixth Street

Tenth Street

Twelfth Street

Fourteenth Street widened

N

0    50   100

**Proposed Plan for Downtown Area**

15

12

# ACKNOWLEDGEMENTS

This book acknowledges the people of The SWA GROUP, and before that Sasaki, Walker, Associates, and Sasaki, Walker Roberts who now and in the past have made my journey so fulfilling, exciting, sometimes frustrating but ultimately sublime. I also acknowledge the incredible contribution of Tom Fox and the other SWA GROUP photographers who brilliantly bring our work to life, and to Andrea Hansen for her editing that has made my story more compelling.

The plans and designs throughout this book would not have been possible without the collaboration of the architects, engineers, economists and environmental scientists who enriched our work beyond all my expectations. And our amazing clients gave us the opportunity to reach our goals and became true collaborators in the process.

I must give most thanks to Janne, my wife of 53 years, who was and is my first line of support along with my children Andrea and David. Watching our grandchildren Jenna, Daniel, J and Devin grow and thrive has made this all worthwhile.

I acnowledge Gordon Goff and his publishing team at ORO EDITIONS and Pablo Mandel's brilliant graphic design that brought this complex story together so elegantly. Finally and most importantly, I thank all those who work every day to make a difference in how cities, communities and places are planned, designed and built better for people and the environment.

**Opposite Page** Downtown Plan for Richmond, California.

# 1

# Learning about cities, architecture, construction and planning

## 1931–1959

## Growing Up in the Big City
## (New York, 1931–1948)

I was born in 1931 in the Bronx, New York City during the great depression. I went to kindergarten near the Grand Concourse but left school the first day and walked home since they "were just playing games" and I already could read. This is a good example of how I approached my education all my life, from a very early age I was very serious about learning. I was curious about what was going on around me in the big city and excited about all the exotic things I could learn from books. My interest in ideas was fostered by the spirited dinner time discussions led by my father, who was an avid reader and observer of many topics.

I went to an elementary school in my neighborhood, which had a rich mixture of Irish, Italian, Jewish and Puerto Rican children. I was advanced in reading and did very well on tests, so I wound up in a rapid advanced class and finished a year early. I went on to Junior High just after World War II had started and great influxes of people had come to work on the war effort. . My school was in an adjacent neighborhood, where many kids came up from the segregated schools of the rural south. The place was a real "blackboard jungle," with police lineups every morning and all kinds of crime. I was accosted every day at lunch, so I brought unappealing food and pens and carried no money.

The school had an abundance of violence, and was uneven in educational standards. I was again put in an advanced class where the teachers so welcomed our eager brains that they locked their doors so we could get their whole day's academic energy. Even better, since we were an oddity and a source of school pride for our academic achievements, our class was considered "off limits" in the violent wars between classes that happened every day. My PE teacher, Monahan, literally threw bowling pins at rowdy students—sharp contrast to the sport he chose for us: throwing deflated balls at each other. He was amused that I stood behind lockers and chose not to participate. I came away from that difficult school with a better understanding of people.

**Opposite Page** A view in the 1950's of Central Park and the surrounding New York skyline.

**Right** New York in the 1930's with the Empire State, Chrysler and Rockefeller Center buildings.

Being a great test taker, I applied for New York's premier science public school in Manhattan, Stuyvesant High School. I not only got in, but was also assigned to the advanced class. Humility was not my strong suit going in, though Stuyvesant quickly changed that, much to the benefit of my further education. I no longer needed to be the smartest kid in the school, giving talks in the auditorium and acing all the tests. From then on, I simply wanted to learn with the smartest people, like those in my Stuyvesant class where I was challenged every day. I sometimes struggled to keep up, but loved every minute of it. My classmates in Junior High showed me that dead ends for people were not inevitable, and Stuyvesant unveiled the joy and infinite possibilities of education by working hard and with the best minds. I did not forget this in my choices in later life as this book tries to illustrate.

High School was when I began realizing that not all education is done in school. Since I was such a quick learner in those days, I did not have to study much, even at Stuyvesant, and I could do my homework quickly in the evening. Due to the aftermath of the war, Stuyvesant was on two shifts so I took the Third Avenue El before the sun rose from the Bronx and finished school by 1pm. That allowed me to take a job to earn money for college as a Red Arrow uniformed messenger in midtown Manhattan. Based at Saks Fifth Avenue, I rode my bike to all the great luxury stores and took taxis or the subway to deliver packages to hotels and apartment buildings along Central Park, Fifth and Park Avenues, and the riverfronts. I saw how dramatically different this New York was it was from the ethnic villages I grew up in the Bronx. I began to understand what New York City was to the world and just what made it tick.

**Above** Old Stuyvesant High School on 15th Street between First and Second Avenues where I went to school is now a technical school with new Stuyvesant relocated to Battery Park City.

**Opposite Page** The Biltmore Hotel is a landmark and sets the architectural reference for Coral Gables, Florida.

## Moving to "The City Beautiful" and Studying Architecture (Florida, 1948–1953)

As I finished high school, my family moved to Florida, a long- time dream of my father made possible with the end of the war. My sister came to New York after my graduation and we took the bus south to an entirely different way of life in Coral Gables, a beautiful garden suburb of Miami that rightfully called itself "the City Beautiful." I learned to love these two different places, for each had aspects of humanity and place that intrigued me.

At Stuyvesant I had taken a Beaux Arts architectural drafting class that the science curriculum of the school used to introduce students to the arts and culture. I was intrigued by the possibility of making the physical environment of the city better for people. This course inspired me to follow up in Architectural studies at college. Since we were technically not residents of Florida yet, I would have had to pay out-of-state tuition to go to the University of Florida. So, I enrolled for one year at the University of Miami. They did not have an architecture curriculum so I enrolled in a Civil Engineering program and took some math that continued my work at Stuyvesant, as well as general engineering courses that were helpful later on.

I was only sixteen and a half years old when I entered college, which was an eye-opening experience in several ways. Considering Stuyvesant was a boys-only school with no social functions, the University gave me the chance to notice girls in my classes, and this was the start, though mostly a very slow start of an entirely different phase of my education. My family lived only a

**Above** Coral Gables street trees provide an arbor of shade and a people friendly character in the subtropical climate. **Right** Coral Gables overall landscape provides a public garden character for the city with tree lined streets, gateways, trellises and fountains.

**Pages 20–21** The Frank Lloyd Wright sketch for the unbuilt Zeta Beta Tau Fraternity House at the University of Florida for which Ken Treister and I as architectural students provided the on-site tree survey.

10-minute bus ride from the University so I was a commuter with no car and my social life that year did not amount to much. In 1949, when I was almost eighteen, I transferred to the University of Florida in Gainesville to finish my second year of general studies so I could enroll in the three-year architecture program. Florida was not much of a challenge in the lower division studies, but it was a chance for me to get away from home and continue to mature since I was one to two years younger than my classmates and a decade younger than the significant number of GI Bill students in my classes. It was also a time to learn about money.

In Coral Gables, my dad opened a hardware and artist supplies store with a businessman he knew from New York, but it became a real problem for him. His partner proved to be in serious debt, misused my Dad's money and committed suicide in the back of the store one evening. Because of these troubles, my family was having great difficulty coming up with the money for tuition, even though it was only fifty dollars a semester, and my dorm costs were equally low. Even so, my mom saved her change and said she could give me forty dollars a month for my food and other expenses. I knew how hard it was for her, as she had my younger sister and brother at home to take care of. But she always wanted me to go to college, and I was glad for the help.

Living on forty dollars a month, I decided to set a strict budget. This meant I would have one dollar and thirty cents per day to live on, period. Since I had basic clothing, a place to live, and school to keep me busy every day, the challenge was food—no small thing for a growing teenager! Luckily, the university cafeteria had fifty-cent lunch and dinner specials that were quite complete, and the coffee shop had a cheap breakfast. Putting together breakfast of coffee, a donut or cereal, and juice (22 cents), the lunch special with extra bread (52 cents), and the dinner special with extra bread and milk (56 cents), I was able to keep to my daily food budget of one dollar and thirty cents exactly. It was the same every day for the next few semesters. No snacks, no cokes, no clothes, no nonsense.

Besides food, I was helped with schoolbooks and equipment by the wonderful veterans in my class, who would get more books and drafting equipment than they could use each year from the GI Bill. They were generous to this skinny kid ten years their junior, with a no-nonsense budget and a wardrobe of t-shirt, jeans and sneakers that never changed. I didn't know then that I was setting a fashion for college kids, and I surely did not realize I was way ahead on the environment by not washing my jeans but once a semester!

Later on, my budget became more flexible, as I got a job in the cafeteria, delivered dry cleaning, worked for the architecture department, and got a small scholarship. My dad was also able to recoup his earlier losses after several years when he started Rex Art Supplies, which became a very successful business. But those early years instilled financial discipline and the importance of making things work as a family—no matter how difficult—and these lessons stayed with me. I knew how difficult it was for my Dad and Mom: they were doing all they could so that I could keep going where I wanted to go in my life, so I did whatever I could to stay in school and worked in my dad's art store every summer or vacation.

Architectural school was a great challenge and I made lifelong friendships with people who shared my ambitions and search for creativity. However, though the school had some good technical teachers, it lacked creative leadership. This left students to seek out architects who opened up new ideas,

which we did with aplomb. At the University of Florida, there were a few new professors like Ted Fearney, whom several of us students latched onto, eager to make a difference ourselves. When Paul Rudolph came to Sarasota to practice, we all visited his office and got involved, and a number of our group ended up working with him. We also traveled farther afield, for instance to North Carolina State to visit with Matthew Nowiscki during his brilliant but short career there, and welcomed visitors, like William Lescaze, an accomplished Philadelphia architect with great sensitivity to city planning, who got me very interested in how architecture could become city planning as he described how he placed his famous PSFS modern building in the context of Philadelphia's street pattern.

We welcomed another famous visitor when my classmate, Ken Treister, got his fraternity to hire Frank Lloyd Wright for their new house in Gainesville. Ken and I did a complete site survey plan locating all trees for Wright. Because of this commission, he agreed to come to Gainesville to see the site and give a university-wide talk—but he made us promise that no professors would be involved! Several of us excitedly arranged for his trip and lecture. He ended his visit with us architectural students listening at his feet—literally—as he lectured us under the campus trees, porkpie hat and cape and all. It was truly inspiring. Although the fraternity house was not built in the end, the beautiful drawings are in Wright's archive of unbuilt work and this firsthand experience with one of architecture's greats has stayed with me throughout my life.

The Korean War started in June 1950, when I was just starting the three-year Architectural program. The draft was immediately reinstated, and we were all classified 1A. I was not at all certain about this war (which was technically a police action under the UN anyway), but more than that, I really wanted to stay in school. So, I set out to join a Naval Reserve unit at the university to avoid being drafted. However, right at that time there was a discussion in Congress about granting students draft deferral, so I delayed signing up. Despite pressure from the unit and amidst much worry that I would be called by the draft, I waited until the deferment law was passed. As it happened, that reserve unit was called up the next year, so I was glad to have taken the risk.

Thanks to my deferral, I was able to stay in Florida and finish architectural school. Before I was set to graduate in June 1953, I wrote to the Harvard Graduate School of Design about continuing my education in City Planning, which I had come to decide was going to be the next part of my professional practice based upon my desire to broaden my understanding on how cities worked. I received a reply from William Wheaton, the Dean of the School suggesting that I should consider MIT or Penn rather than Harvard. I was surprised, but later learned Wheaton was leaving Harvard. Wheaton's discouragement mattered little, however, as I soon learned that the door to continuing my education in the way I wanted was closing. On the verge of losing my college deferment, and knowing that a masters degree program would not qualify for further deferment, I received word from my draft board in Miami that I was classified 1A and would be called up after graduation. I was heartbroken not to be able to finish my education, especially later that year after I heard from Reginald Isaacs, who took over from Wheaton at Harvard, apologizing for Wheaton's letter and encouraging me to apply. It pained me to let him know of my draft status and decline his invitation, but even so, I was determined to keep on learning in my chosen profession and follow my interests, regardless of where I had to go.

If I had to serve, I decided it would be in the Navy Civil Engineer Corps (CEC) to further my training in designing and building things and to avoid wasting years of my time in the army. So, in March of 1953 before I graduated, I applied for Naval Officer Training. About two months later, right around the time of graduation, I was notified that I didn't get into the CEC and was rejected for Line (ship) duty, as I wore glasses. My two friends Ken and Dick were also rejected by the CEC, but at least they got in on-ship duty officer training. That meant they would have to spend their time on ships, but as the Navy liked to say, they would get to "see the world."

After graduation, I reported to Miami and received orders to go to Georgia by train in order to take my pre-induction physical. I reluctantly left for this awful town and was subjected to subhuman treatment in the company of other men, many of whom were unable to read or write. I returned home convinced that the army was not for me. Thus, my interest was piqued when I was called by an Air Force recruiter asking if I wanted to join Air Force Intelligence (I had done so well on my written exam at the army physical that I was selected to go to Officer Training in the Air Force). I asked the recruiter if I could have some time to find out what that entailed, and he told me he could put in a hold at my draft board—boy did that sound good! After learning more, I was surprised to learn that the job would be to fly in small reconnaissance planes behind a pilot and gather information on ground activities. I couldn't see how their idea of intelligence would mesh with my idea of intelligence, so I contacted the Army Corps of Engineers, whose duties better matched my interests, to see if the exam opened any doors there. It didn't.

Fortunately for me and all my friends, not to mention the country, right around this time the UN and the U.S. signed an agreement with North Korea, creating an armistice in the Korean War on July 27, 1953. Unfortunately, the draft would continue, since the U.S. was still concerned about renewed hostilities. It was now August, and I knew the Navy would open a new CEC school term in September. So I used every excuse I could think of to delay making a decision, but it was no use: I received a call from the Air Force recruiter, who said that the following week he would take the hold off on my draft status and expedite my induction into the army. I asked if I could come down to see him early that week to finally give him my answer and he agreed.

That morning I got ready to take the bus downtown. I had no idea what I would decide—the army or the air force—as they were both far from what I was interested in doing with my life. I didn't subscribe to the "get it over with" belief that many of my peers held, which meant taking the two year army service option since hostilities had ceased. I thought I would learn nothing of value that way, and much preferred the option of serving three years in the Air Force or Navy if it meant being able to add to my learning. In my heart, I still felt the Navy was the only fit for me.

Before I left that day, I checked the mail and there it was! A letter from the Navy saying I was accepted to the November session of Officers Training for the Naval Civil Engineer Corps. Elated, I phoned the Air Force recruiter to let him know I would not be coming down. He was upset, but I was as happy that day as any in my entire life! Maybe then I could make use of my time in the military to keep learning about planning, designing and building.

## Learning Construction from the Navy Civil Engineers (Charleston, 1953–1957)

With orders in hand, I boarded the train from Miami to Newport, Rhode Island wearing a corduroy jacket, the only coat I owned. It was November and cold and rainy in Newport. When I received the Navy Pea Coat, white hat, blue jumper, tie and the 13 button bell-bottoms, they felt good. Wearing a real sailor suit was a revelation—it imparted a sense of freedom, as no one expected you to act with any decorum or responsibility whatsoever. A good example occurred in Boston, where I reunited with my Florida classmates Ken and Dick, who were still in their "Ship Navy" school. One night, we all went on leave to hear the Boston Symphony, which was free to servicemen. In the cab from symphony hall, Dick, who had a cold, carried a huge box of Kleenex, and we argued about who had written one of the pieces in the concert. The cab driver turned toward us and said, incredulously, "Are you guys really sailors?" It was a very perceptive question.

After graduating as an Ensign in the CEC, I was off to Seabee school at Port Hueneme in Southern California. The LA basin in 1954 was relatively smog-free, and you could see the snow-covered San Bernardino Mountains way across the basin from the beaches of Port Hueneme. We went skiing one weekend at Big Bear, hit the beach another, and went to the strip in Las Vegas, with one more weekend in San Francisco. What was not to like about California? I would find out as so many servicemen did that California was a magnet I could not resist for long.

Bernie, a classmate in CEC School, was from LA and said the best way to meet girls was at student meetings at UCLA, not far away in west LA. What could stop four Navy Ensigns from going where the girls were? We would

**Opposite Page** The Dock Street Theater, originally commissioned in 1736 by King Charles, where I provided set, lighting and graphic design during my Navy career.

**Above** View of the East Battery in Charleston, South Carolina in 1953 with my green Chevrolet convertible in front of the 1845 William Ravenal House, where I lived on the upper story during my Navy service.

soon find out: the meeting Bernie got us invited to was for a politically in-correct "fellow traveler group", a term used at that time to loosely cover any organization that might be sympathetic to communist or socialist ideas. This was the McCarthy era, and the House Un-American Activities Committee was in its heyday. I pulled Bernie aside and reminded him that just three months before, we were put under the Universal Code of Military Justice, meaning our judge and jurors had just spent the last few years fighting com-munists in China and North Korea. Not a good place to be so we left swiftly—but not before looking back at the girls (who were in fact incredible).

Following Seabee school, I was assigned to the District Public Works head-quarters of the 6th Naval District in Charleston, South Carolina. After a week at the Bachelor Officer Quarters I left the base to join my architectural school classmate, Newt Sayers, who had gone through the CEC School six months earlier and lived in an apartment in the historic part of the city. As two young Naval officers, we became roommates in the remodeled slave quarters on the top floor of an historic Charleston mansion on the East Battery. With a view of

the river and Fort Sumter, and an attic that still showed signs of cannonballs fired from the fort to answer the shots that began the Civil War (by our predecessor Naval Officers, coincidentally) it really felt like we were living history.

Charleston seemed like it was another world, still adjusting one hundred years later to its fall from antebellum grace. The city retained its cultural and architectural quality and uniqueness, however, and living "south of Broad Street" in the beautifully preserved historic district, you could sense how remarkable a place this was and continued to be. At times the tension between the city's past and its present was evident, coming to a head in 1954—a decade before the civil rights movement and the great changes to come—when the Supreme Court affirmed school desegregation in the famous *Brown vs. the Board of Education* decision. At the time I had just moved off base, but was put on "red alert" and asked to return to the base until the authorities could be sure there would not be any violence. Given the city's place in history as the start of the Civil War over slavery, it was an anxious time, but Charleston showed its class: there was no trouble and we returned home to a friendly community.

In the mornings, Newt and I would drive north to the "modern world," in other words, the busy shipyard and headquarters where we were building naval facilities around Charleston. I was given the task of a Resident Officer in Charge of Construction (ROICC). This was very fortunate as I learned contracting skills with civilian builders and became immersed in the day-to-day activities of my role supervising the construction of a pier for submarines, a rail spur and a highly complicated building complex at the Ammunition Depot far up the river. The things I learned from my civilian superintendent and the contractor's manager stuck with me throughout my career, and I still

**Above** The William Ravenal House where I lived in Charleston lost its portico and four Greek columns in the late 19th century great earthquake.

often think back to those days when I am building projects today. Incidentally, years later we would all learn that this facility housed the ultra-secret Polaris Missile Nuclear Submarines. Although I suppose we had some inkling when the sub showed up and the motley crew was unconcerned about the millions of dollars we had spent carefully spark proofing every part of the facility to protect against gunpowder explosions. That was the Navy!

After a long day's work on base, Newt and I drove back to the historic district at the tip of the peninsula, leaving the modern world in favor of an elegant, walkable city filled with scented gardens and beautiful buildings, whether museums, churches and synagogues, the Market, or fine civic, educational and shopping places. Arriving home on the East Battery, I could take off my uniform and change into civilian attire from the Porgy and Bess shops on nearby Church Street, free to roam the city and discover its secrets.

Eager for something to do to balance my military duties, I joined the Dock Street Theater, which was originally begun by King Charles in 1736 and was the first theater in the colonies. I was glad to have an outlet for my creative side, and quickly became a set designer, technical director, and graphic artist for all the programs and flyers. But what really kept me coming back to the theater day after day wasn't the sets or the plays, but the people involved who quickly became my friends especially the girls! I fell under the spell of Charleston's belles, especially those with a love for the theater. Celia Brown had a southern purr and a lively laugh, and we were both 23 and in love with each other and this romantic place. Evenings and weekends when I wasn't on duty were spent with her and our friends from the theater, as far away as I could get from my military work. With Celia, I discovered a world of culture, love, friendship and living in this elegant city reminiscent of another time, though we both understood the drawbacks to the relationship, since I still intended to finish my education after the Navy and she was intent on remaining in the Carolinas.

After New York and Coral Gables, Charleston was the third place that would have a profound and lasting effect on me and my professional work. I spent much time in Charleston looking, learning and feeling how a special place works and to trying to discover if and how such a place could be made through planning and design. With this challenge in mind, I inquired again near the end of my service about enrolling in City Planning at the Harvard Graduate School of Design (GSD). This time they were ready for me.

## Becoming an Architect (1958)

I left Charleston in January 1957 and returned home to Coral Gables to work for my architectural license with Reginald Caywood Knight until Graduate School began. Reg was a great architect and won an international competition for the Enrico Fermi Memorial in Chicago while I was there. While he was negotiating for the memorial, he left the two of us in the office in charge of finishing a complex set of working drawings. When the other architect left me on my own, I was forced to learn quickly, but thanks to my years in the Navy building from complex sets of drawings I could complete the set for an interesting modern church in Sebring, Florida. With my experience in the Navy and with Reg Knight I was eligible to take the exams and received my architectural license from Florida before I left for Cambridge!

## Studying City Planning at Harvard, (1957–1959)

When I arrived in Cambridge, I checked into the new dormitories designed by Walter Gropius in the Bauhaus style he brought from Germany, and went to see Reginald Isaacs, the Chairman of the City Planning Department. He had encouraged me to come to the GSD, and we discussed my two-year program. He had me taking studios and courses, but put the Planning Theory course by Professor Meyerson in my second year. Considering that my service had put me out of school for three-and-a-half years, and with Meyerson being known as a profound theorist, I asked if I could start with the theory course in my first year as it better fit my thinking process. He seemed unwilling to go along with my request, and when I expressed my disappointment he seemed irritated and said "well this is really up to Professor Meyerson."

At that moment Meyerson was in the hall outside Isaac's office and I quickly excused myself, walked out, asked the Professor if my idea was possible. To my relief, he quickly replied that it was fine. When I returned to Isaac's office he had no choice but to OK my request—and to add me to his list of "impertinents." Though it didn't help me with Isaacs, an enormous amount of understanding of city planning came from that course, and the early exposure to Meyerson shaped my whole approach to the social and political aspects of planning, in contrast to, (and in meaningful addition to), my education in architecture and building.

As for Isaacs, we had an up and down couple of years after that which was fine with me, as I always considered education to be disruptive and painful as much as enlightening. In my second year, I asked for his permission to go to the Littauer School of Government (now the Kennedy School) to take a

**Above** View of the new wing of the First Baptist Church in Sebring, Florida where I did the working drawings under Architect Reginald Knight in 1957.

course in governmental planning. Isaacs was hesitant, since he recently had a planning student do poorly in the difficult course by Professor Maas, our school's official Ph.D sponsor (there were no Ph.D's in the School of Design). However, he knew I was doing well in my courses and finally gave his permission. I finally managed to get back on his good side with that class: after receiving the only "A" in the class (which included ministers from U.S. and foreign governments), Isaacs held a sherry party happily toasting Professor Maas and I. Looking back I was hard on my professors, but I do appreciate Isaac's role in creating a great planning program at the school.

Harvard introduced me to Hideo Sasaki, head of the Landscape Department, who taught a course that included City Planning students. He was a revelation and gave me a real appreciation of his view of this profession that made so much sense in designing and building cities. Little did I know then that he and Peter Walker, his new partner in their consulting firm, would figure so strongly in how my career developed a decade later.

In the summer between my two years at GSD, I was an intern in the Portland, Maine Planning Department, where I worked on a Downtown Study. Maine opened my eyes to three important things—first, I learned how to eat a lobster right at the boat dock. Second, we four interns from different schools rented one of the twenty-four cottages on Little Diamond Island, ten minutes by ferry from Downtown in Casco Bay. Little Diamond was a "wheelbarrow island," meaning that there were no automotive vehicles (or horses as in the old days) so you had to use the community wheelbarrows at the ferry dock to carry your luggage or groceries to your home, and then return them to the dock after you were finished. Thirty years later I used a similar system in Sausalito to carry things to my houseboat and the end of a long pier.

It was the experience on Little Diamond that was the most important, for it introduced me to the use of information technology in planning. One of our interns was a business technology student at Rutgers who used IBM business machines for data collection and interpretation. This was twenty years before the personal computer, and in that era, "computer" meant large, room-sized research computers with vacuum tubes. On this project, we got together and combined techniques about data collection that some of us knew. With this guy's expertise with the punch card and sorting techniques, we were able to put all the Downtown Portland data on punch cards and use them to summarize a number of critical planning parameters. This 1958 study was later published as the first computing machine planning study for an American city. It was exciting to be part of such a landmark study, and I would build upon this work in my plan for Santa Ana, California in 1964, still then working with punch card technology, and later with new computer technology as it became available.

While I was at Harvard, I tried my best to take full advantage of the resources of the University, and so I audited three lecture courses at Harvard College with Robert Frost, economist Kenneth Galbraith and the sociologist David Reisman. Just being in the halls with these great men and a raft of young Harvard and Radcliffe students was worth the additional course load—they could take you places and make you think and feel things you hadn't before.

I enjoyed the Gropius dormitories and dinners at the Harkness Commons, where the large round tables allowed our diverse group of Masters and Ph.D students to have discussions on the Arts, Science and the Law—always provoked by my neighbor and planning classmate Sol Rabin, a recent philosophy

**Above** The Gropius Dorms at Harvard where
I lived as a student. **Middle** The Harvard
Yard has always been the center of the
University's activities. **Bottom** Robinson Hall
was the location of the Harvard Graduate
School of Design when I was a student.

graduate from Reed College. In our second year, with my classmates Sol Rabin and Steve Staples, I rented a coldwater flat (no hot water or heat supplied by the landlord) owned by Harvard next to the campus. Luckily, the flat below was rented by a wealthy law student and his family, and they had put in a heating system that contributed much to our comfort in the old wooden three-decker. The upper floor was occupied by an elderly woman who had come from Ireland as a child and lived all her life in Cambridge. She had lost her husband many years ago so we helped her out as we could but were astonished when she said she had never left Cambridge even to go to Boston.

The Graduate School of Education was nearby to our flat and had afternoon tea open to the University. We would visit frequently since that is where the women were, and the Design school was almost all men in those days. One afternoon, while sitting at tea with an affable gentleman, I noticed a beautiful young woman sitting alone. I excused myself with a comment that I was here to meet women, and he smiled. I went over and talked to the woman, Ivonne, and she asked me what I was doing sitting at the table with the Dean of the School of Education.

Ivonne was from Buenos Aires and was involved in innovations in teaching English without translation. She was a warm and wonderful person and we both shared a memorable year at Harvard. On bright cold winter weekends, I would retrieve my Chevy convertible, put down the top, role up the windows and turn on the heater full blast as we drove up the north shore to Marblehead for lunch. We would go to the Isabelle Stewart Gardner Museum to see the paintings and hear the chamber music concert in the courtyard. And with an Argentine Doctor friend of Ivonne and his wife we went to Harvard Stadium to hear Fidel Castro on his only trip to America. He gave a stirring oration but they said, "he sounds too much like our dictator Juan Peron!" We loved each other but we knew at that point in our lives we would follow our long educations to places that would allow us to put them to good use. We would go separate ways after graduation to begin our careers far apart.

In 1959, I graduated with my Master of City Planning Degree eager to begin the next phase of my life. This long, extensive, and somewhat roundabout education had made me anxious to practice my profession and to use all that I learned in my first 28 years.

# 2

# Finding the right partners and places in life and work- choosing landscape architecture

## 1959–1967

The bayshore holds promise of a more profitable development for the benefit of all of Dade County. The open visual expanse of Biscayne Bay lies unused today (see below). This unique asset could be profitably used adjacent to the most highly developed urban area. (See sketch above)

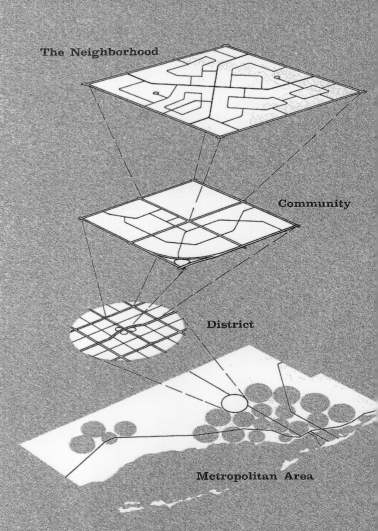

The Neighborhood

Community

District

Metropolitan Area

## Working as a public planner (1959-1962)

After completing my Master's degree in 1959, I was excited to take my first planning job as a Principal Planner in the Comprehensive Planning Division of the Metropolitan Dade County Planning Department in Miami. The Miami Metropolitan Area was one of the fastest growing in the country, and in 1957 it had ratified a charter to create a metropolitan government. The charter gave the new government the authority to plan land use and transportation for the entire Dade County, which was the largest county by both area and population in the State of Florida. Dade County included 27 municipalities, including Miami and Miami Beach, as well as a large, developed unincorporated area, and the unification of such diverse communities was a new experiment in planning and governing. This was an opportunity to address a metropolitan area as a unity rather than as an assemblage of competing and uncoordinated cities, county and other jurisdictions, and it was a planner's dream to be involved in preparing the first overall plan.

The Department's economic planners started with an in-depth Economic Base Study that set the parameters for the rapid growth to be expected within the plan's 25-year horizon. Dade County was to grow from a population of just under one million to two-and-a-half million by that date. At the same time, we began a series of workshop meetings with a prestigious Planning Advisory Board that was set up for the entire planning process.

Noting my familiarity with Dade County and my enthusiastic, "take charge" attitude, my supervisor Reginald Walters and the two other young planners working on the Land Use Plan agreed to let me lead the study process. I began a series of seven Planning Staff Reports that were published in sequence for discussion and review in collaboration with the Planning Advisory Board. The reports included "Planning Objectives", "Urban Growth" patterns in the county from 1890 to 1960, "Service Units" ranging in size from neighborhoods and communities to the entire region, "Movement in the Metropolis" covering automotive, rail, air, water and pedestrian/bicycle transportation, "Land Developability" including soils, fill requirements, water management and environmental sensitivities, and "Amenities" analyzing visual, landscape and urban design elements.

The Advisory Board took their work seriously and contributed much to the discussion about what the future might hold for Miami and Dade County. They particularly liked our decade-by-decade urban growth maps that could be extrapolated several finite ways for the next three decades of the plan. Miami was at a turning point with the great influx of Cuban refugees going on and making all the more feasible the long discussed role of South Florida becoming the major center of trade and culture for all the Americas, North, South, Central and the Caribbean.

Based upon the studies and discussions, a Preliminary Land Use Plan report was prepared in an outline form to be reviewed in well-attended and intensive workshops before the Planning Advisory Board. In 1961, these were followed by workshops with the Metro Planning Commission and Board of County Commissioners, allowing us to publish the documents in an attractive public information format. We were fortunate to have Irwin Partegyl, a master mapmaker and graphic artist on staff and I worked closely with him in creating these very well received documents. They included the "Economic Base Study", "The Existing Land Use Study", "Transportation and Service

**Opposite Page Left** A sample set of sketches from the Amenity section of the Metropolitan Dade County plan showing a before and after better use of the bay front edge. **Right** The plan divided the entire 2.5 million population of Metropolitan Dade County into neighborhood, community and district service areas.

DADE COUNTY

WATER CONTROL

CONSERVATION AREA #3

RESIDENTIAL
ESTATE DENSITY
LOW DENSITY
MEDIUM DENSITY
HIGH DENSITY
COMMERCIAL
TOURIST
INTENSIVE USE
EXTENSIVE USE
INDUSTRIAL
INSTITUTIONAL
PARKS AND RECREATION
TRANSPORTATION
AGRICULTURE
ORGANIC SOILS
WATER

EXPRESSWAY - PARKWAY
EXPRESS STREET
GLADE ROAD

SCALE IN MILES
0    1    2

SEE
LARGE
MAP

ENTIRE COUNTY MAP

EVERGLADES

NATIONAL

PARK

SOUTH DADE
CENTER

HOMESTEAD
CENTER

HOMESTEAD
AIR FORCE BASE

MAGIC
CITY
CENTER

OPA-LOCKA

OPA-LOCKA AIRFIELD

MIAMI INTERNATIONAL AIRPORT

GOLDEN    GLADES    EXPRESSWAY

INTERAMA

BISCAYNE   BAY

ATLANTIC   OCEAN

DADE COUNTY
MONROE COUNTY

Preliminary
## Land Use Plan
for 2,500,000 Population · 1985 Estimate
Metropolitan Dade County                    Florida

Area Studies", and a more refined "Preliminary Land Use Plan to the year 1985" (a year which at the time really seemed far off). A countywide review process was then mounted by the Planning Department.

The plan consolidated the future growth of Dade County into two large urban areas with a greenbelt between them. The primary urban area focused on the twin cities of Miami and Miami Beach as the regional and international serving core while the secondary urban area focused on a new more local serving core under development at Kendall, in the southern part of the county. The two cores had the highest densities in the region, and in order to promote their central roles they were flanked by support communities and neighborhoods that had full urban services and gradually decreased in density as they moved away from the cores.

Our plan placed another greenbelt at the north of the Miami-based urban area, just south of the Broward County line, giving some separation from the Hollywood and Fort Lauderdale urban areas in that county. To the east were Biscayne Bay and the Atlantic Ocean and to the west of both urban areas were very large green areas comprised of agricultural lands, water conservation areas, the everglades, and Everglades National Park. To the far south of the Kendall urban area was a large agricultural area around the Town of Homestead, and further south large lay wetland and conservation areas bordering Monroe County and the Florida Keys.

While the public involvement and review of the Preliminary Land Use Plan was going on in 1961, I was asked to head up a Comprehensive Zoning Study that would produce a new zoning ordinance for the unincorporated county, along with guidelines for a common zoning language, model ordinances and modern zoning procedures for the 27 municipalities in the county. The metropolitan approach was beginning to shape up, and with the enthusiastic support of the Planning Advisory Board, we retained high-powered consultants to do this intense two-year study.

Unfortunately, this was when things began to unravel for the Metro Dade approach. The first shoe dropped when the county assessor began a reassessment of all properties both in the unincorporated and municipal areas. The Board of County Commissioners had the Metro Charter and all the authority they needed, but the political will was not there. Under severe pressure from cities and businesses, they cancelled the reassessment process thereby allowing the old inconsistent local assessments to stand and to carry on the local interest group politics that the Metro Government was formed to change. The second shoe dropped quickly after that, when the zoning study was cancelled for the same reasons. I realized that Florida still had a way to go to get past unplanned sprawl that had made many wealthy but had produced chaos for the residents. Thus, in early 1962, I began to look elsewhere to continue my career.

With the Florida experiment, a great opportunity for better government was only partially successful. To the credit of Reginald Walters, who was my supervisor and later became Planning Director, in 1963 a good "Land Use Plan for Metropolitan Dade County" did emerge from our efforts, and this plan contained many but not all of our concepts. Gradually, Walters and some of my colleagues like Bill Kuge patiently made Metro planning better every year, step by step. When I returned in the late 1970's and 80's to prepare plans in the region for my SWA GROUP clients, I was impressed with the quality of the Metro planning they had struggled to develop with some help from the State of Florida's changing attitudes and forward thinking in land use, environmental and development control legislation.

**Opposite Page** The first Preliminary Land Use Plan for Metropolitan Dade County and its 27 municipalities including Miami and Miami Beach, with urban centers, greenbelts and large conservation areas.

## Starting a Family and Moving to California (1962)

My two years at Metropolitan Dade County as a planner had solidified my feeling that I had begun my life's work. My long and useful education had given way to the next step and, besides finally having a chance to test my passion for urban planning, the period between 1959 and 1962 saw me through extremely important decisions that would resonate for the rest of my life. First, having returned home from graduate school to Miami to work as a public planner, I needed to convince my dad that I would not take over the family Art Supply business. I had waited long enough to start my career, and could not afford any more diversions. Luckily, he graciously understood and was able to offer the business to my sister Rita and her husband Mel, who went on to great success, much to my dad's joy.

Second, and perhaps more importantly to my going beyond my single minded career track to becoming a more mature and well rounded person, things began to happen when in 1960 my coworker Marianne introduced me to her friend Janne. At almost thirty years of age and having experienced love with two wonderful women in Charleston and Cambridge, I could recognize those feelings beginning again as we started to see each other. But there was something more this time, or I should say a *lot* more between me and Janne Staller, who was a special education teacher and recently divorced with a 5-year-old daughter. We were in love, but we also had the right mix of being alike and different that just made being together so natural. For the first time, my tendency toward postponing non-career matters began to evaporate.

It was obvious to both of us that we had found "the one." And so, we married in 1961, though not before I had also "proposed" to her daughter and then adopted her at six years of age. We loved the leafy old village quality of Coconut Grove where we lived and it was not long before our son David came along. Our little family, which became the joy of my life, had begun so quickly and so well. Looking back after more than 50 years of marriage and with four grandchildren now in college, I realize that finding Janne meant finding a partner who, more than anyone, has helped me and sustained me through both life and work.

Realizing the job at Metropolitan Dade was not going to give me the future I needed, Janne and I soon faced the first of many critical decisions about where my career would take our young family. I started contacting friends and looking around the country for where that could be, since recent political developments in Florida made my career difficult there. Graham Finney, who had been Planning Director in Portland, Maine during my internship there, suggested I join him at the Philadelphia City Planning Agency, the premier public agency of that day under Ed Bacon.

Another friend, Sol Rabin, who was my roommate at Harvard, suggested I join him in working at an impressive private planning consultant practice in Northern California. Little did I know then, but this decision would mark a turning point in our lives. Would it be Philadelphia, a city whose planning legacy I greatly admired, which was close to New York City and close to Janne's home in New Jersey? Or across the country to California, where I had been so impressed during my Navy school experience and where exciting new things were happening in planning? Ultimately, despite geographical factors, the choice was between continuing a career in public work and starting a career as a private consultant.

A trip I took to the agency in Philadelphia raised some doubts about continuing in a public agency where there would be layers between the work and my involvement and a visit to Coconut Grove by one of Sol's associates in California gave us an intriguing glimpse into the dynamics of the planning practice there as a consultant. Finally, with encouragement by Sol who I had established such a close relationship at Harvard, and with much deliberation we were off to California with the promises (and challenges) of a new place and a new kind of work.

## Planning in an Engineering Company (1962–3)

I arrived in California in 1962, and joined Sol Rabin at Wilsey, Ham and Blair, an engineering and planning company in the San Francisco Bay Area. My first assignment as Project Planner was a redevelopment plan for Downtown Richmond, California. It was my introduction to private planning consulting and the methods of California professionals.

Richmond, which was across the Bay from San Francisco, had grown rapidly during WWII, but lost significant employment in the post-war period. The black workers who had flocked to the area's shipyard and war industries from the south and east now had difficulty getting new jobs, and California's complex racial attitudes made their opportunities even scarcer. Thus, while Richmond was growing in its northern sectors, the older parts around Downtown were stagnating. The area was in danger of facing a steep decline without significant new investment and redevelopment in the downtown and surrounding neighborhoods.

Our plan addressed the context and role of the Downtown within the city and suggested ways to change the physical environment to attract the kinds of investment that were needed. The downtown area had good bones: a good basic layout and location, and close proximity to a new major station of the Bay Area Transit (BART) system that was then currently under construction. This transit station also opened up access to Contra Costa County and Sacramento through a commuter rail service, and also created a bus terminal for access to surrounding areas. The transit hub was also the nexus for a new cultural hub, as the Richmond Civic Center and its cultural facilities were close to the other side of the station. Of course, we picked up on all of these strategic assets in our plan.

Wilsey, Ham and Blair led an impressive team of consultants. As the project planner, I could call on excellent support on a number of areas, including economic factors, traffic engineering, architecture and landscape architecture. This support enabled me to put together a very complete plan with specific recommendations, costs, guidelines and plan and sketch graphics. On our team was Bob Royston, the intrepid Bay Area landscape architect who amazed me with his ability to provide ideas on urban design in close collaboration with the architects. Working with Bob was great exposure for me to the landscape profession, which would undoubtedly become significant in my later career. Overall, the agency had a very competent staff, and I felt the Richmond plan could be readily adopted and implemented. I was particularly happy with the final report, which thanks to the guidance of the graphic designer Barbara Stauffacher, was truly beautiful not to mention very easy and compelling to read.

Our plan for Richmond drew upon many of the modern urban design principles of the day, including a major diversion of automobile traffic around the heart of downtown and a greater reliance on the new transit facilities. A large plaza was planned at the key downtown corner with dense mixed-use development around it that would preserve important existing buildings. Additional pedestrian plazas and covered walkways linked those plazas to the central space, which along with new high-density residential development would bring round-the-clock energy to the downtown core.

In preparing the plan, we worked for the Richmond Redevelopment Agency, which was composed of the city council members and therefore had a great ability to act. And act they did. They approved our plan quickly and soon began building some of the planned infrastructure. But at the same time, in what I can only term racial politics, they undermined the basic economic and contextual advantages of Downtown Richmond and doomed the plan. First, they approved a major shopping center at Hilltop near the I-80 freeway—an area in the northern and more affluent, suburban, and white part of the city. Second, they began a process to relocate the civic center toward that same area. These moves undercut the economic basis for reviving the downtown, and after that, all of the infrastructure and small gestures they initiated over the following years could not compensate for those two keystone changes. Downtown Richmond was left behind.

This first major project as a consultant taught me much about how to get a good plan put together. Unfortunately, it also pointed out how a good plan

**The Future Richmond Center**

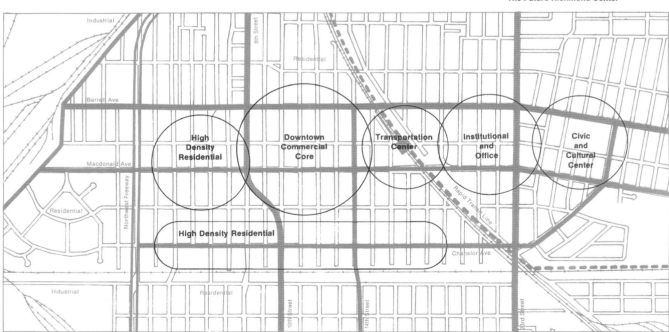

**Opposite Page** The Downtown Richmond central plaza central plaza connects office, retail and residential uses at multiple pedestrian levels.
**Bottom Left** High density residential areas downtown with internal pedestrian and park spaces.

**Above** A diagram of Downtown Richmond in context to the new transit center, high density residential and civic areas.

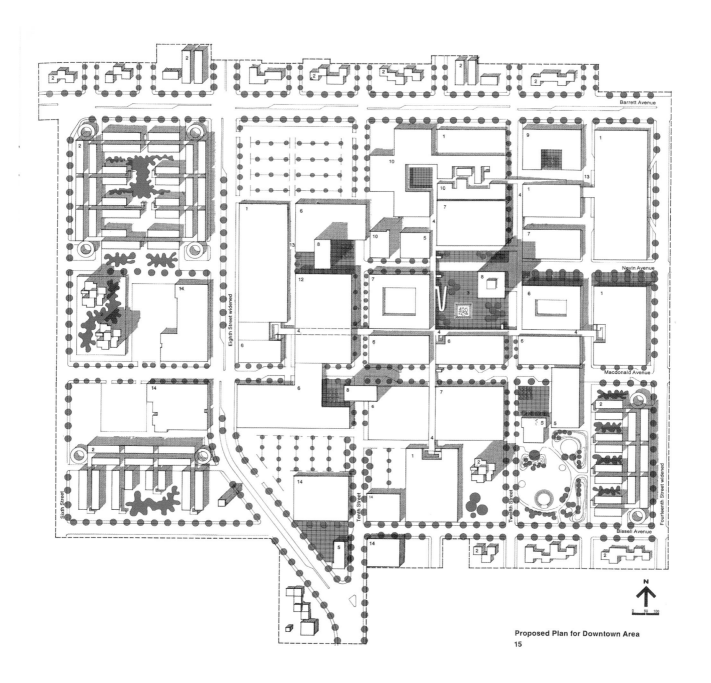

Labels on map (street names):

Barrett Avenue

Eighth Street widened

Nevin Avenue

Macdonald Avenue

Sixth Street

Tenth Street

Twelfth Street

Fourteenth Street widened

Bissell Avenue

N

Proposed Plan for Downtown Area
15

**Above** The Downtown Richmond Illustrative
illustrative plan shows the diversion of vehicular
traffic around the downtown core and a focus
on pedestrian areas with plazas spurring
redevelopment.

could be thwarted by politics in California, just like I had experienced as a public planner in Florida. It was not until more than forty-five years later, when I chaired a Transit Oriented Development workshop on Downtown Richmond for the Urban Land Institute, that a successful first phase of well-designed higher density residential development was finally built between Downtown and the BART/commuter rail station. We were asked to provide advice on getting a second phase going between the station and the Civic Center. The recent "great recession" has kept the second phase from development but I believe the housing resurgence that has begun in 2013, 50 years after the plan will finally begin to round out the potentials we saw in Downtown Richmond. The basic decisions made back then however still means downtown was never given the ability to reach its full potential.

## Working with a City Planning Consulting Firm (1964–7)

I learned much working for Wilsey, Ham and Blair. It was well organized and benefited from its size, but ultimately I felt the planners were primarily there to help get large engineering projects. Thus, when most of the best planners including Abraam Krushkhov who had headed the planning section, Mike McDougall who was planning and designing the New Town of Foster City and then Sol Rabin left to join Ruth and Krushkhov (R+K), an exclusive Planning Consulting firm, I also moved to Berkeley to join them. My new job gave me a chance to dive deeper into the kind of work I had trained for and to work with highly qualified members of my profession. I realized the incredible value of working with and under people I admired, including Herman Ruth, Janet Kourakis and Doug Duncan. as well as Abraam , Mike and Sol.

### *The Santa Ana General Plan Program (1964–5)*

My first large assignment at Ruth and Krushkhov was a multi-year involvement in preparing a General Plan for the City of Santa Ana, the county seat of Orange County in Southern California. What was unique about this process was that Santa Ana was a conservative bastion and did not want to participate in the very popular 701 Program of the U.S. Housing and Urban Development Agency, which provided funding for community master plans. We received many of our projects at R+K due to these federally funded programs, but unfortunately some cities used the programs just to get federal funds, and the planning itself was not their first priority. In this case, Santa Ana wanted a plan to reestablish their City's prominence in Orange County, and in order to have complete control over the elements of such a plan, came up themselves with the significant funds necessary. I liked the direct involvement this funding arrangement created with the city.

I began a process of biweekly trips to Southern California to work with the staff and interested citizen groups. The consulting team included Dr. John Dyckman, a prominent economist from UC Berkeley who worked with the Arthur D. Little organization, and John Forristal of D. Jackson Faustman, Traffic Consultants. Following the approach I used for Dade County, we prepared a series of technical studies that our consultants and I worked through with a special Citizens Planning Advisory Committee and a very active planning staff. The studies had seven parts, including a complete economic and infrastructure base study, citizen generated goals, projections, plans and

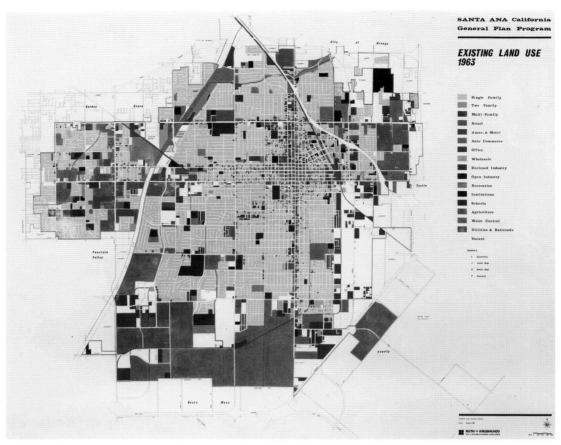

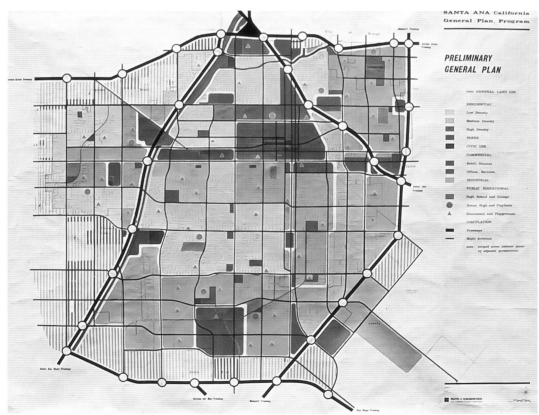

methodology, implementation, city center plans, a capital improvement program, and a summary report. After completing and reviewing the studies, we published them in 1965.

The city, having made this large investment, wanted a plan that could be updated. So we designed the planning process as an information system with explicit methodologies that could be adapted to use with new data over time. We also employed an innovative approach for the land use studies. Drawing upon my experience in IBM machine use for planning data at Portland, Maine during my internship at Harvard, I set up a way to record these data on IBM punch cards and to have the City's finance department process them on their IBM business machines to provide varied statistical analyses. This was done years before the city had computers that could handle this data, but we were aided by an enthusiastic data processing supervisor who provided impressive results. Over time as computer capability expanded, this work was transferred to city planning, as it retained the ability to update the data in-house.

We were fortunate to have Dr. Dyckman and Dr. Ananda Rao of Arthur D. Little help out with sophisticated models including a demographic model to project population, an econometric inter-industry model to project jobs and land requirements by industry, and a construction activity simulation model. Also, Dr. Jack Lessinger of the A. D. Little Company assisted me in using the Development Pressure Model to allocate the projected growth to vacant land resources in 54 sub areas of the city. This model was quite sophisticated for its time, providing the relative attraction of each subarea based upon a recent study he did comparing job and dwelling unit growth in nearby Orange and eastern Los Angeles Counties.

With the allocations of the Development Pressure Model as a base, I could use citizen input to reshape and modify the jobs and dwelling unit allocations according to three growth scenarios: City Center, Urban Corridors and Multiple Centers. Due to the hands on participation of the Santa Ana Assistant Planning Director, Paul Van Stevens, we had earlier taken the citizen goals and related them to the economic and planning data we had collected so we had established a good dialog with the citizen groups. My close relationship with Van Stevens paid off in the realistic land use plans we were able to evolve. Our traffic consultants then took these land use alternatives to input into the Los Angeles Regional Transportation Study model to get up to date traffic projections for our plans. While GIS and computer modeling would eventually become ubiquitous in planning, we were able to create an interconnected series of models for Santa Ana decades earlier, and this opened up a new, far more sophisticated understanding of the relationships between population, economic growth and plan alternatives.

Development in Southern California at that time was primarily composed of sprawling, automobile-centric, and low-density subdivisions, shopping centers and industrial areas. The new freeways that were built around the City of Santa Ana pulled development even farther out to its edges near the major intersections, Since this was a very conservative city where the local newspaper owner was also a member of the libertarian John Birch Society, we struggled with how to enact measures to, if not control growth, to at least shape it toward a more efficient pattern in the city. Our plan addressed this sprawl by organizing new development and higher densities around the existing City Center to support its role as the Orange County government center. We recognized the "polycentric" character that was developing along the

**Opposite Page Top** Existing land uses were surveyed and input into a computerized data base and converted to large colored maps for citizen review. **Bottom** The preliminary plan concept for Santa Ana with center city and urban corridor elements that became the preferred land use plan.

transportation nodes on the periphery and added density and mixed use at these nodes, and also suggested ways to better serve the denser corridors along the major arterials.

During the two intense years I spent working on this plan, I began to feel more confident in my role as a consultant. The client asked that I make the major public presentations, and Abe Krushkhov was happy to let me do that as he was not intimately involved with all the components of this complex study as I was. I found that, not only I was very effective in the formal presentations and quite successful with the public and interest groups who were involved in the planning process, but I also enjoyed being engaged with the community and the highly competent staff.

After exhaustive review by the City and citizen's groups, the plan was adopted in 1963, when Santa Ana had a population of around 130,000. Finally, a plan I had supervised was implemented without political interference! Our plan stayed in place until it was updated in 1982, when the population had grown to 224,000, just short of our projection of 246,000 for 1980-5. Those models had proven to be quite accurate. Later, in 2012 after another General Plan update in 1998, the population of Santa Ana had grown to 350,000 and it remains the largest city and county seat of Orange County.

*The San Francisco Downtown Zoning Study (1965-7)*

In 1965, recognizing my growth as a consultant on the Santa Ana Plan, I was given the role of Principal Planner for a study of great importance to Ruth + Krushkhov. We were named Resident Consultant for a study of San Francisco Downtown Zoning, along with Ladislas Segoe of Cincinnati (a pioneer in American zoning) as General Consultant, and Walter Bogner, (Professor Emeritus in Architecture at Harvard) as Design Consultant. Jim McCarthy was planning director for San Francisco at the time, and he put Peter Svirsky, a brilliant young lawyer-planner on his staff, in charge of the study. My role involved bringing the various consultants—and their various personalities and working methods—together during an accelerated yearlong process that required analysis, community input, new zoning proposals, reporting and community review. The city's desired result was the timely adoption of a completely modern zoning code for Downtown San Francisco.

The citywide zoning ordinance of 1921 was revised in 1960 without much study of Downtown San Francisco—not unusual in those days of obsessing about suburban development. As an expedient measure, they merely sanctioned a very large area around the existing downtown as one district, the 377 acre C-3 Zone, or Commercial Zone 3. Though it might be hard to fathom today, the land uses allowed at this time were the same for the entire downtown area, with no parking requirements and one very permissive control on the size of buildings. The San Francisco Board of Supervisors knew this ordinance did not make sense for the complex, multi-functional and varied topography of downtown. To avoid catastrophic development proposals that the current ordinance might foster on the Bay Area's most expensive real estate, the board ordered a new Downtown Plan in 1963, reduced allowable bulk in 1964, and in 1965 commissioned our study which allowed them to impose a temporary moratorium on downtown development. And that was the reason for the intense schedule: as we began the study, the stakes were high for all who were concerned.

FUNCTIONAL AREAS
DELINEATED IN THE
1963 DOWNTOWN GENERAL PLAN

Principal Downtown Areas
Other Areas

Boundary of Existing
Concentrated Core

Our first working paper published for public review covered goals and
issues, as well as identifying the different functional areas that comprised
downtown, the existing characteristics of space use and activities, and urban design aspects. Our study showed that, unsurprisingly, the present zoning did not make any sense. The Financial District with its high rises had the
same bulk regulations as the narrow streets of low rise Chinatown, the historic three story Jackson Square district, the Union Square retail district, the
Broadway entertainment district, and residential areas! In order to begin the
process of rezoning for these diverse districts, we used this document to subdivide the downtown zone into its respective functional areas. We also noted
that the rebuilding of the Municipal (Muni) light rail and the construction of

**Above** The plan shows downtown functional
areas that were used to create the new downtown
zoning districts.

45

**Above** The new zoning districts with their densities shown by color gradation, focusing on the financial district and the new transit. **Left** The five new BART transit stations on Market Street and their walking distances were used to create zoning density bonuses around the stations.

the Bay Area Rapid Transit (BART) subway, both of which were underway on Market Street at the edge of the C-3 District, would provide a whole new transportation capability and dramatically affect the type, location and intensity of land uses in these areas.

A major component of this stage was trying to accommodate the complex reality of downtown with bulk controls—not a "one size fits all" solution as had been in place, but not an endlessly customized one either. To accomplish this, we used Floor Area Ratio (FAR), a hallmark of modern zoning ordinances, to determine how much building space could be built on any one property. Floor Area Ratio is the amount of total building area relative to the amount of total building site area—in other words, it is a measure of a parcel's density. The ratio allows bulk and height to be controlled in a flexible and understandable way. For example: if a property was 10,000 square feet in size and had an FAR of 12:1, 120,000 square feet of building would be allowable, with the shape and height of the building varying to best suit the site. This might mean anything from a twelve-story building that met the property lines on all sides and had no setbacks, to a taller building that stepped back as it rose up from ground level.

The original 1960 C-3 District was assigned a uniform 20:1 FAR, with corner lots increased to 25:1. The Board of Supervisors had recently reduced that in 1964 to a uniform 16:1, with 20:1 on corner lots. What was startling to discover was that our studies showed that the densest block in Downtown San Francisco did not exceed a Floor Area Ratio of 13:1. Even the 1964 reduced ordinance allowed for all of the properties over the huge C-3 district to have a bulk ratio much in excess of the densest downtown core. This excessive FAR provision could potentially result in the "Manhattanization" of San Francisco, with huge new buildings allowed on locations as unsuitable as steep hillside streets, narrow streets or alleys, near public parks, near historic districts, or on the waterfront. In a city where hills and fog already cast dark shadows, and commercial blocks were interspersed with bustling residential and shopping districts like Chinatown, Union Square, Broadway, North Beach, this was dangerous indeed. Yes, intense density could be a good thing, but it needed to be limited to its proper place.

The second of our working papers studied zoning controls in major downtown areas across the country to determine how the provisions might be applied in San Francisco. We focused on how to develop an ordinance that reflected San Francisco's unique activity centers, space use, topography, sun and wind conditions, urban design, and transportation modes. After intensive consultation with the business and development community, we also did studies of development economics and devised ways to test zoning provisions with regard to their economic impact. We knew we would need the support of the business community if this were to have a timely adoption by the Board of Supervisors. We visited major downtown developers like Walter Shorenstein and others who had a great stake in the outcome of the study. We went a long way toward getting their support by assuring them we would review the economics and effectiveness of our proposals with them before making them final. They knew something had to be done to rationalize downtown zoning.

As expected after the findings of our first working paper, our second set of several different districts with varying FAR was a more appropriate model for Downtown San Francisco than one large district with a uniform FAR. With more diverse zoning, we could also better match intensity of development to the new reality of BART and Muni transit access: downtown San Francisco was a walking district, and we wanted to improve walkability by increasing access to public transit and increasing sidewalks. Where possible, parking was to be located on the periphery of downtown, in parking "belts" set on the perimeters of downtown and in the support areas near the Freeways where larger garages could be built. Large public garages had been built to support the Union Square retail district and Chinatown. Moreover, though newer buildings were requesting substantial on-site parking (parking had not been required in the original zoning code), we felt strongly that parking should be limited in the new core districts In this way, we could fully utilize the excellent new transit infrastructure that was being built and reduce congestion on the limited street network. The new code set stringent limits on the amount of accessory parking that would be allowed in buildings in the core of downtown—providing only for critical service and business needs. In the core districts, parking garages would be by conditional permit only and would be limited or outlawed in congested areas.

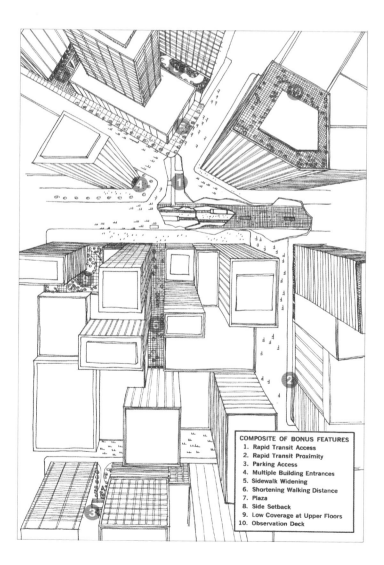

**COMPOSITE OF BONUS FEATURES**
1. Rapid Transit Access
2. Rapid Transit Proximity
3. Parking Access
4. Multiple Building Entrances
5. Sidewalk Widening
6. Shortening Walking Distance
7. Plaza
8. Side Setback
9. Low Coverage at Upper Floors
10. Observation Deck

**Right** The sketch shows the 10 bonuses available in the new zoning to promote public benefits in new development.

To accomplish many of these land use and transportation goals, we recommended using a set of basic FAR bulk limits tailored to each downtown district and then allowing additional square footage of buildings only for specified public benefits. Each district would have a maximum FAR including all bonuses. Development bonuses like these were first devised in the New York City ordinance, and allowed cities to give a developer more floor area in return for specific design elements that provided public benefits to the city. We carefully evaluated how successfully the New York ordinance bonuses worked and how well they might work in San Francisco. We also saw the opportunity to shape new bonuses unique to San Francisco's need. We proposed 10 bonuses for enhanced transit access, parking on the perimeter of downtown, sidewalk widening and new plazas, shaping building to increase air and sunshine and new observation decks. Bonuses were not enough to protect downtown's existing public squares and historic districts so special height and historic districts were set around them to protect their character, sunlight, air and particularly in San Francisco, their direct sunshine.

To test the viability of these incentives, we set up a special evaluation of each potential bonus provision with a respected economic consultant: Development Research Associates. They helped us by ascertaining ways to measure whether a private developer would find that a particular bonus made economic sense as well as improving the project. When we had established these basic zoning provisions, we then revisited recent projects and a few that were in the pipeline to make sure that they could be done under the new provisions. We followed through as we had promised with the business and political decision makers—that the new ordinance would work.

In addition to defining new sub-districts within the downtown core, our study recommended expanding the downtown to include areas south of Market Street as well as north of Market (where they were concentrated in the old ordinance) that would be connected via the new BART and Muni subway. As proposed in the 1963 Downtown Plan, Market Street would finally be realized as the new "spine" of downtown. This would also pave the way for moving higher-density development off the steep hills and into the flatlands south of Market. Now, the 101 Freeway and Bay Bridge access ramps became the new southern border of downtown.

In December, 1966 we published our final report that reconfigured the existing C-3 District into four commercial and two new residential districts with the range of allowable FARs ranging from 14 to 24 with bonuses in the compact financial core to 7 to 12 with bonuses in the south of Market support district. The Zoning Study was adopted a year later in 1967, and the ordinance was rewritten and adopted soon afterward. In subsequent years the ordinance had additions and refinements, but the basic premise of reconfiguring the monolithic C-3 district into a series of smaller districts that reflected the variable character of downtown San Francisco remains, as does the general structure of districts and the use of bonuses to provide workable densities and amenities for light and air and walkability. This historic study left behind a legacy of encouraging growth suitable for Downtown San Francisco, increasing walkability and access to transit, creating new public plazas and street amenities, promoting better building design, protecting unique and historical areas, and reducing the impact of the automobile that continues today.

## Why I Chose The Transition to Landscape Architecture (1967)

A year after heading west to California, it was in Berkeley, living right near the University of California campus, that we started to recognize that the San Francisco Bay Area would become our permanent home. The work was exciting and Berkeley itself was equally exciting as the Free Speech movement was going on right near us. From the R+K office on Telegraph Avenue we could walk to the campus at lunchtime to hear Mario Savio speak. We loved going into San Francisco with the family, taking trips to Monterey and Lake Tahoe, and staying with friends in the Napa Valley. By 1967 I was established as a planning consultant, but I still felt I was not where I could do my best work. I missed being able to use my architectural training, and now that I better understood City Planning and to some degree Urban Design, I became anxious to move beyond planning and get to designing and building places.

During my time on the San Francisco Zoning Study, I had the opportunity to work with Peter Walker and Dick Law of Sasaki, Walker Associates, as Herman Ruth had a close relationship with Pete. I remembered Pete from his association with Hideo Sasaki at Harvard, as they started Sasaki, Walker Associates in nearby Watertown while I was a student there. I had come to appreciate the approach this fine firm had established, integrating planning and urban design within its landscape architectural practice in the building of cities and places. And so, though I had studied and practiced architecture, city planning and civil engineering, it was with Landscape Architects that I found the practice that put all of these so effectively together.

In a somewhat serendipitous confluence, my long education, personal background, and professional experience over eight years of practice since graduate school jointly pointed me toward landscape architecture. Beginning with a love of the big city and the garden city that was instilled during my childhood in New York and Coral Gables, through high school years that introduced me to architecture and gave me the desire to work at the intersection of science and art, to college and architecture school in Florida, Navy construction experience in Charleston, graduate school in planning at Harvard, and finally my time as a public and consultant planner, it seemed like my combined experience was almost singularly suited to landscape architecture.

Growing up in a Bronx tenement, I understood what it meant to go to the Bronx Zoo and Botanic Garden as a child. Before I knew who Frederic Law Olmsted was, and before I knew what that founder of American landscape architecture believed about the civic and social purposes of Central Park, I rode my delivery bike through the park in the evenings and understood what made New York so livable.

When I moved to Coral Gables, I found that I also loved living in this garden suburb that was itself a reflection of Olmsted's work at Riverside and elsewhere, not to mention influenced by the American "City Beautiful" movement as well as the English "Garden City" movement. Both New York and Coral Gables were uniquely American, one built on the technology of the skyscraper and subway, the other built on the technology of the automobile and trolley.

My studies at Florida introduced me to Frank Lloyd Wright, the other American genius who deeply influenced me with both his "Organic Architecture," which emphasized design with nature, and with his plan for Broadacre City, which embodied the spirit of American individualism

50

through its embrace of the single family home and the farmstead. Olmsted and Wright were my earliest heroes.

Charleston, where I spent my brief Navy career, immersed me in the European roots of our American towns and villages with its common use of the riverfront and a delightful integration of architecture and gardens that clearly expressed its unique natural environment. I was reminded of this European influence during my 1961 honeymoon "grand" tour with Janne, during which we visited London, Paris, Amsterdam, Copenhagen, Munich, Zurich and finally to Milan, finishing with a drive through Italy to Rome. One could really see how the public realm of streets, parks, waterfronts and civic places worked with each city's unique architectural vocabulary to make them great. I wanted to participate in the creation of that public realm, and came to realize that landscape architecture was where it happened.

More recently, living in the San Francisco Bay Area had accentuated how wonderful the contrast between urban environments and their natural settings could be. San Francisco gloriously spilling over the hills between the contained bay and limitless ocean, the Golden Gate Bridge connecting the sparkling "white city" to the green headlands of Marin, the Bay Bridge connecting to the fog cooled Berkeley Hills and through the tunnels to the hot valleys. It is no wonder that this was the center of the ascendance of the environmental movement in the 1960's.

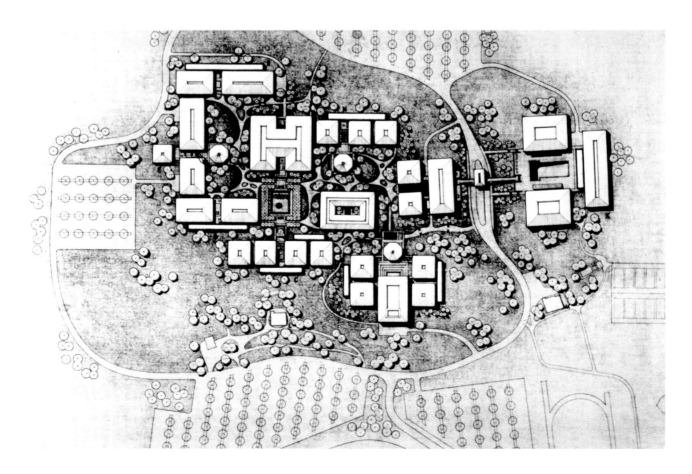

This led me to remember that landscape architecture, the design profession that brings nature and culture together, had originally been the home of city planning in academia. The strong ties between physical city planning, urban design and landscape architecture had once existed at Harvard, having evolved from the practice and teaching of Fredrick Law Olmsted Jr. Something had been lost when physical planning, the translation of policies and politics into the essentials of the natural and built environment, first became secondary to policy and politics, and then disappeared entirely from the curricula. In fact, as a graduate of both the School of Design and the School of Government at Harvard, I saw firsthand the tensions between planning, design and policy. After seeing how mired in policy and bureaucracy planning could be in academia, I was determined to seek out the physical relationships between urban design and the public realm in the real world.

Also, even though my work at Ruth + Krushkhov gave me experience and confidence in my abilities as a planning consultant on various kinds of public work, it was apparent that the planning and the building of American cities in the 20th century involved both public and private enterprise, with the private sector leading the way in many cases. City building was an economic, environmental, sociopolitical and physical process. I realized that none of the physical design professions, whether architecture (including architect/planners and architect/urban designers), engineers or government or consulting planners put together the key elements of building places in cities as well as landscape architects. Landscape architects, unlike the others, embodied an environmental approach to the planning and design of the public realm in cities and communities. They also took leading roles in campus planning, not only for educational institutions but for the complex groups of buildings and facilities for employees that new business typologies brought to the information economy. As a planner, I saw how this could make enormous differences in how people lived in urban places.

Landscape architects also had a scope of work that was far broader than other professions. They worked for the private and public sectors (and sometimes both!), on both large and small projects in urban, suburban, rural and open space contexts. I wanted to expand my role to include the private as well as public sectors and working with landscape architects would open that opportunity to me. The public realm of streets, public buildings and works, parks, waterfronts, open space reserves and conservation areas was expanding via the construction of large and complex private developments that created substantial public use and open spaces on private land to meet city criteria or enhance their amenities for people in those developments. Though not understood well by the public, landscape architecture went far beyond the soft elements of plantings and trees and included the planning and design of hard elements including sidewalks, plazas, and vehicular pavements, walls, steps, fences, shelters, fountains, outdoor furnishings for seating, lighting and orientation all within the public realm.

This was powerful community building, and landscape architects were taking the lead. From contextual master planning to site planning to site design, all the while working closely with the architects, engineers and contractors, landscape architects really did design "everything outside the buildings." This kind of site land based design involved not only the design of the spaces but working closely with the architects it set how the entire site would be configured including the arrangement, grades and even configuration of the

buildings. Most importantly, landscape architects recognized that the spaces between and outside buildings could become as important or even more important in creating a sense of place and making cities more livable than the buildings themselves.

Having come to this realization, I saw that no landscape architects merged physical planning  urban design and built work in both the public realm and private sectors as well as Sasaki, Walker Associates. This firm had revitalized the stodgy landscape profession, which had moved away from Olmsted's pioneering private sector work since the depression and the world wars, taking refuge in public work instead. This aversion to private development work even continued into the boom years of the 1950's and 60's. Sasaki, Walker Associates brought the great potential of the profession back into its historic and rightful role as a central player in physical planning and the design of cities, communities and places, in both the resurgent private sector *and* the public sector. They sought out architects and developers and businesses that shared their passion for good planning and responsible development increasingly through public/private partnerships, and worked with non-profit conservancies, and environmental and citizen organizations.

To put it simply, Sasaki, Walker Associates was where I wanted to be. So I walked over and talked to Pete Walker at his house near mine in the Berkeley Hills, and joined the firm in August 1967. I had finally found the right place to do my life's work.

**Opposite Page** The upper plaza gardens, built over parking garages served office workers and residents at the Golden Gateway in San Francisco. **Above** The lower Crocker Plaza has shops and restaurants and leads to an underground transit station. **Bottom Left** The street level Crocker

Plaza ornamental steps and fence are places for lunch breaks and people watching. **Bottom Right** The multi level Crocker Plaza is at a key intersection of downtown San Francisco and was designed to fit into the new Market Street improvements.

**Page 56-57** The 20 acre Golden Gateway redevelopment in downtown San Francisco added office and residential towers as well as low rise residential, retail and publicly accessible private parks and plazas.

58

**Opposite Page Top** Sidney Walton Park in the Golden Gateway became a favorite green oasis for downtown workers and residents in San Francisco. **Bottom Left** Residents had a community club as well as shopping and employment centers within the Regency community.

**Above** Regency was a large mixed use residential and commercial community, added to the perimeter of the City of Omaha at the new freeway interchange.

# 3

# Planning, designing and building cities, communities and places at Sasaki, Walker Associates

## 1967–1974

Sasaki, Walker was the perfect place for me to finally use my whole education and experience. Pete Walker had assembled a talented and highly motivated team of professionals. He ran the office as a design studio, where he was the lead designer on each project. He was then supported by key Associates , including planners like me and Ed Kagi, project managers like Gary Karner, designers like Dick Law, George Omi on production of working drawings, and Gene Rosenberg on field operations. It was an exciting place to work.

Because of my professional experience, I was immediately involved in a variety of projects. This was in sharp contrast to my experience in planning consulting, where one focused for a long time on a single project. I began to learn how to fit in and work with the designers, production and field people. My analytical skills in land developability from my previous work were immediately useful in studying alternative massing schemes for the Weyerhaeuser Headquarters building near the Seattle-Tacoma Airport to see how well they fit upon and impacted the wooded site. I much enjoyed being able to provide technical drawings and studies supporting the site-sensitive design by Pete and Chuck Bassett of SOM that was eventually selected and built.

On urban or downtown projects, I called upon my training and experience in the three "P's": Politics, Planning and the Public Interest. On public projects, I would perform outreach to public interest groups in our plans and designs. On private development projects, I used my previous studies of market-driven development economics to explain the value-added content of our plans and designs to our clients. The designers liked this kind of support, and appreciated my help in explaining and getting approvals from our clients or public entitlements as well as in managing the projects. In return, I liked the fact that they encouraged me to add my ideas during our intense design and planning charettes.

Not having formal training in landscape architecture, I found I shared a lot with my new colleagues. Like them, I looked to the site to give me clues about how it should be transformed following Wright's Organic Architecture concepts. I found the site visits stimulating and could not wait to see the ideas come out on paper. I was comfortable having my architectural and city planning training and experience enhanced by this site specific and natural systems approach. By performing careful site analysis and building an understanding of natural systems, the landscape architects could achieve development goals without destroying the integrity of the site.

Unlike architects and engineers who might cause unnecessary or awkward site grading and vegetation removal for a new development, the landscape architects would locate homes or businesses to retain the site's natural character, or cluster buildings, leaving pristine stands of native oaks, streams, woodlands or wetlands to be enjoyed by people. These professionals could make streets into greenways and link together private and public open spaces to make breathing spaces for people in dense urban places. It was a very effective way to better design cities, communities and places. Given my training in architecture, I also enjoyed working closely with architects as clients and collaborators. Even my Navy experience in contract and construction supervision helped me work closely with our field people in getting the projects built.

Because of my ability to be involved in all project stages, I was quickly promoted to Associate in 1968. In 1969, having arrived there at a propitious time, I was added to the five key Associates (aforementioned) as we six were then named the first Principals other than Pete Walker of the San Francisco

Illustrated on pages 60-63 are projects I contributed to soon after joining Sasaki, Walker Associates.

**Opposite Page** The linear park ran several miles in Albany and El Cerrito, California under the new elevated Bay Area Rapid Transit tracks.

**Above** The linear park had pedestrian trail connections to the residential communities as well as to the El Cerrito BART station.

office of Sasaki, Walker Associates. Around then, we needed more space, as our Commercial Street office in San Francisco was now quite cramped. Gary Karner, who lived in Marin County, found an interesting building in the old shipyard in Sausalito located just across the Golden Gate Bridge from the city. Pete became interested in the offbeat character of this area, with its fancy sailboats and beat-up old houseboats. And so at that time, he asked Mike Gilbert to join our firm as a business consultant, but also to help us look into buying our offices. Mike quickly found a good way to make the deal work, and we took the leap of leaving the City for Sausalito, where we still are to this day. Pete moved to Tiburon, not far from Sausalito, and most of us soon followed him to Marin County. My family moved to Mill Valley, right next to Sausalito, where our children grew up and where we still live today. We love the place!

## Future Urban Transportation Systems (1967-8)

In 1967, a few months after I joined Sasaki, Walker Associates, we were asked by the Stanford Research Institute to work on a pioneering study for the U.S. Department of Housing and Urban Development (HUD). In 1966 the U.S. Congress asked for this research as part of the Mass Transit Act to see how these mass transportation systems could improve American cities, reduce pollution and costs, and increase access to a larger segment of the population. SRI had carried the transportation systems study through economic, technological and engineering phases, but needed outside help to evaluate these prototype transportation systems for their impact on future urban life and form. That's where we came in. Our team worked closely with two architects, Don Crosby of Crosby, Thornton, Hill; and Scott Danielson of John Carl Warnecke. Our areas of study covered four transportation levels and technologies:

1. Extended Area Travel that would provide fast links between metropolitan areas. These Fast Transit Links or FTL would be equal to or faster than modern-day High Speed Rail as seen in places like Europe, Japan and now China.

2. Area-Wide Networks or NET systems for use in relatively longer trips within metropolitan areas,. These systems would consist of automatic vehicles on guideways with stations at major urban activity centers and transportation nodes. They would be more flexible than current heavy or light rail systems, and much faster than commuter buses on HOV lanes.

3. Public Automobile or PAS feeder and local distribution systems, for local area travel or to serve lower density areas. These would include small electric vehicles that could run automatically without drivers in caravans on guideways, with some of them able to be removed from the caravan at stations, so that a driver could take them short distances on city streets. The PAS vehicles could then be returned to the guideways at stations and re-linked into the caravans once more. The alternative would be shared cars available at NET stations, which could be returned to curbside stands or designated parking lots throughout the neighborhood or district. Another alternative PAS would be "Dial-a-Bus." This was a futuristic technology at that time, though the concept seems quite realizable now with the advent of smartphones sensors and GPS systems. Many of the schemes imagined at the time are actually

**Above** The pool area at Cedar Riverside was one of the shared community facilities.
**Bottom** Cedar Riverside in Minneapolis adjacent to the University of Minnesota was a "New Town in Town" redevelopment focused on student and faculty housing, retail and community facilities.

**Opposite Page** The formal visitor entry to the Weyerhaeuser headquarters emphasized the company's roots in forestry and care for the environment. **Bottom Right** Weyerhaeuser world headquarters in Tacoma, Washington was a "high rise set on its side" with planted tiered terraces, a forest setting and a reflecting lake.

under development now: self-regulating spacing of autos or driverless cars and many types of car sharing with remote payment systems have already appeared in our cities.

4. Major Activity Center or MAC systems, for moving people around high activity or high density mixed use centers. These would be electric "people movers," or airport-style trains, monorails, moving sidewalks, and a specific form of PAS-type small share vehicles

Our studies first applied these systems to hypothetical metropolitan and city areas, using plans, diagrams, sketches and design guidelines to link the systems together and integrate them into the cities. The Fast Transit Link systems would connect different metropolitan areas to one another as well as interconnecting each area's major city centers, future New Towns, and major airports by creating large central transportation hubs that included links to NET stations, and MAC systems.

The stations built along the area-wide or NET systems, which would be sited at major civic, institutional, medical, retail, commercial, entertainment and business centers, would spur Transit Oriented Development (TOD), higher-density development that would include a mix of residential, commercial, and recreational uses. These NET stations would also serve as connection points for other types of transit such as PAS, and more traditional modes such as buses and bicycles. Depending on the density of development around NET stations, different types of transit links would be provided.

Figure 21

VIEW FROM MAC VEHICLE OF MALL ACTIVITIES IN METROPOLITAN CORE

Figure 22

TRANSIT-ORIENTED DEVELOPMENT OPPORTUNITIES IN THE INNER CITY

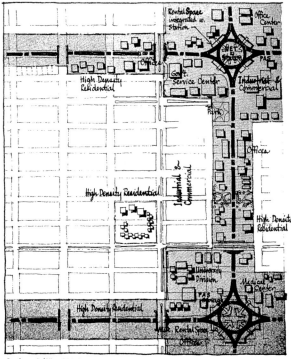

The plan diagram in Figure 22 indicates how the NET system might serve this portion of the metropolitan city and encourage its redevelopment. A grid of NET service with stations less than a mile apart would serve much of this area. Pedestrian activity would be a major means of

Scale    3/4" = 500 feet

The sketch in Figure 24 depicts a station-interchange complex from the viewpoint of a traveler on the NET system. The two center NET guideways are shown entering and leaving the station at subgrade, while the outer guideways are shown elevated as part of the interchange function. The station itself is at the center surrounded by buildings of various ages and character.

PAS and Dial-a-Bus services are provided to fill this need. Curbside PAS stands are provided throughout the neighborhood at several block intervals, and PAS storage is provided near the NET station. Figure 27 shows PAS, Dial-a-Bus, and pedestrian access to NET at a station. The NET cars passing overhead in the illustration are making turns on the interchange, which is incorporated with the station.

Figure 24

NET INTERCHANGE, STATION, AND GUIDEWAY WITH
INNER CITY DEVELOPMENT

Figure 27

NET STATION WITH TRANSFERS TO LOCAL AREA TRAVEL MODES

The Public Automobile Systems (PAS) would serve lower density nodes and neighborhoods and would be available at most NET stations, while the Major Activity Center (MAC) systems would only be used in the most intensely developed Metropolitan Centers, and at major facilities such as airports, sports venues, downtowns, regional commercial and entertainment centers.

Our conclusions from this transportation study found that these innovative systems would be able to create new development opportunities for cities, especially when linked together in a web that connected lower-density suburbs to higher-density urban nodes. By adding these four new mass transit typologies to the automobile-dominated roads and highways that proliferated in the 1960s, inner cities could be more effectively planned with appropriate densities, types of development, and transportation assets in order to reduce pollution and energy use and increase access to a larger segment of the population. Moreover, this broader range of transit facilities would enable more sustainable, higher-density Transit Oriented Developments in urban cores and inner-ring suburbs, providing a mid-scale buffer to connect to the auto-centric, lower-density outer suburbs.

Unfortunately, when the study was presented to Congress in 1968, it came up against the powerful oil and automobile lobbies who insisted that more and better transit was not needed in metropolitan America. These lobbyists instead promoted automobile and bus transit only, touting it as cost effective since it used the road infrastructure and the then cheap gasoline. As a result of this pivotal decision, much of today's development proceeded to be constructed without adequate transit, resulting in irreversible atmospheric pollution that only becomes magnified as global temperatures rise and inefficient as gas prices soar exponentially. Sadly, HUD and Congress lost an opportunity to make America a global model for sustainability and urban innovation, and now we face the high costs and difficulty of retrofitting our cities for more sustainable transportation and land use systems.

## The Kohala Coast Resort, Hawaii (1967-9)

After working on the theoretical Future Transportation Study I made a dramatic shift in work. These shifts were a characteristic of the practice at Sasaki Walker Associates that I really liked. Having to think about many new places, clients, and kinds of planning in quick succession kept you sharp. This time, we were retained to work on a 3800-acre property around the existing Mauna Kea luxury hotel on the Kohala Coast of the Big Island of Hawaii. The clients were an interesting combination that included Dillingham, a Hawaiian heavy construction contractor, Laurance Rockefeller's Olohana and Rockresorts Corporations, which had developed and operated the Mauna Kea, and Eastern Airlines, which had recently filed with the FAA for routes to Hawaii from the mainland. The client was thus named Dilrock-Eastern, a portmanteau of each of the company's names.

On our team, we had a local planning firm, Belt Collins of Honolulu, and a hotel architect, William Tabler of New York. The year was 1967, and at that time Pete Walker and I were intensely interested in the newly available resources and techniques that were coming out of the growing environmental movement in the form of a growing number of natural scientists who were concerned about land use and development issues. Drawing upon the firm's

**Opposite Page Top Left** This view is from a Major Activity Center (MAC) elevated people mover in a downtown area. **Top Right** This plan shows Transit Oriented Development opportunities of the proposed public transportation systems, three decades before TOD became a popular concept. **Bottom Left** This sketch shows the Area-Wide Network (NET) system guideway in the inner city. **Bottom Right** The sketch is at a NET station with transfers to dial a bus and personal area transportation (PAS) electric cars.

longstanding reliance on site analysis, these natural scientists working with our young professionals at SWA like Ray Belknap and John Furtado were applying watershed and biological analysis and planning to sensitive sites like the forested Weyerhauser Headquarters site near Tacoma, Washington, but the Kohala site seemed like the perfect place to study these methods at a larger scale.

The Kohala Coast was particularly sensitive to flash flooding even though it was in a semi-arid climate, as tradewind-induced tropical storms would hit the mountains high above the site and produce torrential flows through the steep, dry gulches. These floodwaters moved so quickly and with so much volume that they would destroy anything in their path down to the ocean. The ranchers who worked the site when it was part of the historic Parker Ranch understood this, but they only had to concern themselves with cattle. The prospect of bringing throngs of people to enjoy the relatively rain-free climate with its salubrious sunshine, however, raised serious issues. To begin to tackle these issues, we knew we first had to address watersheds, so our studies divided the site into land units bordered by the drainage channels. Rather than trying to defeat the natural systems, the approach was to work with them. We studied each unit's soils, geology, drainage, vegetation, slopes and orientation to try to get a full understanding of how different areas reacted to both wet and dry conditions.

We put all the information about each land unit together to analyze the site of the new hotel to be built at Hapuna Beach, just down the coast from the Mauna Kea hotel. Hapuna Beach was a beautiful swimming beach, but the gulch running down the mountain to the beach would empty onto the hotel site. While not as large as the Waiulaula Gulch, which ran through the middle of the entire Kohala site, the Hapuna Gulch still presented a formidable engineering challenge. We were concerned about the safe use of this site for a large hotel, yet the architect insisted that the hotel should still be built in this location.

In those days Mainlanders were led to believe by the media that Hawaii was a "green jungle paradise" throughout, and the resorts felt they had to reinforce this widely held view even though the actual environment and climate were much more variable. At the Kohala Coast, for instance, recent lava flows produced dry rocky soils, and the trade winds flowing against the huge volcanoes Mauna Kea and Mauna Loa controlled rainfall to create an arid, desert-like climate. True, the area had abundant sunshine, beautiful beaches and

mountains, but not nearly enough rain to make it fit preconceived notions of a tropical paradise. Meanwhile, areas higher up on the mountains or on the rainy side of the island were lush and green, but far wetter than tourists desired. Thus, the resorts sought to create a happy medium, even though it was somewhat at odds with the true microclimates on the island.

The golf course around the Mauna Kea hotel cost a fortune to build and given the dry climate, maintaining the green fairways was equally expensive. The internationally famous golf course architect, Robert Trent Jones, Sr., who designed the original course, told us how the construction had required grinding tons of rock on site to create soil for the fairways and expensive irrigation systems to maintain them. The changes in soil and water also meant that native plants such as the magnificent Kiawe trees and other groundcovers, shrubs and trees, which flourished in the dry rocky soils on the site required adjustments to fit the jungle aesthetic. These plants were striking in their own way and fit well into the ecology, but were not what the "paradise hungry clientele" expected to see.

We were working with a much larger site than the golf course, however, and as such would not have the luxury of creating new soils and water sources for the 3800-acre resort and its variety of residential villages, hotels, commercial areas and employee housing as well as luxury home sites. In any case, we sought to demonstrate a more environmentally responsible and economically practical approach, beginning with the Fairway Homes sites that were to be built adjacent to the Mauna Kea golf course as the first phase of the resort. Our goal was to have green gardens for the homes but to limit their extent and integrate them into the overall native landscape.

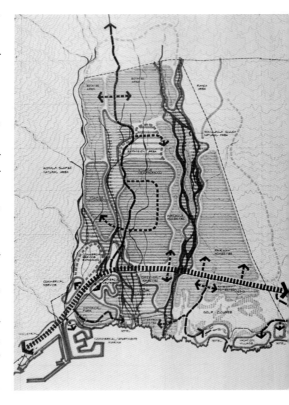

**Opposite Page** The Mauna Kea Beach Hotel on the Kohala Coast of Hawaii with the golf course and Fairway homes beyond.

**Above** The Plan shows the Kohala Coast in Hawaii at the Mauna Kea Hotel and the surrounding Parker Ranch, indicating how new development would relate to key environmental drainage corridors.
**Left** This illustrates concepts for the Fairway Homes project built around the Mauna Kea Hotel golf course showing limited building envelopes within each large lot for houses and irrigated exotic plantings, and the remaining larger areas of the lots in native and non irrigated plantings.

To do this we defined a series of home sites on the rocky outcrops around the course, siting each site to ensure great views to the horseshoe beach and bay below the Hotel. For each large home site, we defined smaller envelopes of land immediately around the home that could be irrigated and lushly planted with exotic plants. This left the vast majority of the home sites to be planted using the native palette, which did not require long-term irrigation. This simple move allowed homeowners to have their green gardens close by, while easing the transition to the natural ecology and hopefully, instilling an understanding of the unique beauty of the area's natural environment. We believed that these kinds of small steps could eventually promote an appreciation of sustainable principles and the true character of this special part of Hawaii.

Unfortunately the Kohala Resort did not move forward on the scale intended by the three-client partnership. Eastern Airlines did not get the routes to Hawaii, which were tightly controlled in those days, and the partnership dissolved. However, the Fairway Homes were built following our design guidelines with much success and acceptance by the homeowners. Instead of the large new hotel at Hapuna Beach, modest additions were built for the Mauna Kea close to the main hotel and it became a Prince hotel.

In the ensuing years, new developers built a Hapuna Beach Prince Resort not at the gulch where our architect wanted it, but at the extreme edge of Hapuna Bay. This change occurred for two reasons. First, a large storm occurred on an otherwise sunny day at the Mauna Kea Hotel, and flash floods racing down the gullies washed out large parts of the main access highway to Kona and seriously damaged hotel support facilities and parts of the golf course. The Mauna Kea itself was not severely damaged as it was away from the major gulches, but the storm still served as a reminder that building a hotel across one of these gullies was not a good idea. Second, there were few sandy swimming beaches along the rocky Kohala Coast. The Mauna Kea laid claim to one and the Hapuna Hotel would have dominated the other, which was much larger. To conserve public access to these beaches, the state and county insisted that Hapuna Beach become a public beach with direct access rather than the indirect access that existed to the Mauna Kea beach. Fortunately these circumstances contributed to a solution that was much better both socially and environmentally, as they preserved a valuable amenity to be enjoyed safely for many generations to come.

## Oakland City Center, Oakland, California (1972)

By the early 1970s, I had been made a Principal at Sasaki Walker, along with five other Associates at the west coast office, and as one of firm's planning specialists, I quickly became involved in a series of HUD (US Department of Housing and Urban Development) Urban Design projects. We had previously worked with HUD on the future mass transportation systems project with Stanford Research Institute, and I had also assisted Pete Walker in a HUD demonstration study of the Bay Area Rapid Transit Linear Park under an elevated guideway in Albany and El Cerrito. In San Francisco we worked on creating the Buchanan Street pedestrian mall in a HUD redevelopment project, and in 1970 at Cedar Riverside we worked on a HUD "New Town in Town" redevelopment project in Minneapolis. So it is safe to say that by the time the Oakland project came around in 1972, we were familiar with the way HUD worked.

Opposite Page The mid level plaza and fountain at Oakland City Center are always popular at lunch time. Bottom This plan shows the first phase of the Oakland City Center with the Clorox and Wells Fargo Buildings along Broadway and the plazas and entry to the City Center BART station below. The shopping center later became a mixed use government, office and commercial development.

The Oakland City Center project was HUD-sponsored for the Oakland Redevelopment Agency under the direction of John Williams, its dynamic director. We worked with Cesar Pelli of Gruen Associates, Architects and with Hal Ellis of Grubb and Ellis, developers for the first commercial portions of this mixed-use project. At that time, the Bay Area Rapid Transit (BART) lines were under construction and the City Center station was the hub of the San Francisco and East Bay lines. This project brought to bear much of my previous experience in downtown planning and transportation systems, especially with regard to the connections between land use and transportation in cities.

I worked with Pete and Dick Law to prepare urban design studies that would place this City Center project within the context of downtown Oakland and in particular the main street, Broadway. Much like Richmond, downtown Oakland had become rundown in recent decades and there was an economic and social stigma to the site. Newer development such as the Kaiser Center had migrated north toward Lake Merritt and the better neighborhoods at Grand Avenue. Our studies emphasized the City Center project as the beginning of a reinvigorated Broadway from Lake Merritt to Jack London Square.

Our firm had recently ramped up its photography and print graphics capabilities by acquiring The Gnu Group and we took advantage of these capabilities to communicate our urban design ideas to a public audience through bold graphic posters widely distributed and covered in the press. I leaned on my experience in the public sector to couple these graphic communications with clear and persuasive public presentations to move our work toward understanding and approval. For these presentations, Pete and I would work as a team. I would lead with a two-projector slide presentation while he would watch for audience reactions. He would then provide additional comments and answers to questions after I had finished.

We took care to emphasize the City Center's location along the most important BART hub station, 12th Street, Oakland City Center, as well as its nearby freeway access and position as the center point of the mile-long Broadway strip in downtown Oakland. This strip connected the popular Jack London Square on the Oakland Estuary to the Kaiser Center and Lake

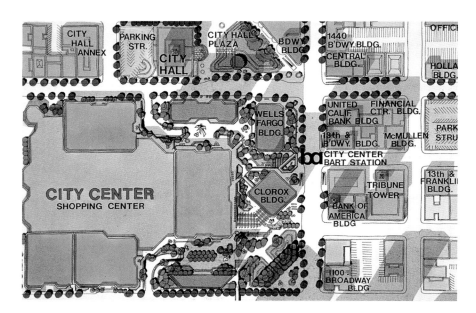

Merritt. The City Center could not have had a better location than the "100% corner" of Broadway and 14th Street, which was the east-west link between the site of City Hall and City Hall Plaza to the west and the Alameda County administrative buildings and the Oakland Public Library to the east. In addition to the BART hub, the site was also a hub for many AC Transit bus lines, which radiated out to the rest of the city at street level. We saw the City Center as having the potential to singlehandedly catalyze the revitalization of Downtown Oakland.

Once the overall plan received support, we complemented Pelli's architecture with landscape that would provide a striking new image for this part of Broadway: we widened sidewalks to become brick plazas at street level and designed a lower-level brick plaza with sculptures and supergraphics that connected directly into the City Center BART station mezzanine. I worked directly with the BART engineers to design the access port into the underground station structure, and we added elevators, escalators and stairs to provide access to all levels. These hardscape elements were complemented by waterfall fountains and trees placed at the different levels to soften the impact of the city and create a lush pedestrian respite in the middle of downtown Oakland. The foliage also served to create visual continuity between the upper and lower levels to draw them down to the lower level's restaurants and shops.

Our efforts at City Center spurred a new energy along Broadway that included the opening of the Clorox Headquarters and Wells Fargo office buildings along with plans for major commercial development extending deep into the site. Over the years, while the shopping center was not built, the project has grown to include a robust mix of office, shopping and other commercial uses, a major Federal Building complex, and even several private universities. Today, it is a vital part of Oakland's downtown, keeping convention facilities, hotels and residences full and significantly contributing to the renewed vibrancy of the urban core.

## The Central Ranch Plan and the Village of Woodbridge, Irvine, California (1972)

Working with Pete was exciting, as he was always quick to come up with big ideas that we new Principals could take and develop into plans and designs. He also genuinely encouraged us to offer up our own ideas, however, and I soon gained confidence to fully participate in Pete's idea rich process he used to move from idea to plan to design and then to built landscapes.

One project on which we had the opportunity to practice this approach was the prototypical community of Woodbridge, in Irvine, California, for our long time client The Irvine Company. Sasaki, Walker Associates had worked on the Ranch at Fashion Island in the Newport Center nearby, and I was involved at the University Park Community bordering the Central Ranch, so we were quite familiar with the area. Ray Watson, the Irvine Company's Vice President for Planning and soon to be the new Ranch President, asked us to first provide an overview study of the entire 20,000 acre Central Ranch with the goal of deciding where the first new community should be built. Then we were to provide a development plan for this first village. Pete asked me to join him on this assignment and to manage this complex community planning and design project.

**Opposite Page** Coming from the office uses in the center of the site to the mid level plazas and looking toward Broadway in the Oakland City Center. **Bottom** Looking out from the BART station mezzanine to the water stair fountain and mid level plazas of City Center.

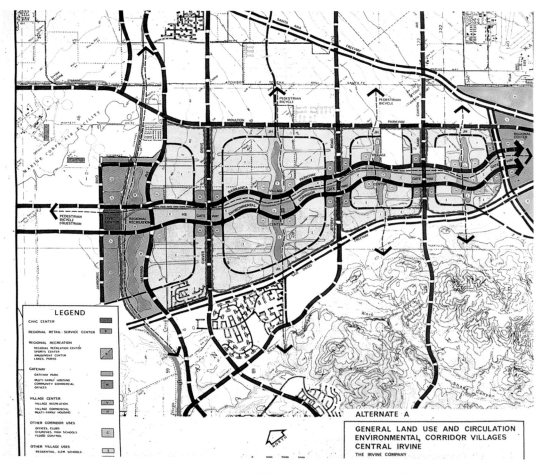

ALTERNATE A

GENERAL LAND USE AND CIRCULATION
ENVIRONMENTAL CORRIDOR VILLAGES
CENTRAL IRVINE
THE IRVINE COMPANY

**Above** The plan for the central Irvine Ranch was a series of four villages running along the new San Diego Freeway with an environmental corridor and parkways at their center that connected to regional commercial centers on the west and east ends. The largest village was built first and became Woodbridge. **Bottom** The illustrative plan for Woodbridge shows the central corridor, the two lakes and the loop road that connects the varied neighborhoods.

**Opposite Page** Steps and fountain at the Woodbridge lake edge where it meets one of the parkways along the corridor. **Bottom Right** A view of the upper lake at Woodbridge showing the recreation center, pedestrian bridge and several neighborhoods.

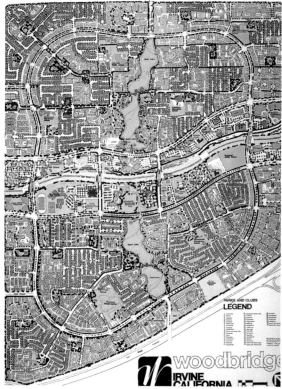

PARKS AND CLUBS
LEGEND

woodbridge
IRVINE CALIFORNIA

The master plan for The Irvine Company's 88,000-acre Irvine Ranch properties had begun development in the coastal sector of the ranch around Newport Center in the City of Newport Beach, including the new University of California campus at Irvine. In the early 1970's, the company began the process of expanding the development to the large agricultural areas of the Central Ranch. This was an attempt to broaden the housing market and also to take advantage of the construction of the new Interstate 405 San Diego Freeway, which increased access to the part of the ranch between the 405 and the older Interstate 5 Santa Ana Freeway.

The team of Pete, Dick Law, Jim Reeves, and myself considered the regional scale first. At the western end of the Central Ranch was the City of Tustin and the Tustin Air Base, while the southern portion of the ranch to the south of the base, contained existing business and industrial areas that were planned for expansion. The east end of the Central Ranch was a large triangular section formed by the merger of the I-5 and I-405 freeways and the interchange with the Laguna Canyon Freeway, and given all of this adjacent vehicular access, it was well suited for a major regional commercial center.

Our plan for the Central Ranch therefore, was a series of residential villages between the I-5 and I-405 freeways with the industrial and business parks to the west and southwest and the potential regional commercial center in the east.. Connecting these villages to the jobs and commercial centers would be an east-west "activity corridor" formed by two parallel parkways running through the Central Ranch. This corridor would contain many local commercial and civic uses for the villages, and the San Diego Creek running through the center of the corridor would be transformed into a linear park and trail system.

With this regional framework in mind, we jointly selected the first village to be developed. It would be located between two planned north-south major

arteries, Culver Drive and Jeffrey Road. These roads would connect the proposed village directly to the University, Newport Center and the Coast. Thus Woodbridge Village, as it finally became known, was the beginning of a new part of the Ranch that would establish the structure for the remainder of the development. Woodbridge was also particularly important since it was the first major development by the Irvine Company in the brand-new City of Irvine, which was incorporated in 1971. Before the city was established, we had designed and implemented the plan for University Park, which upon becoming a part of the new city, was where many of the new city officials lived. They wanted everything they liked at University Park to become the standard at Woodbridge, and in fact, after Woodbridge was approved by the city they established many of its attributes as the new standards for further city development.

Woodbridge comprised 1750 acres and was planned for 27,000 residents. Its planning included two manmade lakes that ran perpendicular to the regional activity corridor, which contained the Village Center, civic buildings, schools, churches, offices, and commercial uses. To encourage pedestrian connections between these uses, parks were designed along the creek, and continuous pedestrian and bicycle trails along both lakes were connected by grade separations to the Village Center and activity corridor. In total, Woodbridge included forty parks, all linked by trails and greenbelts to subdivide the village into small clusters of housing specifically designed to appeal to families, seniors, empty nesters or singles. This was a significant break from the large, uniform subdivisions that populated most of Orange County, and the finer grain of development gave a more diverse feeling to the community.

To serve these mini-neighborhoods of thirty to forty homes each, the plan used a grid system of narrow local streets in each of the four quadrants formed by the central activity corridor and the two lakes to the north and south. The plan connected the quadrants with the Yale Loop Parkway, which had an innovative design: the typical collector street at Irvine was lined with walls to shield the adjacent homes from noise, but this created a barrier in the community. We wanted the village feeling to continue on the Yale collector so

**Above** The village center commercial and community uses rise above the south end of the upper lake at Woodbridge **Bottom** The upper lake pavilion, and multifamily homes sited above and along the shoreline trail at Woodbridge. **Bottom Right** Water oriented housing reflected by the lake is a hallmark of Woodbridge.

**Opposite Page** The Boca West Resort Community has a series of mixed use villages within four golf courses and clubs.

that it would be friendly to pedestrians as well as cars. To do this, we followed the precedent of historic American communities of the 19th century where major collector roads were lined with large estate homes set back from the road. At Woodbridge, lining the Yale Loop with large lots on either side that were graded to roll up from the road resulted in an attractive greenbelt where one would still have the feeling of being in a community. To diversify the program along the greenbelt, multi-unit residential structures were designed to look like large estates and were served by rear alleys and single driveways through the setback. We established complete design and development guidelines and villagescape criteria for Woodbridge to guide local landscape architects in implementation and designed key projects on the Lake edge and the Town Center.

We planned Woodbridge during the deep real estate recession of the mid 1970's, but despite this, when it opened in 1976 it sold 900 units a year and reached full buildout by 1990. The Central Ranch became a key part of the fast-growing City of Irvine, and a combined with the Irvine Ranch a formidable player in New Town development in America. The Woodbridge project, meanwhile, has received many awards, including a ULI Urban Land Institute Award of Excellence and Pacific Builders, American Society of Landscape Architects, and Urban Land Institute Awards for project excellence. Most importantly, however, it is beloved by those who live there. Its tiered homeowner associations have maintained the quality of the community and built a fierce loyalty to the village. In fact, in the 1990's the then-mayor told me that the politics of the City of Irvine are simple—as Woodbridge goes, Irvine goes.

## The Villages of Arvida, Boca Raton and Other Planned Communities, Florida (1972 to 1995)

In 1972, our client Chuck Cobb became CEO of the Arvida Corporation, which had extensive real estate holdings in Florida. Chuck was previously in charge of master planned communities for Kaiser Aetna in California, and we had worked with him on Rancho California and Amberton, both in Southern California. I was working on a small project in Florida when we got the call from Arvida for our interview in Boca Raton. The office contacted me immediately, and Arvida was quite impressed when I called back and scheduled the interview early the next day. At the interview they took note of my roots in Florida where I studied at the Universities of Miami and Florida, worked for the Metropolitan Dade County Planning Department, and where my family still lived. Even better, Chuck and his Arvida team were recent transplants from California and enthusiastic about a California firm that they had previously worked with, so combined with my Florida experience, we got the job.

Chuck Cobb was an ideal client for me because his successful experience at Rancho California and McCormick Ranch in Arizona taught him the benefits of carefully planned communities, and he sought to use master planned communities rather than conventional subdivision or parcel development that could turn a quick profit but would not achieve the best use of the company's large landholdings over the long run. This type of planning and development was of continued interest to me as environmental, social, and political trends throughout the nation were adding complexity, time, and cost to the government regulatory processes. More and more, enlightened consumers were seeking a better quality of life, and they increasingly looked to superior physical environments, among other things, to satisfy their lifestyle expectations and create rising values for their homes.

Arvida's 5,000-acre site for The Villages covered the western part of the City of Boca Raton, extending into Palm Beach County and including the landmark Boca Raton Hotel and Club on Florida's Gold Coast. The history of this hotel was intertwined with that of the City of Boca Raton itself, which was incorporated in 1925 when Addison Mizner, an architect and developer, founded the Mizner Development Corporation and launched his audacious dream of transforming a small agricultural community between Palm Beach and Miami into the "Greatest Resort in the World." Mizner planned and developed gracious tree-lined boulevards, the hundred- room Cloister Inn Hotel (later the Boca Raton Hotel and Club), and thirty homes in the Floresta area. In all of these properties, Mizner employed the dramatic Mediterranean architectural style that had won him acclaim and clients in the Palm Beaches. In just the first year of its incorporation, wealthy patrons began wintering in Boca Raton, thereby giving the new community its luxury feel and unique identity.

While Mizner was a gifted architect, his timing as a developer could have been better. In 1926, the Florida real estate boom was turning into a bust. Banks were failing, and investors and homebuyers avoided Florida properties, no matter how well located and planned. To make matters worse, that September a powerful hurricane swept up the Florida coast, damaging Miami, Palm Beach, and Boca Raton. The following year, Mizner's development company went under, and development stalled throughout the Great Depression. The Boca Raton Hotel became a training facility for military officers during World War II.

Arthur Vining Davis, the founder of Arvida and the Alcoa Corporation, purchased the hotel and large real estate holdings in the late 1950s. He then initiated the hotel's renaissance and, directly across Camino Real from the hotel, developed the 500-acre private Royal Palm Yacht and Country Club with a yacht harbor and golf course by Robert Trent Jones, Sr. In 1962, Davis died at the age of 95 and corporate ownership shifted, with Arvida managing the existing properties for almost a decade without any new large developments.

**Bottom** The Millpond village bike trail connects to a system of parks and trails throughout Boca Raton.

**Opposite Page Top** The Boca Raton Hotel and Club anchors the physical and social character of downtown Boca. **Bottom Left** Adjacent to the Town Center, the Boca Center has hotel and office uses mixed with pedestrian oriented retail and entertainment uses. **Bottom right** The Boca Raton Hotel includes and builds upon the original Mizener designed Cloisters hotel.

When we joined in the Arvida planning under Cobb's management and his excellent team of project leaders, we jointly were interested in using the historic precedents created by Mizner and Davis to highlight Boca Raton's uniqueness and value. It was particularly important to once again make Boca different from the fast-moving, formless, suburban sprawl that was beginning to dominate Florida's "Gold Coast", a seventy-mile stretch of sub-tropical beaches extending from Miami to the Palm Beaches. The older parts of Boca Raton around the hotel retained their unique character, but the lands to the west, a good portion of which were controlled by Arvida, were still undeveloped, and in our plan strategies for this land, we set about re-establish Boca Raton as a "special place." We knew that a market had once existed for this kind of distinctive and high-quality development, and it was our job to help Arvida bring it back. We were aided in this by two key developments: the advent of efficient air conditioning—which made year-round living in Florida comfortable—and the imminent completion of the I-95 freeway connecting Boca Raton to Miami and Fort Lauderdale in the south and the Palm Beaches in the north.

After establishing these overarching principles, we prepared a coordinated City/County plan for the hotel and the extensive western properties that would meet the "special place" challenge. The plan first devised ways to emphasize strong connections between the landlocked Arvida lands several miles to the west and the signature waterfront properties: the legendary Boca Raton Hotel and Club, the marinas, and the new Beach Club on the Gold Coast. Some of these new connections were physical, such as improved east-west circulation, while other connections were social, such as opening up hotel and club membership to residents of all Arvida developments in the west. The Boca Raton Hotel and Club could then in turn benefit from

reciprocal arrangements with the new and underutilized tennis facilities and golf courses in the Arvida western communities, allowing hotel guests and club members to gain access to these excellent facilities. This was a win-win situation: the Boca Club activities and the hotel's improved facilities provided prestige, identity, and real access to the Florida oceanfront and waterways for guests as well as residents of all the Arvida Villages at Boca Raton.

To further strengthen the links between the various communities, the Boca Raton Hotel and Club shuttle buses carried people on a frequent east-west schedule to Arvida's Boca West Resort Community. Arvida also funded an innovative program to provide a full landscape treatment for Florida State Road 808 (Glades Road) the city's major east-west arterial, which connected downtown Boca to I-95, the Florida Turnpike, and the western part of town. It was the first time in Florida history that a private company fully landscaped a state highway.

The site plans, detailed design guidelines and landscape designs that my colleagues, John Exley, Jim Reeves, John Wong, Bill Callaway, Danny Powell, and I prepared for the new Beach Club, Hotel, and Villages of Arvida at Boca Raton drew upon these connection strategies as well. The plans consisted of diverse residential villages, resorts, and recreation, transportation and civic facilities, as well as commercial shopping and business developments. This master planned community was subdivided into smaller units in order to be complementary to the existing heritage of development within the City of Boca Raton. Such a comprehensive planned community designed to integrate into existing city fabric was unique in Florida, but did inherit some of its character from Chuck Cobb's work with Kaiser-Aetna at the McCormick Ranch in Scottsdale, Arizona as well as my recent experience in planning the Central Irvine Ranch and the Village of Woodbridge in the City of Irvine, California..

To best achieve a design that was truly integrated into the historic Boca Raton fabric, our plan adopted basic building blocks consisting of a highly diverse series of residential villages varying in size from one hundred to three hundred homes. Each residential village had a distinctive character appropriate to its site and location, and included landscaped roadways in addition to pedestrian and bicycle trails. Each village also had landscaped entries that used a combination of earthen berms and walls with thematic graphics that provided both privacy and identity. The villages were landscaped further with

Opposite Page Bottom The character of the Sawgrass Country Club Resort community near Jacksonville, Florida includes residential villages in the natural forest, golf and marsh preservation areas and beach, golf and tennis swim clubs.

Above The beach and condominiums at the Sawgrass Beach Club. Bottom The Tournament Players Club headquarters at Sawgrass Players Club.

amenities such as lakes, golf courses, parks and school playgrounds. As the new South Florida water management guidelines required numerous water retention and detention sites, we worked closely with the engineers to pioneer the use and design of these water bodies as amenities, as well as needed hydraulic facilities.

While some of the villages were freestanding under the overall master plan, others were part of larger city or county approved Planned Unit Developments such as Boca West, Via Verde and Broken Sound. This meant there could be a competitive diversity of housing products available in the overall community, although more so in Arvida's County lands as Boca Raton limited overall densities . The commercial and industrial developments meanwhile were planned as high quality business parks or commercial centers with several coordinated elements to assure that they also contributed to the sense of a "special place. These included the Arvida Park of Commerce, an 810-acre planned development that included a championship golf course, and the Executive Center, an 84-acre campus for offices around a central lake and park. These facilities, along with various corporate headquarters situated around the Town Center, established Boca Raton as the primary corporate center in Palm Beach County.

High-end retail meant that Boca Raton was also a prime shopping destination, with Neiman Marcus, Saks, Nordstrom and Bloomingdales, as well as Macy's and Sears located at the Town Center at Boca Raton. Finally, pedestrian-oriented recreation commercial centers and higher-density housing helped to promote a sense of inclusion. These larger commercial developments served the region in addition to local residents, and therefore could be developed in early phases in conjunction with the residential villages, thus providing high standards of commercial service to new residents.

By 1982, the Arvida work was taking up the majority of my time and providing significant work for the firm to boot, so I moved to Boca Raton to start a branch office that would handle our Arvida work as well as projects for other clients in Florida and Latin America. When I left in 1984 to return to the Sausalito office, SWA GROUP Principals Roy Imamura and Eduardo Santaella and then Joe Runco took charge of our efforts in South Florida. By this time, the once-skeptical city officials and local residents began to see the superior quality of Arvida's developing communities, and more frequent channels of communication opened. Two former opponents formed a working partnership to guide future development, and the city added many of our planning and development standards into its own codes. As a matter of fact, many of our developments of in adjacent Palm Beach County were subsequently annexed to the City because of their high overall quality.

In 1970 before the new Arvida plan, Boca Raton had approximately 30,000 residents and a small job base—that is, before IBM invented their personal computer and opened a facility on Arvida land. By 2010, the city had reached almost 90,000 residents and even with the dramatic reduction of IBM employees, retains 90,000 jobs, amounting to a labor surplus of 50,000 jobs for residents of surrounding communities. This surplus of employment has contributed to a robust tax base for the city that has helped to maintain the high quality of development and landscape. This remarkable transformation would not have been possible without the Arvida developments, and it can be assumed that Addison Mizner and Arthur Davis would have been proud that their dream of making Boca Raton a "special place" came true.

**Above** The Park of Commerce in Boca Raton is an 810 acre high technology, office and business park built in part around a championship golf course.

**Opposite Page Above** The Cocoplum club activities encourage neighborhood gatherings.
**Opposite Page Bottom** The Islands of Cocoplum in Coral Gables with its waterways and mangrove preserves in a view toward Biscayne Bay and downtown Miami.

The Villages of Arvida at Boca Raton became the symbol of "Arvida Quality," which Cobb saw was in most cases directly related to our work in the community. The principles of Arvida Quality were:

1. A comprehensive plan and enhancement of natural resources
2. Image setting entryway and controlled access
3. Complete design of streets, landscapes, graphics and signage
4. Community character and product diversity
5. Resource management and energy conservation
6. Recreation facilities and resort and club operations
7. Stewardship responsibility and community management
8. Marketing and sales promotion events

This approach used by us at The Villages of Arvida at Boca Raton, set the stage for the 1980s, when the corporation had over twenty master planned communities under development in Florida, Georgia, North Carolina and California, many of which we planned and designed. A brief summary of three of the Master Planned Communities; Sawgrass, Cocoplum and Weston follow. A more complete summary of these communities and a number of others can be found in my previous book published by the Urban Land institute in 2011, Master Planned Communities, Lessons from the Developments of Chuck Cobb.

1. Sawgrass was a 2300 acre Master Planned Community in the Ponte Vedra Beach area of Metropolitan Jacksonville. In the plan by Principals Roy Imamura, Rick Pariani and I, we transformed the patterns of high quality residential development in the Metropolitan region by bringing high quality residential development to St Johns County. It also established Jacksonville as a prime national destination for golf, attracting the Tournament Players Club national headquarters and world class stadium golf, and tennis facilities. It featured planned neighborhoods set into the beautiful woodlands and adjacent to significant marsh preserves at Sawgrass bringing the "River City" to the beach.

2. Cocoplum was the last large waterfront properties in the garden city of Coral Gables located adjacent to the historic Coconut Grove district of Miami. Our plan for the 350 acre property followed the historic plan for the "City Beautiful" by George Merrick. The "Islands of Cocoplum" implemented Landscape Architect Frank Button's 1925 City Master Plan of four islands and their waterways with a yacht harbor near the point where the Coral Gables Waterway meets Biscayne Bay. We followed Coral Gables' precedent of a "public garden" for all of Cocoplum created by tree shaded streets to accommodate pedestrians with limited pavements for automobiles. We added modern environmental ideas of protecting all existing mangroves on the property for habitat and hurricane protection purposes.

3. Weston was a 10,000 acre New Town on the western edge of Broward County developable land sitting between three freeways and the everglades to the west. Using a community development district, affordable infrastructure was created for a family oriented community with neighborhoods on a system of waterways with riparian habitats. Along the freeway frontage were planned commercial areas and the Florida major campus of the Cleveland Clinic creating a balance of 25-30,000 jobs for the 60,000 person town. The

**Opposite page** The Cleveland Clinic chose the City of Weston for its main Florida facility.

**Above** The main entry to the City of Weston with its extensive waterway system, employment centers and residential villages.
**Bottom** A view of the walkable downtown in the City of Weston.

neighborhoods planned by Principals Roy Imamura, Joe Runco and I have central school and parks and there is a walkable mixed use town center and community wide recreation facilities. In 1996 Weston became a city, annexed an adjacent existing community and agricultural and conservation areas adjacent to the everglades increasing the city to 16.000 acres. During the 2009-2013 "great recession" Weston was rated the number one real estate market in the U.S. by Businessweek as properties during that time did not decline in value as most areas of the country but actually showed a modest increase!

## Sun Valley Master Plan and Elkhorn Village, Sun Valley, Idaho (1973)

In our practice at Sasaki Walker Associates, we preferred to work first on master plans and then carry them out as design projects, rather than picking up where other planners left off. Beginning with planning allowed us to shape the landscape from the ground up and fully utilize our skills in creating places within larger contexts. Sometimes, however, this worked the other way around, and we would be brought in to work on a project only to then expand to the larger scale context. This was the case at Sun Valley, Idaho.

The historic 1936 ski resort at Sun Valley was famous for having the first mechanized ski lift and for its charming Hollywood-inspired alpine architecture. The resort grew along with the popularity of skiing in the 60s and 70s and so resort owner Bill Janss asked Ed Killingsworth, a prominent Southern California architect, to help him plan a new ski area in the 2500-acre Elkhorn

Valley, a part of Sun Valley that was not yet developed. Ed in turn asked Pete and I to join in the venture.

Our team at Sasaki, Walker took the lead in analyzing the pristine valley and in deciding where development should (or should not) occur. We were all struck by the beauty of the valley, and so it was unanimously decided that we should not spread development over the many surrounding hills but rather take a more sensitive approach and locate a dense, European-style walking village at the base of the valley. Ed immediately went to work designing beautiful condominiums that could be arrayed like an alpine village.

Bald Mountain, a fine ski mountain with a peak of 9,400 feet, was located just outside Sun and Elkhorn Valleys and was conveniently accessible via a

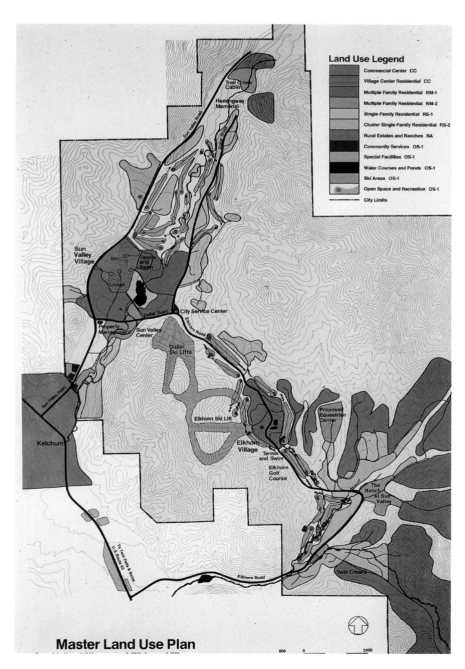

**Land Use Legend**

Commercial Center  CC
Village Center Residential  CC
Multiple Family Residential  RM-1
Multiple Family Residential  RM-2
Single-Family Residential  RS-1
Cluster Single-Family Residential  RS-2
Rural Estates and Ranches  RA
Community Services  OS-1
Special Facilities  OS-1
Water Courses and Ponds  OS-1
Ski Areas  OS-1
Open Space and Recreation  OS-1
City Limits

**Master Land Use Plan**

**Opposite Page** The Elkhorn Village and golf course in the summer season.

**Bottom** The plan shows the Sun Valley and Elkhorn Villages making up the expanded historic resort of Sun Valley, Idaho.

regularly scheduled, year-round bus. Therefore, we designed a central plaza in Elkhorn Village that would be serviced by the bus to connect to the mountain and to Sun Valley Village. We also wanted to .capitalize on the rising popularity of Sun Valley in the summer, and thus worked with Robert Trent Jones to wind a second championship golf course through Elkhorn Valley over a narrow saddle and into Sun Valley.

Dollar Mountain, another ski mountain with beginner and intermediate slopes, was located between the new Elkhorn Village and the Sun Valley Village. Skiers taking the existing Dollar lifts from Sun Valley Village or the new ski lifts close to Elkhorn plaza would have the option to ski down to either Village. This would mean skiers could choose to travel between the valleys on skis, ski lifts or the frequently scheduled ski buses. In the summer season, golfers could also use golf carts to get between the two villages, and more active visitors could hike, bike, or ride horseback between the villages as well. Having so many options greatly helped us in our goal of reducing automobile use in the resorts.

The Elkhorn plan also included luxury home sites along the golf course and only the lower hillsides, since we wanted to protect the upper slopes and ridges of the valley from development and keep homes and road construction from visually intruding on the pristine setting for the Elkhorn Village. To do this, our design Principal John Exley performed a careful viewshed analysis by examining the topography and orientation of the lower hillsides and then selecting individual homesites that possessed views and privacy but were not noticeable when one looked up at the slopes and ridges from the valley below.

Bill Janss was so taken with our plans for Elkhorn and the multiple connections that could be made between the two valleys that he then asked if we would look at the entire Sun Valley Resort. We relished the opportunity to apply our environmental planning approach to such a large and beautiful site, and so of course we said yes! For the larger study, we prepared an environmental and planning analysis for Sun Valley, adding it to the Elkhorn analysis and plans. In the remaining few areas of Sun Valley that had potential for home sites, we applied the same process as in Elkhorn to carefully locate homes and still protect the valley views. All said, in the overall plan we dedicated three quarters of the land to undeveloped open space, thus protecting the entry to Sun Valley, the mountainsides, and the integrity of the Sun Valley Village. Another important goal of the project was keeping Sun Valley Village as a primarily pedestrian area, utilizing the excellent bus system year round, and downplaying the use of the automobile in the entire city. This was important since the rapid growth had begun to endanger the original quaint character of the Sun Valley Village.

We worked closely with the City of Sun Valley—an incorporated entity—on preparing a Master Plan for the entire City including Elkhorn Valley. SWA Principal Tom Adams and I felt good as we came through a snowstorm to present the final plan to the City Council. The next morning as we set up to make the presentation in the Sun Valley conference room, however, we discovered to our embarrassment that we had brought the Sun Valley Plan carefully wrapped around a roll of beautiful analytical studies of Squaw Valley! We were working at the time on a number of ski resorts, including Sun Valley, Squaw Valley in California, and Loon Mountain in New Hampshire and had performed analytical studies for all. The studies we were looking for were inadvertently wrapped around the wrong roll in our office back in Sausalito.

**Opposite Page** Catching the bus in the Elkhorn village center to the close by the Baldy ski mountain. **Bottom** Summer in the Elkhorn village center.

The presentation was scheduled to begin in a half hour, and we had no studies to make the points I had carefully prepared for each of the eight analytical maps to convince the council they should adopt the plan. Could I do that without those impressive graphics? Then I remembered that Bill Janss had a beautiful aerial photograph in a picture frame behind his desk that was the same scale and size as our plans. I ran down the hall, burst into his office, saw the framed aerial fixed to the wall and, telling Bill what the emergency was, pulled it off, frame and all. I knew Bill would understand the urgency, and he did.

So, with just a aerial photograph and our beautiful plan I proceeded to make eight different analytical presentations about soils, vegetation, slopes, drainage, orientation, road networks, land uses, development sites, all from the aerial, and then explained how these were accommodated in the plan. Fortunately, we had done our homework with the council in previous meetings, and they followed the rationale and then enthusiastically adopted the plan. Planning improvisation had worked for me but as far as I was concerned, from then on I would personally check all drawings I was bringing to presentations!

As we began implementation of our plans, one of our Associates took the job as in-house landscape architect and planner for Sun Valley, as he was an avid skier. He moved to Elkhorn for the next decade and was able to see the implementation of our plans through to completion, ensuring that Sun Valley-Elkhorn remained a world class, year-round resort. Losing a fine professional and some consulting work over time was unfortunate, but having the right person there when key decisions needed to be made was worth the sacrifice.

## Monterey Conference Center and Custom House Hotel, Monterey, California (1973)

I had always enjoyed visiting the Monterey Peninsula for its unique beauty and history, so when we were asked by the Monterey Redevelopment Agency to prepare an urban design and full landscape services for the historic Custom House area of Monterey's downtown, it was a great opportunity to contribute to this wonderful part of California.

The City Redevelopment Agency had hired Van Bourg Nakamura, an Oakland architecture firm, to design the conference center, and they brought in a developer and architect to build a hotel next to the conference center. We were to work with both architects to guide the overall urban design and landscape development.

The site was bounded on the north by the historic Monterey Custom House and its park and plaza, which led to Monterey's waterfront and Fisherman's Wharf. Del Monte Avenue, the main access to downtown from the freeway, formed the southern boundary of the site. It ended at Pacific Avenue, which formed the western boundary. The eastern boundary of the site was formed by the entry to a vehicular tunnel that ran under the Custom House Park and connected to Cannery Row to the north. Alvarado Street, the main commercial street of downtown, ran up toward the center of the site and terminated at Del Monte Avenue. Another important downtown street, Calle Principal running parallel to Alvarado also terminated at the site.

Working with our Principals Dick Law and Roy Imamura on the urban design, we saw the opportunity to use the conference center and hotel site to create a strong connection between downtown Monterey and its historic waterfront. In conjunction with the architects, we located the conference center at the western edge of the site facing Del Monte Avenue and downtown.. Then, working with closely with the developer and his architect, we located the main building of the hotel directly next to the conference center, but set back from Del Monte Avenue in order to create a large, European style plaza at the terminus of Alvarado Street. Pedestrians would have access to the entire brick plaza surface. The plaza would allow limited bus, delivery, taxi and automobile drop-off to both the conference center and hotel on a portion defined by bollards and a park along Del Monte Street  The park was covered in part by a large planted trellis and contained a fountain with a bus shelter, seating and planted areas.

We located a smaller, linear portion of the hotel to the east of and separated from the main hotel building, creating between the two hotel elements a brick-paved pedestrian mall that extended Alvarado Street through to the Custom House and Fisherman's Wharf beyond. This pedestrian mall between the two hotel elements had shops, restaurants, offices and a museum with hotel suites above. The smaller hotel element was also used to screen the plaza and pedestrian mall from the hotel parking structure at the eastern edge of the site and to buffer the vehicular tunnel entrance that formed the eastern site boundary. The overall urban design of the site thus continued the downtown activities along Alvarado Street north through the site via the pedestrian mall to the historic activities of the Monterey Harbor.

The Monterey conference center had landscaped pedestrian terraces off the conference rooms along the streets and the plaza. Later, a pedestrian bridge was built from one of the conference center terraces across Del Monte

**Opposite Page** Elkhorn Village condominiums set on the Dollar ski mountain slopes.

to connect to a large Marriott convention hotel on Calle Principal. The scale and detail of both the conference center and hotel buildings were designed with tile roofs and other details that complemented Monterey's historic, mission-style architecture and mediated the transition from the higher buildings of downtown toward the low-rise Custom House. The hotel was stepped down in height where it directly bordered the Custom House State Historic Park, and we used landscaped terraces and pedestrian entries on that side to soften the overall hotel development. The hotel was originally a Doubletree, but is now the Portola Hotel and Spa, a fine tourist and business meeting hotel that shares meeting space with the conference center.

Working with the two architects and clients, we were able to use urban design, architecture and landscape architecture to create a unified development for this strategically located site. The overall conference center, hotel complex and the public plaza with its pedestrian mall, shops, and museums became the key connection between downtown Monterey and its historic Custom House and waterfront. By using the configuration, scale and materials of the architecture and landscape together, we provided a harmonious transition to the historic area and reinforced the appealing character of Monterey for residents and tourists alike.

**Opposite Page** A view of the plaza and fountain at the entry to the conference center. **Bottom Left** The pedestrian mall leading from the plaza through the two elements of the hotel to the historic Custom House and waterfront.

**Bottom** A view of the plaza and trellis looking through to the hotel adjacent to the conference center.

# 4

# Sasaki, Walker Associates becomes the SWA Group, and I become a leader

## 1974–1980

The mid 1970's were transformative for the firm and for me. After nearly two decades practicing together, Hideo Sasaki and Pete Walker decided it was time for the two linked firms to become separate companies. Both the east coast office led by Hideo and the west coast office led by Pete had expanded from regional practices to national ones, and it was becoming confusing for our clients. Each of the two offices had different Principals, separate accounting systems, and a different professional makeup. In Watertown, Massachusetts, Hideo had shaped the office to his ideal of comprehensive service that included architecture as well as landscape architecture, with strong in-house engineering, environmental and economics support. He had changed the name of his office to Sasaki, Dawson DeMay incorporating Stu Dawson, a landscape architect, and Ken DeMay, an architect.

Meanwhile, in Sausalito, Pete enjoyed the group of strong architectural clients that we worked with and did not want to compete with them with in-house architects. He had in 1973, however, joined with an environmental firm, James A. Roberts, and created Sasaki Walker Roberts (SWR). The Sausalito office also included engineering and communications support groups, but did not include an architectural component. So, in consideration of these different approaches, it made sense to end the partnership between Hideo and Pete and to open the door to new ownership in each firm, which was an important thing as we had named many new Principals in both offices. It was agreed that Hideo's firm was to become "Sasaki Associates", and we were to come up with a new name that did not use "Sasaki".

Besides the differences in leadership styles and office makeup, another major factor that drove the decision to create separate firms was the deep recession of the mid 70's. This recession was the worst in decades and put both firms into survival mode. We found it was no longer viable to keep all of the Sasaki Walker Roberts practice areas together under one roof, and in 1974 and 1975 in the first step in creating our new identity the firm separated into three distinct firms. Guided by the invaluable assistance of Mike Gilbert, who had joined us earlier as a business consultant and had become a Principal, the environmental group became LSA Associates, a very successful firm to this day, while the graphics and communications group became the Gnu Group, led by Rich Burns, which still practices today. As for us, we went back to focusing on what we knew best: landscape architecture, urban design and planning.

Illustrated on pages 92-99 are select projects as the firm transitions from Sasaki, Walker Associates to SWA Group.

**Opposite Page** The IBM West Coast Programming Center for 2000 employees sits in sharp contrast to the brown summer hills of its 1150 acre site in Santa Teresa, California.

**Bottom** The patterns of buildings, pavements, sculpture and trees of the IBM programming center catch the winter light against the green rolling hills.

The experience we gained with the environmental scientists during the firm's short time as SWR firm did provide me with a better sense of how to make our plans more sensitive to these issues. I had of course been interested in environmental issues and had used this kind of information and analysis in practice for several years already, especially as it became more widely available. However, I was able to delve deeper into these methods at SWR while working directly with biologists, foresters, soil scientists and others on the Monoplan for Mammoth with Mono County and the U.S. Forest Service as clients. This plan was done after the "Friends of Mammoth" had sued about a development for a ski village, and the suit was used to create the California Environmental Quality Act, a pivotal law that required all private projects in California to produce an Environmental Impact Report (EIR) before any approval would be given for development. CEQA was admirable in its aspirations, but the problem was that the law worked backwards: all the environmental studies were to be done after the plan for development was prepared and submitted. It was a lawyer's, not a planner's approach.

Despite the challenges, however, my experience with this process gave me a better sense of how to use the environmental specialists on the Monoplan as well as all our other plans from then on out. We decided we would call for the environmental specialists to perform preliminary surveys of their disciplines before we prepared the plan. In this way we could use the plan as the major form of mitigation, in essence allowing for pre-mitigation of the key environmental issues. This required a little negotiation with the scientists, as they considered their findings preliminary and were reluctant to draw conclusions. But as planners, we always understood that the process by necessity moved from preliminary data and ideas to more complete ones. If a particular issue became important and needed more study, we would authorize a more complete survey during the planning process. Eventually, the environmental scientists became comfortable doing it our way and so this became our approach to development planning.

**Opposite Page** A family enjoying the Refugio Valley Park in Hercules. **Middle** There are places for all ages at Refugio Valley Park. **Bottom** The Pavilion and lake are a focal point of the Refugio Valley Community Park in Hercules, California.

**Above** The ARCO (now City National Bank) plaza is designed to attract people and make them comfortable in the desirable climate of Los Angeles. **Bottom** The ARCO (now City National Bank) plaza and fountain in downtown Los Angeles.

After SWR disbanded, we continued to use LSA as consultants, given our close working relationship. The result of this partnership was that when the required EIR was prepared, we had all the major issues addressed. Our clients liked that they had a good idea of what would be necessary for mitigation early on, and it certainly helped make the trying political process a little bit more tractable.

Once we had settled on a firm model we liked, we shifted our attention to identifying and structuring the new firm. To clearly demarcate the rebirth of both Hideo and Pete's practices, Hideo's firm had taken the name "Sasaki Associates" and we then adopted the name "The SWA GROUP". That name came from our frequent use of "SWA" over the years, but also reflected discussions between Pete and I about creating a group practice that recognized the Principal group who were fast becoming sought out by our clients on their own merit. The idea of a group practice was no small thing to me. The seven years between the time I joined the firm in 1967 and the time we became The SWA GROUP in 1974 had coalesced my view of what our practice could be. The group of us worked together so effectively to make the world a better place; I wrote once that I felt like "it was us against the world."

When the dust settled, Pete surprised me by asking me to become the President of the new company—he would become Chairman. I was reluctant at first, as I was just hitting my stride as a professional and I did not want to interrupt that process after having come so far. He insisted, however, and I knew I would have to accede to this new role. He had brilliantly brought the firm to where it was, but needed help taking it to where we wanted to go. Pete wanted more flexibility in his project involvement, and it was no longer possible or even desirable to have him as the key designer of all this work. He wanted to focus on specific projects that would allow him to hone his interests, but also have time to pursue his great interest in art and teaching. So, I accepted his offer, but not before giving much thought to how I could responsibly lead the firm through the difficult times of the mid 1970's, take it to the next level, and still continue my practice as a professional.

I took over as President in 1974 and with the invaluable help of Mike Gilbert on the business side and the hard work of all the Principals, we did make it through the economic crisis, and new opportunities awaited us on the other side. We emerged leaner but stronger, and set out to create a new structure for the SWA GROUP. We wanted to create a true group practice where we would attract only the best of the best people and to do this, we had to create a working environment where they would have the support and freedom to create. But we also wanted those who proved themselves to stay on and be proud to call the firm their own, and this could only be accomplished by giving employees real ownership. Thus, the Employee Stock Ownership Program (ESOP) was born, and today each and every employee owns a small part of the company.

Another structural ingredient we believed was essential for the future of SWA GROUP was to make the firm more resilient by adding offices in high growth areas. I asked Dick Law as a Senior Principal in 1976 if he would join Orange County-born Don Tompkins in establishing an office there to serve our long time client, the Irvine Company and other clients in this vital region. Next, in 1978 Ed Kagi, another Senior Principal, agreed to go with Houston-born Jim Reeves to establish a critical base in that region, which was experiencing explosive growth due to the oil industry. That left Gary Karner and Bill

Callaway to head up the Sausalito office. These six outstanding professionals became our first group of Managing Principals, and worked closely with me to form the base of our future growth and vitality, establish the firm's ability to provide regional expertise, and maintain the highest standards of quality across a national practice.

The processes of building a group practice, structuring the firm and expanding to multiple offices and a global practice are covered in more detail in Chapter 8, Shaping the Firm: Lessons from 55 Years of Practice. In that chapter, I discuss my 23 years leading SWA GROUP through many challenges to set it up for where it is today, with a lot of help from my friends!

**Opposite Page** A Calder sculpture at the entry plaza to the Security Pacific National Bank Headquarters (now Bank of America) in downtown Los Angeles.

**Above** The concourse level of the Bank of America in Los Angeles with its waterfall fountain spilling from the plaza level and willows is cool and refreshing. **Bottom** The garden quality of the Bank of America upper plaza in downtown Los Angeles is accentuated by pots of seasonal color.

**Opposite Page** People at a concert enjoying a picnic on the grass slopes as well as in seats within the Performing Arts Pavilion at Concord, California. **Bottom** The Performing Arts Pavilion in Concord, California by Frank Gehry is contained within an earthen sculpture and landscape creating a sense of arrival, privacy and acoustic control.

**Above** The Promontory Point complex has magnificent views to and from the marina in the Newport Beach Harbor. **Bottom** The Promontory Point apartments in Newport Beach, California are built like a Mediterranean Hill Town.

**Pages 100-101** The Golden Gate Bridge connects the San Francisco and Marin sections of the Golden Gate National Recreation Area (GGNRA).

## Golden Gate National Recreation Area, Marin County, California (1975)

For generations, the pristine cliffs and bluffs fronting the Pacific Ocean and the spectacular Golden Gate entry to San Francisco Bay were a conglomerate of military facilities, parks, watershed lands, ranches, a few small communities and the City itself .The Golden Gate Bridge spanning the waterway between San Francisco and Marin Counties was constructed in 1937 tying them together and drawing resident and tourists to these scenic resources but frustrating their use by their different access and ownership characteristics. Congress created the 100,000-acre Golden Gate National Recreation Area in in 1972, comprising 10,000 acres in San Francisco and 90,000 acres in Marin County to be administered by the National Park Service (NPS). The unique concept of the GGNRA was a new type of National Park, as it contained these diverse land holdings, and combined federal, state and county as well as private lands directly adjacent to a large metropolitan area.

Upon establishment of the GGNRA, the National Park Service began work assembling the parkland's properties and scoping out a strong organization for planning and implementation. Since this type of park was a first for NPS, Sasaki, Walker Associates were retained by the Park Service to prepare a General Management Plan for the 90,000-acre Marin County portion of the GGNRA, which ranged from the Golden Gate Headlands, Angel Island, and Muir Woods to the Point Reyes Seashore. Sasaki, Walker Associates had recently merged with an environmental science firm, and so our numbers included several professionals with national park experience, including Principal Terry Savage. With his help and that of Principals John Exley as designer, forester Jim Culver, engineer Bill Clarke and environmental planner George Kurilko, I coordinated our work closely with Royston, Hanamoto, Beck and Abey, who were studying the 10,000-acre San Francisco portion that included The Presidio and Alcatraz.

I was particularly delighted to work on the GGNRA, as I had a brief and difficult experience six years earlier when my then-employer Ruth + Krushkhov was asked by Paul Zucker, Planning Director of Marin County, to help his beleaguered staff deal with the county's preliminary approval of Marincello, a 30,000-person city to be built on the Marin Headlands adjacent to the Golden Gate Bridge. I was conflicted about the project from the start, as the client was Thomas Frouge, an irascible developer backed by Gulf Oil who paid no attention to our detailed comments about the plan's flawed access, environmental issues and size that was completely out of proportion with adjacent Marin towns. Fortunately, a courageous citizenry and an outstanding grassroots effort convinced Gulf Oil and the County to remove their support and spurred Congress to acquire the critically located lands for the new National Park. This decision hit close to home, as I now lived in Mill Valley, a beautiful historic town of 15,000 that was adjacent to the proposed Marincello development. I knew our quality of life was made far better thanks to my Mill Valley friends Marty Rosen and Doug Ferguson, who formed the Trust for Public Land, and Marin County Supervisor Michael Wornum, who fought to create the GGNRA.

At the time we began work on the GGNRA, the Park Service had just come off two difficult and minimally successful planning efforts, at Yosemite and at the Point Reyes National Seashore in 1962, which was plagued by public

**Above** People reviewing alternative plans for the GGNRA during the public workshops.

**Opposite Page** The draft management plan for the long term use of the GGNRA.

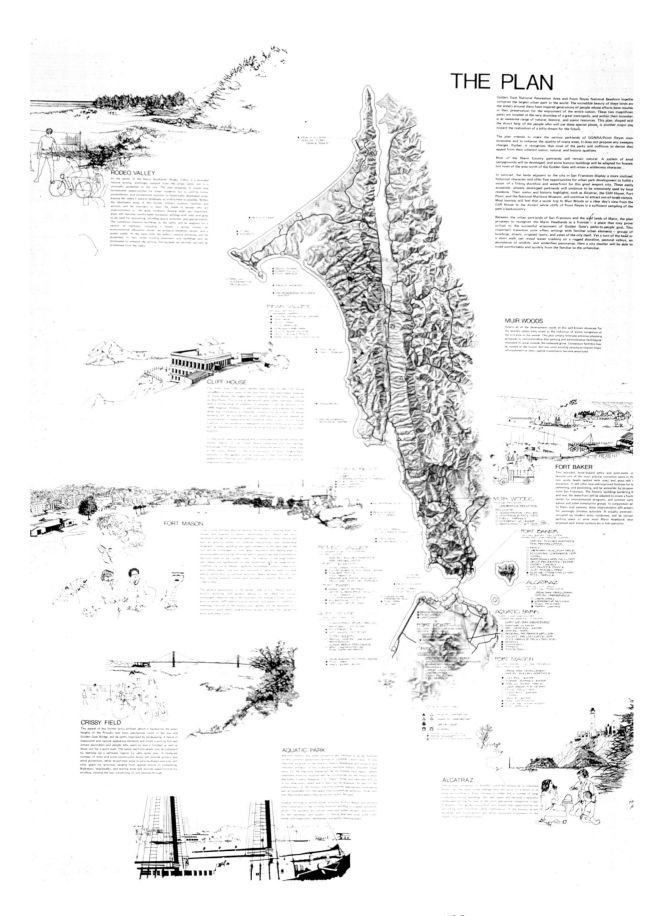

# THE PLAN

Golden Gate National Recreation Area and Point Reyes National Seashore together comprise the largest urban park in the world. The incredible beauty of these lands and the waters around them have inspired generations of people whose efforts have resulted in their preservation for the enjoyment of the entire nation. These two magnificent parks are located at the very doorstep of a great metropolis, and within their boundaries is an awesome range of natural, historic, and scenic resources. This plan, shaped with the direct help of the people who will use these special places, is another major step toward the realization of a lofty dream for the future.

The plan intends to make the various parklands of GGNRA/Point Reyes more accessible and to enhance the quality of many areas. It does not propose any sweeping changes. Rather, it recognizes that most of the parks will continue to derive their appeal from their coherent scenic, natural, and historic qualities.

Most of the Marin County parklands will remain natural. A system of small campgrounds will be developed, and some historic buildings will be adapted for hostels, but most of the area north of the Golden Gate will retain a wilderness character.

In contrast, the lands adjacent to the city in San Francisco display a more civilized, historical character and offer fine opportunities for urban park development to fulfill a vision of a fitting shoreline and waterfront for this great seaport city. These easily accessible, already developed parklands will continue to be intensively used by local residents. Their scenic and historic highlights, such as Alcatraz, the Cliff House, Fort Point, and the National Maritime Museum, will continue to attract out-of-town visitors. Most tourists will feel that a quick trip to Muir Woods or a clear day's view from the Cliff House to the distant white cliffs of Point Reyes is a sufficient sampling of the park's backcountry.

Between the urban parklands of San Francisco and the wild lands of Marin, the plan proposes to recognize the Marin Headlands as a frontier — a place that may prove critical to the successful attainment of Golden Gate's parks-to-people goal. This important transition zone offers settings with familiar urban elements — groups of buildings, streets, irrigated lawns, and views of the city itself. Yet a turn of the head or a short walk can reveal ocean waves crashing on a rugged shoreline, pastoral valleys, an abundance of wildlife, and wilderness panoramas. Here a city dweller will be able to move comfortably and quickly from the familiar to the unfamiliar.

## RODEO VALLEY

At the center of the Marin Headlands, Rodeo Valley is a secluded natural setting seemingly isolated from the urban scene, yet it is unusually accessible to the city. The plan proposes to create new recreational opportunities for urban residents here to confirm scenic conservation and recreational facilities to historically developed areas, leaving the valley's natural landscape as undisturbed as possible. Within the developed areas of this former military reserve facilities and services will be provided to meet the needs of people who are unaccustomed to the great outdoors. Several small but important areas will become comfortable recreation settings with trees and grass to be used for picnicking, schoolbus special activities, and special events. The numerous historic buildings in the valley will be adapted for a variety of facilities, including a hostel, a group rental, an environmental education center, an artists-in-residence center, and a public stable. At the same time, the valley's natural amenities will be protected. In turn, some existing pavement and buildings will be eliminated to enhance the setting. During peak-use periods cars will be prohibited from the valley.

## CLIFF HOUSE

For more than 100 years people have come to the Cliff House headlands to enjoy views of the Pacific, the wave-swept expanse of Ocean Beach, the rugged Marin coastline and the hills high in the Seal Rocks. This is one of the world's great ocean overlooks, draped with a strong sense of tradition. It exemplifies a will be restored in 1896 elegance. However, a good balance must be achieved to confine these new necessities is a necessary to improve. However, additional services will be eliminated in accordance with several features of this area. Here development and structures will be protected. A widened reservation for the overlook or roadways, it will enhance the ambiance of this area as a public enjoyment. The purpose is to create a widened edge along the coastline in this popular environment. The last and its environs will be a place to enjoy a full spectrum of activities.

## FORT MASON

Fort Mason is a well established urban area, with more than its prominent role inside. The site commanding view of the harbor and the Golden Gate Bridge, represents one of the most dramatic opportunities for the development of an urban open space with the utmost public utility. Several historic buildings are here, and the surrounding land and water provide an exceptional setting for active and passive recreation. For the historic and natural properties at the waterfront's edge, the best approach will be to develop these grounds and the buildings for a variety of active and passive recreation, cultural activities, education, and public enjoyment, while capitalizing on the area's historic structures and natural environment.

## CRISSY FIELD

The appeal of this former army airfield, which is backed by the green heights of the Presidio and faces spectacular views of the bay and Golden Gate Bridge, will be vastly improved by landscaping. A blend of manicured and natural-appearing elements will create a setting that will attract picnickers and people who want to toss a football as well as those out for a quiet walk. The sandy lagoon beach may be enhanced by opening up a saltwater lagoon for safer water play. A moderate number of trees and some constructed dunes will provide privacy and wind protection, while broad lawn areas in varying shapes and sizes will offer space for activities ranging from special events to sunbathing. Walkways, boardwalks, and resting areas will provide opportunities to strolling, viewing the bay, socializing, or just passing through.

## AQUATIC PARK

Aquatic Park's special appeal to residents and visitors is in its function of this former waterfront setting along a sweeping cove. The maritime museum is the historic Haslett Warehouse will provide an intensive ambiance of the historic buildings. Another major focus for the maritime theme will be the Hyde Street Pier, where additional historic vessels of various types will be contributed by the historic ships foundation. A waterfront park will be developed on to an extension when it then can be adapted to part of the enhancement of the historic maritime activity. Improvements are to be expanded into the great new enjoyment to enhance. Here the bay bosom where they can enjoy within the bay.

Golden thinking of active water activities to Fort Mason will prove a convenient relocation for the sailing museum building to a more accessible center. The building will capture important visible elements and restore for fair operation and locate a historic ship and small water craft along and surrounding attractions, and public viewing space.

## MUIR WOODS

Nearly all of the development needs at this well known showcase for the world's tallest trees relate to the reduction of visitor congestion at the entrance to the woods. This plan simply reiterates previous planning proposals in recommending that parking and administration facilities be relocated to areas outside the redwood grove. Concession facilities may be moved in the future, but not until existing structures require major refurbishment or when capital investments become amortized.

## FORT BAKER

This secluded, bowl-shaped valley and open water will become one of the most popular recreation spots in the new sandy reach backed with lawn and grass until its attraction. It will offer new and improved facilities for boating, swimming, and picnicking, and be accessible by proposed transit from San Francisco. The historic buildings bordering the parade ground and near the waterfront will be adapted to create a hostel center for environmental programs, and summer camps for seminarily-limited activities. A visually oriented parking space to serve most Marin Headlands destinations until proposed park transit systems are in full operation.

## ALCATRAZ

The strong attraction of Alcatraz Island will always be its infamous prison, but the sheer scenic beauty felt by visitors to the island is an overwhelming offer. A fine mixture of visible and a number of large collections prison buildings. This open space will become a beautiful wildflower setting. Fine use of the most panoramic viewpoints to San Francisco. The guided tours will inspire new opportunities for interpreting the history, the excitement and emotions while inhabiting the buildings, providing a connection to the history of the building, and fortification will allow continued enjoyment of the island's long and varied history.

process issues. Many of both plans' opponents were environmentally active Bay Area residents, which made it even more important that we were sensitive to public input from the outset on the GGNRA project. With this in mind, we began working with Bill Whalen, the n ew superintendent of the GGNRA, and his Park Service Planner, Doug Nadeau. They looked to us to help them plan a park in the midst of this highly active citizenry. For my part, I brought with me experience planning sensitive and highly contentious projects along the California Coast and in the Bay Area, having recently worked on the Monoplan for the U.S. Forest Service and Mono County, which evolved out of the Friends of Mammoth court decision that gave rise to comprehensive environmental review in California.

We strongly advised Whalen and Nadeau to set up a planning program for the GGNRA that could deal directly with environmental and political sensitivities, and to ensure maximum transparency, we recommended that the majority of the work be done not out of the Park Service's Denver center but right in the Bay Area instead. They supported this arrangement, and so together we set out to catalog all of the natural and cultural resources of the park properties. At the same time, the Park Service undertook a complete survey of the historic resources in the GGNRA, which included myriad military facilities dating back to the Civil War. In fact, the Park Service determined that the GGNRA lands contained the largest collection of historic resources of any National Park. In short order, we were to find that our joint cataloguing efforts would become the most complete atlas ever compiled during the planning of a National Park.

We knew that having detailed information about the park's resources would help facilitate discussions with concerned participants, but also knew that, as proven by the difficulties of the Yosemite process, the traditional linear process of collecting data, preparing plan alternatives, and presenting them to interested citizens would never work. Rather, we made it clear to the Park Service that we needed to establish a direct and early outreach to the many interest groups while we were compiling the data and analysis. Even more importantly, we wanted to ask them for their information, ideas and

**Bottom** The GGNRA extends from San Francisco Bay to the spectacular shorelines, beaches and inlets of the Pacific Ocean.

**Opposite Page Above** The Marin hills of the GGNRA form a fascinating contrast to the city of San Francisco. **Middle** A simple but inspirational hike not far from the city of San Francisco along the rugged Pacific coastline north of the Golden Gate.

input as early on in the studies as possible. This emphasis on community involvement allowed us to incorporate vital information that many local, state and national groups in the Bay Area had collected into our studies. In fact, this was to become the most participatory process for any park ever!

To achieve our desired level of transparency, we scheduled an extensive series of workshops at convenient venues throughout the entire Bay Area, and invited neighborhood organizations, interest groups and stakeholders that had vital information we could use in the studies. We particularly wanted to understand what they wanted and expected from the park that we were planning right in their backyard. The first round of workshops was well attended, and we reaped great basic information, questions, preferences and ideas that were catalogued and then widely disseminated. The Park Service, initially skeptical that this level of transparency would encumber the process, quickly came on board once they saw the benefits. During the first round every workshop was attended by Park Service employees and consultants who described to the community how and where they could see accessible portions of the park, and how they could provide feedback and ideas during the planning process.

Through the workshops, we began to get a good idea of what kind of plan would be supported by various groups. Time and again, three questions came up at each workshop: where is the GGNRA, how do we get there from here, and what is there to do when we get there? After all, this wasn't like other National Parks, which one flew or drove several hours to as a discrete destination.. This was a National Park that you could literally walk to, hike or bike to, take the bus or ferry to or drive to in ten to thirty minutes! Even from the most remote places in the Bay Area, the park could be accessed in about an hour and a half. To explain these benefits, we gave people in Chinatown, the Mission, West Oakland and San Jose flyers and detailed information on where different features were, which parts of the park had been acquired and were accessible, how to get there and what was there now. Even though the planning was in progress, the GGNRA already offered easy access from these dense urban places to incredible getaways and spectacular natural resources.

It is hard to overstate the importance of increased access to these natural resources. Since much of the GGNRA historically consisted of military facilities and agricultural or watershed lands, access had been restricted or had limited availability to most people. However, the military bases that lined the coastline lands of the GGNRA already had access roads, infrastructure and many structures suitable for adaptive reuse, making the task of increasing accessibility less challenging that it would have been if new roads and infrastructure needed to be designed. At the same time, the presence of certain active uses within the parklands could actually be to the park's benefit. This concept had a precedent at the Point Reyes Seashore, where families were allowed to maintain their ranching activities even after their ranch lands were acquired by the Park Service. This provided a beautiful pastoral setting for the roadways to the beaches and hiking trails along the coast, but also allowed the families to preserve their livelihoods and to continue their stewardship of this large land area.

Among both the public and the planning team, there was a general feeling that overall, the park should act as a contrast to the urban areas as a means of providing respite from the cities. As such, we privileged conservation over development. Key resources of the park in that were closer to urban areas, such as the Presidio and Crissy Field, Alcatraz, and Forts Baker and Mason, would naturally have more intense visitation. Thus they were slated for special uses and events. In addition, it was predicted that these well-known and well-loved landmarks would draw not just high numbers of visitors, but would also foster community involvement and generate financial support from donors. An example of this was the Presidio Trust, an oversight corporation in partnership with the National Park Service, which became self-supporting over time with revenues from adaptive use and limited new development within the Presidio. Given the size of the park and the limited resources of the Park Service, the concept of limited development in a few appropriate areas—with the remainder of the parkland being reserved for conservation and open space with hiking trails, beaches, and camping—was very much in line with the long view of the citizenry and the practicality of managing such a complex resource.

By the time we reached a point where we were able to produce planning concepts or express alterative policies and ideas on paper, we had already discussed almost all of the options in the workshop process. By 1976, after several rounds of workshops, alternative proposals were prepared for the projects, and these were assessed in 1977 with even more public participation. This was followed with the publication in 1979 of summary of the General Management Plan and Environmental Assessment. There was an overall good response to the plan and much support, and after a few details were patiently worked out, the final management plan was successfully published and implemented.

Throughout the multi-year planning process, the sequence of informational workshops followed by scheduled workshops and organized involvement proved to be the critical factor in the creation of plans that were enthusiastically supported by the public. The work of the GGNRA Citizen's Advisory Committee, the more than 200 workshops used in the planning process, and the incredible amount of public participation made our team's efforts pay off in the form of a truly great National Park. Amy Meyer a founder of the "People for a Golden Gate National Recreation Area," a citizen's group that led the initiative to establish the GGNRA, includes in her 2006 book, New Guardians of the Golden Gate, a quote from Doug Nadeau, the project's Park Service Planning Coordinator:

"As far as precedent-setting work is concerned, the bottom line is that Golden Gate (GGNRA) carried out the most difficult, extensive and effective public involvement process ever accomplished by the National Park Service. The process set the standard for the rest of the Service and many other agencies."

Following the planning of the park, the establishment of the Golden Gate National Parks Conservancy in 1981 set up a mechanism for citizen participation that has continued very effectively over the park's four decades of existence. As a measure of its success, the Conservancy has been involved in over one thousand park projects, recruited 250,000 volunteers and raised 250 million dollars in support of the GGNRA. With over 17 million visitors in 2012, the GGNRA is now the most visited National Park in the nation, and it consistently holds the record for the most volunteer participation. It is truly is a park for the people by the people, and to commemorate this, the GGNRA was awarded the Landmark Award by the American Society of Landscape Architects in 2005.

**Opposite Page** The Long Beach Shoreline Plan defined the uses and character of the city's diverse waterfront.

## Long Beach Shoreline Plan, Long Beach, California (1975)

In 1975, Sasaki, Walker Associates (we changed our name during this time to SWA GROUP) were asked by the City of Long Beach in Southern California to create a Coastal Plan for the city. Ed Killingsworth, with whom we had worked so well at Sun Valley and Boca Raton had referred us to the city. Ed was a leading architect in Long Beach and had been contacted by several prominent Long Beach businessmen who were concerned when the California Coastal Commission shut down development along the city's ten-mile shoreline. The Commission was concerned that Long Beach was granting large development projects along the coast with no specific Coastal Plan as required by the law. To help mediate this dispute, we were asked to propose how the City could solve this difficult problem in a way that allowed development of the City to continue without harming the sensitive coastline.

We began a study that could satisfy the Commission and get Long Beach back to issuing permits to develop its coast along the lines of the recent Coastal Act. The Long Beach Harbor District, which operated one of the largest ports in America, was not included in our study as it was working directly with the commission on a plan for their maritime uses. We would just address Pier J near downtown Long Beach, since it housed the Queen Mary and was thus considered a special recreation district. The major area of our study then consisted of the remainder of the city shoreline from the edge of Pier J, extending toward downtown Long Beach and Pacific Terrace, a recent land-fill area, then eastward toward the Bluff Communities and the East End, a

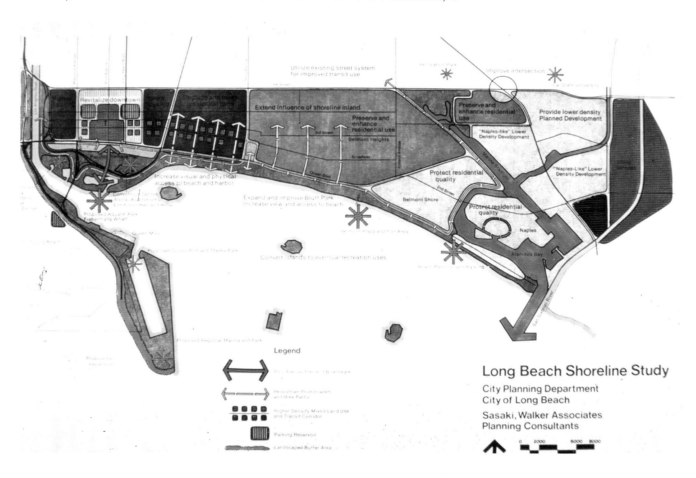

**Long Beach Shoreline Study**
City Planning Department
City of Long Beach

Sasaki, Walker Associates
Planning Consultants

complex of residential communities along the coast and Alamitos Bay. The East End in particular, with its beaches, estuaries and large pleasure boat marinas, had become a battleground given the many large new development proposals it attracted, and this was a major cause of the shutdown by the Coastal Commission.

It was apparent to us that there was a basic breakdown in communication between the citizens and the City that needed to be addressed. So, in addition to the environmental and planning studies of views and access to the coast that were called for by the Coastal Commission, we instituted a series of citizen workshops where we encouraged local groups to voice their concerns and to show them how our process would incorporate their ideas into the plan. Our ability to communicate data, analysis and planning concepts quickly and clearly to a diverse set of stakeholders made the Long Beach public meetings and workshops very effective.

Early on in the process, our photographer Gerry Campbell and I traveled around Long Beach taking photographs, including many panoramas that required multiple slides. We used these photos and panoramas in our public meetings and workshops, incorporating two synchronized side-by-side projectors and a very large screen to visually immerse the audience in the issues involving their community's plans and designs. At the end of the workshops, we left time for the citizens to ask questions, define the issues and hear relevant public response. In follow-up meetings, we showed plans and sketches created by our Principal Jim Reeves on one projector next to slides of existing conditions and precedent photographs on the second projector.

Having literally accumulated a million slides from our design projects and examples in cities around the world—a real treasure chest of visual resources

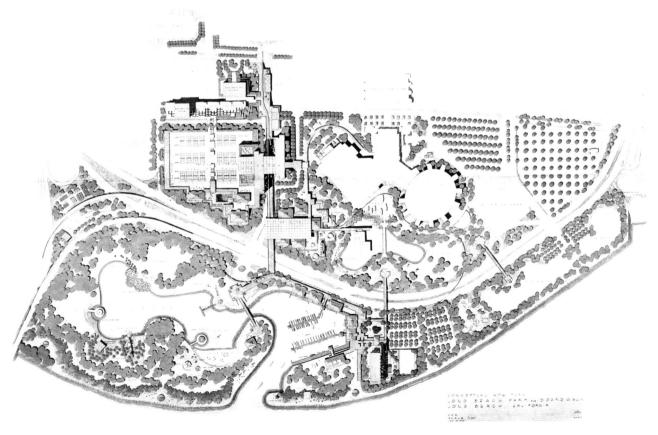

that set us apart from our competition—we were able to explain our ideas and recommendations with great specificity. Of course, this was before the time of computer file systems, but nevertheless we became adept in finding the exact right photograph to explain our idea. The audiences always left engaged—most times in a very positive way. Using so many photographs of their hometown made them feel more involved, and this involvement provided us with very helpful responses and critiques that we could use in the final Urban Design Plans.

Our public participation approach was not all smooth sailing for the City administration however. The Coastal Commission was very sensitive to this level of public input, since its mandate had come about through citizen action and a state ballot measure that had recently been passed to protect the coast and provide better coastal access for all citizens. Therefore our study was set as a transparent process to give us credibility with the citizens and Coastal Commission. As the plan progressed as an independent study and the citizens and Commission staff got behind it, there was increased scrutiny of the City staff's previous actions. We later learned that there was rampant criminal corruption in issuing development permits for years leading up to the showdown between the City and the Coastal Commission that halted the permit process based on non conformance to the Coastal Act. As a result, the City Manager, Planning Director and several other officials went to prison.

Through our research, we were able to determine the different needs of each district in the plan. It was apparent that downtown Long Beach even with its excellent regional access had experienced a long decline, and was in deep need of renewal and an increased intensity of activity. The Bluff Communities meanwhile were in better shape, but still had some areas that needed development and also neighborhoods needing view protection. Furthermore, in this area it was critical to preserve valuable open space to provide amenities to communities that were farther away from the shoreline but also to maintain an ecological corridor for stormwater management. The preservation of Bixby Park and the Bluff Parks were integral to this plan. Finally, the East End communities of Naples and Belmont Shores were charming coastal communities, but needed protection to ensure that any new development would maintain and enhance their character rather than detracting from it, and to not have their limited regional access overwhelmed by huge new developments.

The major policy change that our plan recommended was to move this development pressure and greater density from the East End, locating it instead in the downtown and western shoreline districts, where development was much needed and with its excellent regional access could be readily accommodated. This policy protected the positive character of the East End that was strongly supported by the citizens. It seemed like an obvious solution, but had evaded the city due to their misguided (and as we found out later corrupt) focus on large development proposals that would have negatively changed the East End. The adoption of this policy ensured that new development in the East End would be limited, following the low-key character and access to Naples and Belmont Shore. Similarly, we recommended that building heights along the Bluff Communities be limited at the shoreline to maintain view corridors from to the interior blocks that were to be redeveloped. These policies emerged from our work with the citizens and gained their strong support.

Opposite Page Boats at Pacific Terrace with downtown Long Beach beyond. **Bottom** The Pacific Terrace plan indicates civic, commercial recreational and park uses for this waterfront addition to downtown Long Beach.

**Above** An aerial view of the Shoreline Village, park, hotel and convention uses of Pacific Terrace connected to downtown by a pedestrian boardwalk. **Middle** People in the Shoreline Village at Long Beach Downtown.

In addition to tailoring density and development to the character of the city's neighborhoods, our plan also considered how to improve access to the coast from different points within the city. To enhance redevelopment of downtown and Pacific Terrace, we proposed a major new pedestrian spine that would link downtown to the bay. Along this spine, new high-density office and residential uses could be built downtown and hotel, entertainment, and parks could be built on the new land that had been created by landfilling Pacific Terrace. As a precedent, we looked at the historic Pine Avenue Pier that, early in Long Beach history, extended out from downtown to the bay as a boardwalk entertainment area.

Despite the tension between the Coastal Commission and the City, our plan was approved by both agencies thanks to its sustainable approach to increased development, and the city was able to reopen the permitting process and get Long Beach moving again. After the corruption scandal, we followed up with the new City Manager and City Planner who began the amazing transformation of the city. Over the years, we did more detailed urban design studies of downtown development, which made the pedestrian promenade connecting Ocean Drive with Pacific Terrace a reality, and connected downtown to the new convention center arena, performing arts center, Hyatt Regency hotel, and the Shoreline Village, a restaurant and shopping center fronting a luxury marina. We also did concepts for the development of the entertainment district of Pacific Terrace, which included the Aquarium of the Pacific and the fifty-acre Shoreline Aquatic Park. With this development underway by local landscape architects and architects, new office buildings and mid-rise residential units were added downtown and we, with Ed Killingsworth, designed a new City Hall, Library and park to add to the urban character.

**Above** Downtown Long Beach and the Shoreline in 2013 showing 'a city apart' from the sprawl of the Los Angeles Metropolitan area.

**Opposite Page** Navy Field was transformed into a park, marina and shoreline promenade directly in front of Downtown San Diego. **Bottom** The San Diego Embarcadero Plan covered the City's central bay front from the airport to downtown.

The important recommendations we made are still evident today in the distinct qualities of Long Beach's downtown and shoreline neighborhoods. Freda Moon of The New York Times Travel Section on March 18th, 2012 describes this multi-faceted character:

"At the mouth of the Los Angeles River, shipping cranes flex across the skyline—an industrial panorama that suits Long Beach's gritty reputation. But while the city's maritime character remains, its rough edges have been smoothed in recent years—the downtown waterfront transformed by redevelopment, the busy port now welcoming both cargo vessels and cruise ships. Along with its sandy shore, a compact downtown of low rising Art Deco towers, and unassuming neighborhoods, where craftsman bungalows are ringed by tropical gardens, Long Beach has excellent museums, ethnic enclaves and a tangle of Southern California subcultures. Layered, urban and unexpected, it is a city apart from the sprawl and strip malls that define the outer edges of Los Angeles".

## San Diego Embarcadero Master Plan (1974-6)

We were awarded the San Diego Embarcadero Master Plan project in 1974, after I put forth a comprehensive proposal to the San Diego Unified Port District to work with Deems/Lewis and Partners, a local architectural firm, and John Forrestal, a transportation engineer. Frank Hope, a prominent San Diego Architect who we knew, liked what we had recently done with the Coastal Commission on the Long Beach Shoreline Plan. He served on the San Diego Board of Port Commissioners and recommended us to complete a study of the three-and-a-half mile Embarcadero, the downtown waterfront of the city. The linear waterfront extended from the boundary of the port-operated San Diego Airport to the west, encompassing Harbor Island and its hotel and marina, the Coast Guard facility, and the large, crescent-shaped wooden boardwalk and boat anchorage along Harbor Drive. The central area of the Embarcadero included a working area for fishing boats, an historic sailing ship and museum, a restaurant, the County Administrative Building, and

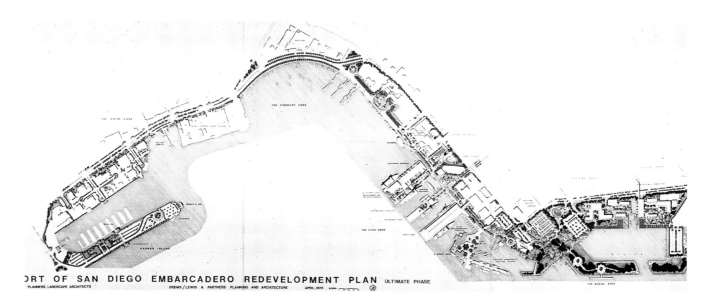

the Broadway pier at the foot of the main street leading into San Diego City Centre. The eastern end of the Embarcadero included the G Street Mole, the Navy Supply Center, the former ferry terminal site, a fish market and the large and now vacant Navy Field.

Phase I of the project had been completed to study the economic, engineering and environmental aspects of the waterfront and its potential for redevelopment. Our work in Phase II meanwhile was to articulate an overall Embarcadero Redevelopment Plan with urban design and transportation recommendations. Our team at SWA GROUP included Pete Walker and Jim Reeves as well as me and our concept was to better connect downtown San Diego to its bayfront, and to make the entire length of the waterfront from Harbor Island to Navy Field more publicly accessible and pedestrian friendly. In addition, we wanted to preserve the maritime aspects of the working waterfront while adding commercial recreation appropriate to the setting to attract more visitors to the Embarcadero.

Many of the features we designed were directly targeted to public access to the waterfront including a public plaza and gateway to Downtown San Diego at the termination of Downtown's main street at the Broadway Pier. Here major cruise ships, sightseeing cruisers and ferries docked along waterfront quays and the adjacent B Street Pier. We included public attractions such as hotels, restaurants, shops, and civic facilities. These facilities were connected to the Maritime Museum, with its historic sailing and steam vessels and adjacent restaurant, by a landscaped pedestrian promenade extending to the west along the Embarcadero. Continuing westward, the pedestrian promenade connected to marine facilities along Harbor Drive and to the planned pleasure boat marinas and resort hotels on Harbor Island. While much of the plan emphasized tourism and recreation, it was also important to recognize the waterfront's role in the livelihood of area fishermen, and we retained

a working area and tie-ups for the use of small fishing boats on the reconstructed boardwalk along the Crescent.

Heading east from the plaza at the foot of Broadway, the planned promenade ran along the bay past Navy Pier, which became the permanent home of the retired USS Midway aircraft carrier museum after the closing of the Naval Supply Center. The G Street Mole, site of the American Tuna Boat Association headquarters as well as a large restaurant and a large, unique fishing boat fleet, provided a dynamic setting for Seaport Village, a specialty commercial recreation and entertainment area we planned on the site of the old fish market. A major attraction to residents and tourists, Seaport Village connects directly to Navy Field, a major redevelopment area where the San Diego convention center, hotels, and commercial complex were built adjacent to a large recreational boat marina and public bayfront parks.

In 1976, the Port District approved the plan and detailed design guidelines, which were also very well received by the Coastal Commission and the City of San Diego. Implementation by local landscape architects began immediately, and over the next 36 years the Port has implemented most of the plan. To the credit of both our plans and the Port in house planning and design team, our guidelines and sketches of various urban design elements were used as references throughout that entire time. The San Diego Embarcadero Plan received an award from the American Planning Association in 1976.

The San Diego Embarcadero is a truly urban waterfront that connects directly to downtown and adjacent neighborhoods such as Chinatown and the Gas Light District. Our plan has stimulated office, commercial and major residential development in these areas, as well as recreational amenities such as the Tijuana Trolley connecting to Mexico and the San Diego Padres ballpark. This comprehensive Embarcadero program provided synergy with the hotel, convention, historic and entertainment areas along the shoreline and the hybrid of a working and recreational waterfront, coupled with recent efforts to complete and enhance public amenities, has made Downtown San Diego a nationally significant destination for tourists and locals alike.

**Opposite Page** Jogging through the new San Diego Embarcadero parks. **Bottom** The new convention center and marina at the former Navy Field make an attractive setting for downtown.

**Above** The Star of India historic vessel along the Embarcadero in San Diego. **Bottom** Walking along the San Diego Embarcadero promenade.

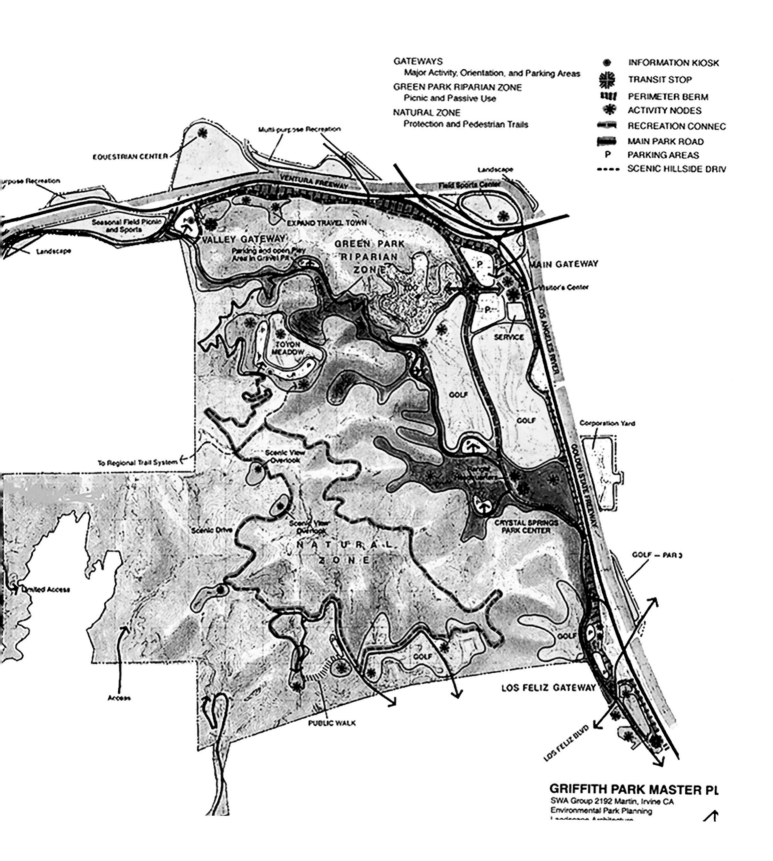

GATEWAYS
   Major Activity, Orientation, and Parking Areas
GREEN PARK RIPARIAN ZONE
   Picnic and Passive Use
NATURAL ZONE
   Protection and Pedestrian Trails

● INFORMATION KIOSK
❋ TRANSIT STOP
▥ PERIMETER BERM
✳ ACTIVITY NODES
▬ RECREATION CONNEC
▬ MAIN PARK ROAD
P PARKING AREAS
---- SCENIC HILLSIDE DRIV

EQUESTRIAN CENTER
Multi-purpose Recreation
urpose Recreation
Seasonal Field Picnic and Sports
Landscape
Landscape
Field Sports Center
VENTURA FREEWAY
VALLEY GATEWAY
Parking and open Play Area in Gravel Pit
EXPAND TRAVEL TOWN
GREEN PARK RIPARIAN ZONE
ZOO
P
P
MAIN GATEWAY
Visitor's Center
LOS ANGELES RIVER
SERVICE
TOYON MEADOW
GOLF
GOLF
Corporation Yard
To Regional Trail System
Scenic View Overlook
Scenic Drive
Scenic View Overlook
NATURAL ZONE
Headquarters
GOLDEN STATE FREEWAY
CRYSTAL SPRINGS PARK CENTER
GOLF — PAR 3
Limited Access
GOLF
GOLF
GOLF
Access
PUBLIC WALK
LOS FELIZ GATEWAY
LOS FELIZ BLVD

**GRIFFITH PARK MASTER PL**
SWA Group 2192 Martin, Irvine CA
Environmental Park Planning
Landscape Architecture

## Griffith Park Master Plan, Los Angeles, California (1978)

We had the pleasure of working with architect Frank Gehry in the early days of his career, before he became world-famous for works such as the Guggenheim Bilbao and the Walt Disney Concert Hall. We worked with Gehry on the Concord Pavilion, the Bixby Townhouses, and the Cochiti Indian Reservation in New Mexico, and so when he was contacted by good friends in Los Angeles about some critical planning issues that had arisen in the planning for Griffith Park, Los Angeles' largest public park, Gehry arranged for us to meet with the city to see if we could help.

At the time, the Los Angeles Department of Recreation and Parks was under great pressure to provide more facilities for recreation in Griffith Park, and they were in the midst of preparing a plan that would dramatically impact the 4000-acre park. The city had gained a large allocation of water that they thought could be used to irrigate and "green up" large areas of the semi-arid, mountainous park. This, however, raised questions of environmental suitability, transportation to and within the park, and compatibility with other large land uses in the park such as the golf courses and the Los Angeles Zoo. Because of these issues, and because of our track record in thoroughly integrating public participation, and harmonizing natural and development goals concerned citizens urged the City of Los Angeles to retain SWA GROUP to study the proposals and come up with a park master plan.

Our team, which was led by Don Tompkins from our Southern California office and myself, undertook intensive environmental and transportation studies of the parklands to better understand the complex issues involved. Griffith Park encompasses much of the headlands of the Santa Monica Mountains, which separate west-central Los Angeles from the San Fernando "Valley" to the north. As such, the park represented a threshold between natural and man-made environments. We learned that the people of Los Angeles greatly valued this aspect of the park as we instituted an intensive public involvement process to complement our environmental and planning studies.

Through this participatory process, both the citizens of Los Angeles and we as a design team benefited from an intensive education about the natural and cultural resources of the park. Together, we learned that the park was naturally a chaparral community, which is characterized by continuous low impenetrable vegetative cover subject to seasonal wildfire. In this kind of environment, the ability to increase moisture content to introduce more temperate kinds of vegetation is limited by the steep hillside slopes, which have thin, dry, rocky, and highly erosion-prone soils, and thus have limited water holding capacity. In the park, in fact, only the flat riverbed valleys and the limited deep canyons possess soils capable of holding moisture and accommodating "greener" plant ecologies. These riparian areas are incredibly valuable for wildlife and as green corridors for recreation and stormwater management.

The park's largest uses—the zoo, Travel Town, the Steamers, equestrian areas, and the golf courses on the flatter lands at the northern and eastern edges of the park—were also the uses most beloved by the public. This indicated that we should protect and increase access to these areas in the plan as much as possible. Parking in the park was poorly distributed: the Zoo had thousands of spaces available even during busy times, while most other facilities had limited parking—this was especially true of Fern Dell, the Greek

**Opposite Page** The overall Griffith Park Master Plan preserves the majority of the upper hill areas as a natural zone, and protects the more intense recreation uses on the lower flatlands.

Theater and the Griffith Park Observatory. As such, we sought to more evenly distribute parking access.

In consideration of the two critical factors that emerged through the participatory process and our research—the delicacy of the chaparral community and the importance of retaining existing uses—we suggested that the park be organized into major use zones and gateways. The largest use zone was the Natural Zone, a preservation zone that would protect forever the steep and sensitive chaparral community lands that comprise three quarters of the park area, prohibiting extensive irrigation to avoid catastrophic environmental consequences. The Natural Zone, with its hiking trails and spectacular viewpoints, would continue Griffith Park as an oasis of nature right in the city. A vegetative rehabilitation program was established for this zone that would replace exotic species with native plants that with low water use could curb soil erosion and foster fire suppression. Meanwhile, in the very limited riparian areas of the natural zone, irrigation could be added to create small passive use "green" areas where appropriate.

For the remaining one quarter of the parkland that was flatter and more intensely developed, the Master Plan added a corridor of lawns, trees and flowing green spaces. This created new picnic areas, which were in high demand, in the Crystal Springs, Park Center, Old Zoo and Mineral Wells areas of the park. Along this corridor, we articulated three high-use gateways, giving each additional gathering places as well as a strong sense of entry, orientation, and activity. The gateways also became key access points for the intra-park shuttle bus system that we designed. This shuttle would use the large parking lot at the zoo and other parking facilities as hubs to serve the underserved activity areas and the natural zone.

We did have one unfortunate episode in our final presentation of the plan. When we met with various interest groups before the plan was finalized, we told the golf groups that we were not going to change the popular golf courses in the park but were considering repurposing a small golf practice area that was currently not in use as a much-needed family picnic area. We secured their understanding and agreement for this aspect of the plan, but when we finished the plan in 1978 and set up a final citizen workshop in a large auditorium, one of the most popular radio station personalities at the time came out with a story that our plan was going to remove all the golf from the park. This happened on the day of the final presentation, and when we arrived that day, the auditorium was packed with angry golfers who were making ugly noises. The Parks Department called in a substantial police presence as this was a potentially explosive situation. We had brought a two-projector slide presentation with a huge screen to present the plan, since we knew it was a large audience. Noting the police presence, the crowd quieted down, and I went up to the podium to begin. To calm the angry golfers, I made sure that the very first slide in the slideshow was a huge blowup plan of the park's golf area. Showing specific parts of the plan in zoomed-in detail was a technique we often used to explain individual parts of the plan, since the printed plan we had on stage was clearly too small for this large audience to see.

The huge projected image showed that all of the golf courses were still on the plan just as they currently existed. I simply stated:

"This blowup from our official Master Plan shows that the radio announcement made today is wholly incorrect about golf at Griffith Park. This is our plan and always has been our plan. We will not change the existing golf

**Above** The green park riparian zone of Griffith Park ensures places for the experience of verdant community park uses for the people of the City.

**Opposite Page** The large natural zone of Griffith Park ensures the lasting experience of the native chaparral community's for residents of the Los Angeles Metropolitan Area.

courses, period. Our overall Master Plan is up here on the stage where you can look at it carefully after our presentation. I am sorry that someone got the story so wrong."

The crowd quieted down, many left, and we went on to present the rest of the plan, to which the remaining audience reacted very well. After the presentation a number of people did come up and look at the plan on the stage, and they were very supportive.

The Recreation and Park Board and the City of Los Angeles adopted our plan in 1978, and plans for overdevelopment of the park were scrapped. However, while we helped define the proper role for Griffith Park for a generation, the overdevelopment of delicate lands continues to be an issue in Los Angeles as the city grows to be a mega-metropolis. To help in overseeing this issue, the Santa Monica Mountains Conservancy was formed in 1980, and the long chain of the Santa Monica Mountains became the backdrop and continuation of the park's Natural Area, reinforcing that portion of our master plan. Much later, Colonel Griffith's great grandson requested landmark status for the park to protect it from a proposal to build aerial trams, hotels and restaurants in the Natural Zone, and this status was granted in 2009. In his request, the great-grandson, Griffith "Van" Griffith, restated his great-grandfather's original intent, "I want it to remain an urban wilderness where people can get back to nature."

## Lakewood Hills, Windsor, California (1979)

I always looked for the opportunity to get involved early in the master planning of land and then to follow up with implementation. This has been true whether the project addresses community infrastructure, housing, commercial or industrial uses. Sometimes the transition from master planning to implementation was a time-consuming process that took years to come to fruition. Lakewood Hills in Sonoma County, California was such a long-term process, and its twists and turns could easily be made into a gripping novel!

In the early 1970's, a United Airlines pilot came to us with a 500-acre parcel in an unincorporated area of Sonoma County called Windsor. He planned to use the profits from the land's growing value and its development toward his retirement. He had already asked an engineering company to come up with a plan for this development, but asked us to review the plan and submit it to the county for a Planned Development Permit. We weren't used to this, as we typically preferred to do the master planning ourselves, but considering the ongoing housing recession, we took the project, adjusting the plan somewhat especially in the hillside portion of the property, where we reduced the amount of development to account for the land's steepness and high utility costs.

We received a preliminary permit from the county in the early 1970's, but as our client was not a developer, we knew the final plan would need to be refined once a developer got involved. Unfortunately, the 1973-1975 recession developed into a long and deep national recession that hit California real estate particularly hard. Unable to get a development partner, our pilot client struggled to keep the venture afloat, and was ultimately unsuccessful, finally losing control of the property. After this, the property was split up and changed hands several times.

It wasn't until 1979 that a developer and a local Savings and Loan gained control of the most developable portion, 140 acres of the flatlands directly adjacent to the 101 Freeway interchange. We got involved in the project again, and went to the county with a revised plan that would develop this part of Lakewood Hills as a master planned community with high-end single family

**Above** The commercial part of Lakewood Hills includes shopping, and professional and medical offices. **Bottom** The two lakes and runnel connection form a setting for the lakeside homes and the larger community.

**Opposite Page** The plan shows mixed residential uses extending around two lakes, a recreation center and park at Lakewood Hills in Windsor, California.

homes on two man-made lakes, condominium developments, an umbrella homeowner association, medical offices, and a commercial shopping village. The developer of Lakewood Hills directed us to plan and build a first-class community that spared no expense to create landscape infrastructure and incorporate innovative landscape designs by SWA GROUP Principals George Hargreaves and Bill Callaway. These features were anchored by two deep lakes connected by a unique channel and greenway.

Windsor is equidistant from Santa Rosa, the largest city in Sonoma County, and Healdsburg, the closest city to the north along Highway 101. Over the years as an unincorporated area, it had become the unwelcome recipient of Sonoma County's low-income housing projects and trailer parks. The local farmers and particularly the fire district had wanted to become a city to control their destiny and improve its prospects for future development. They were supporters of our first plan, but were as disappointed as we were by the long delay in development. So, when they saw the higher-end development proposed in the later plan, they knew they had their opportunity to finally become a city. The large shopping village, offices and luxury housing would give them the tax base necessary to make incorporation a reality, and with this plan in hand, local residents began the long process to become incorporated. In 1992, after a long and sometimes contentious process, the City of Windsor was finally formed.

It gave us great pleasure to see the community unfold and to realize the potential and success that our master plan brought to Windsor. It wasn't until much later, however, that we discovered that the relationship between the

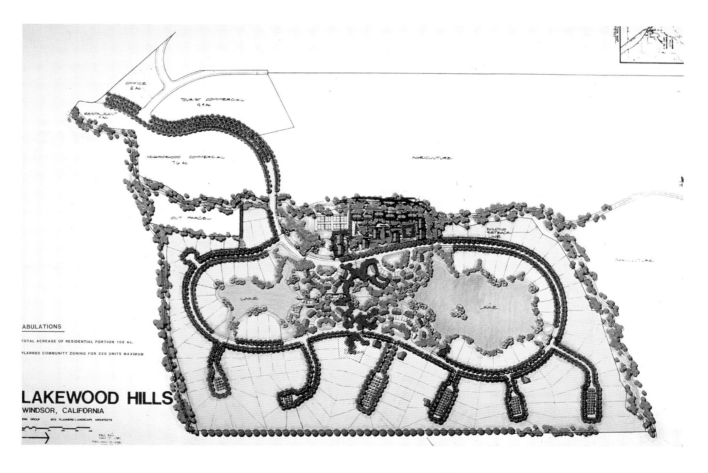

ABULATIONS

TOTAL ACREAGE OF RESIDENTIAL PORTION 108 Ac.

PLANNED COMMUNITY ZONING FOR 220 UNITS MAXIMUM

LAKEWOOD HILLS
WINDSOR, CALIFORNIA

**Above** The runnel between the lakes and its stone walls and waterfalls set a unique character for Lakewood Hills. **Bottom** The loop street around Lakewood Hills is pedestrian friendly and a community link.

**Opposite Page** The plan for Lantern Bay is a mix of uses set upon the bluff tops and lower ranges of a former quarry site in the City of Dana Point, California.

developer and the Savings and Loan was improper, and this corrupt relationship became a notorious part of the Savings and Loan investigations of the 1990's. Fortunately, the development went on as planned and was successful, and after this scandal, we finally finished implementing the community with another local developer in the late 1990's. This later phase involved building the Safeway center on the remaining commercial property, including the Safeway grocery store and several smaller outlets connected by a long landscaped arbor, a medical office building and a health club and spa. By 2010 Windsor had expanded to the other side of the freeway with a neo-traditional town center, and the city had emerged from its lower-class beginnings into a solid middle class suburban community of 26,000 people. The twenty-five years of our on-and-off involvement had achieved the goal of planning and building a sustainable community and there is no doubt that we learned much from the long and involved effort.

## Lantern Bay, Dana Point, California (1980)

The establishment of the California Coastal Commission in 1972 resulted in a large number of coastal planning projects in the 1970s, many of which I had the chance to work on with SWA GROUP, including Long Beach and the San Diego Embarcadero. Another Southern California coastal project came to us when Pacific Mutual Life Insurance Company brought us in after they had taken back the 78-acre property overlooking the Dana Point Harbor from the Smythe Brothers. Chuck Smythe was a high quality home builder who, like many others in his shoes, could not fathom why the Coastal Commission

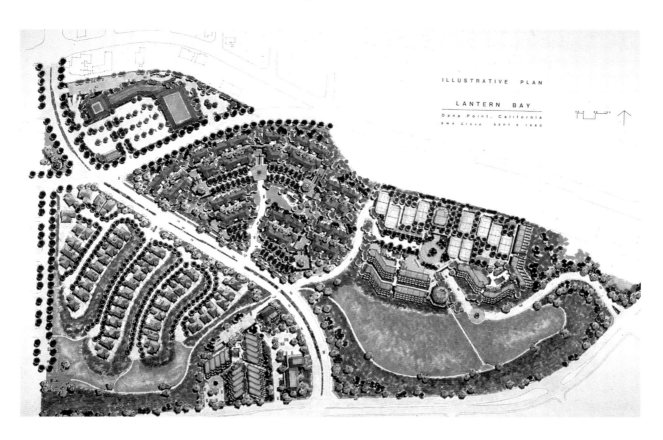

ILLUSTRATIVE PLAN

LANTERN BAY

Dana Point, California
SWA Group  Sept 5 1980

would not let them do what they had for years—build luxury single family homes in gated enclaves on the Southern California coast. In his case he had gotten so upset about his inability to get a permit, he had a heart attack and was convalescing. He was told by his doctor not to get further involved in the development process.

The project, Lantern Bay, was located atop a bluff that had been quarried to build the harbor below, and this had caused the bluff face to begin experiencing severe erosion due to the open cuts made in the quarrying process. Despite this issue though, the site had incredible views down a stretch of coastline famous for the blue and gray whales that pass close to shore every year during their seasonal migration. The Coastal Commission staff explained that their decision to stymie the Smythe Brothers project was because as the Coastal Act mandated they facilitate access to as many people as possible to enjoy this coast. Instead of a private, exclusive enclave of expensive homes they required a plan with the kind of uses that provided access to the largest number of people.

With this mandate as our guiding principle, we began a public outreach effort to find out what the people in the surrounding community saw as issues and solutions. We also visited community leaders in their homes to discuss and include their highly practical considerations in our plans. Through this process we came up with a mixed use plan that allowed for 45 small-lot "view homes" on stepped terraces down the bluff, but also included a hotel site (which later became the Laguna Cliffs Marriott Resort and Spa), a shopping village, moderately priced condominiums, and, at the base of Lantern Bay Boulevard, a motel and restaurant site conveniently located across from the Dana Point Marina and other public facilities.

We also had to address the structural and aesthetic effects of the bluff's serious erosion problem, and for this, Dick Law and Don Tompkins of our Laguna Beach office came up with a mass remedial grading scheme that contoured a major road down the bluff from the Pacific Coast Highway to the Marina, thereby working towards the Commission's goal of increasing public access to that major public maritime use.. The land uses themselves were

**Above** The large resort hotel has commanding views down the coast and sits adjacent to the public bluff top parks of Lantern Bay. **Middle** The long view down the bluff parks with condominium homes and the hotel adjacent to the park. **Bottom** A retail village serves Lantern Bay and the adjacent neighborhoods of Dana Point.

**Opposite Page** The spectacular view down the Orange County coast at the bluff top parks of Lantern Bay.

graded in terraces that re-contoured the bluff and allowed us to treat it with plant materials as an erosion control device. The terracing also allowed us to plan, design and do the landscape development of two public parks on the site, for a total of 24 acres of open space, which addressed the increased public use and access requirements of the commission. These Orange County parks were truly spectacular, with gorgeous views down the coast—especially during whale-watching season—and a continuous walkway and bicycle path that ran along the length of the site and then snaked down the slope to the marina, taking the form of a strikingly sculptural disability access ramp.

The planning of Lantern Bay was a time of tense negotiations with the Coastal Commission, and during this process, Chuck Smythe would sometimes—against his Doctor's orders—visit our internal meetings for progress reports. Having been warned of Chuck's condition, I accented the positive parts of the process. But in reality, there were some real difficulties, which I always later conveyed to Pacific Mutual—after Chuck had gone home. In the end, however, we were fortunate in that the citizens we involved in the planning of Lantern Bay helped us in the approvals processes at Orange County and the Coastal Commission. These citizens went on to incorporate the area around Lantern Bay into the City of Dana Point in 1989, with the Dana Point Marina and our project as their centerpiece. The Lantern Bay Project received awards from the Pacific Coast Builders in 1985 and the American Society of Landscape Architects in 1986 and 1988.

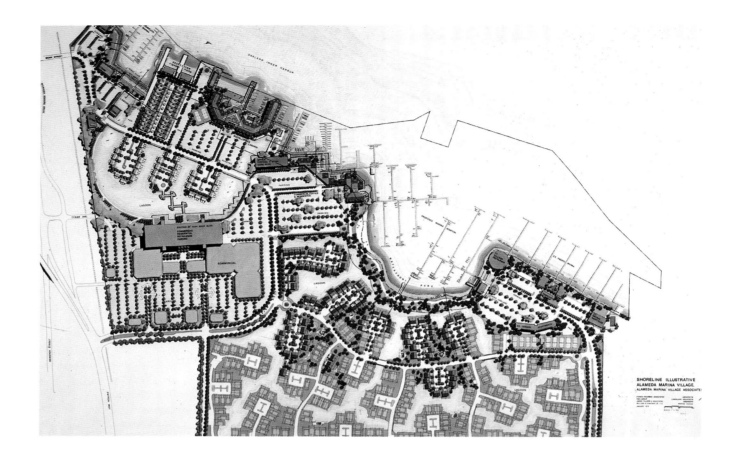

Chuck recovered after the project was approved, and became one of the happiest clients I have ever had. For years afterward, Chuck, as healthy as I had ever seen him, would tell me stories of people begging him to build them a house at any price at Lantern Bay, and of him obliging but taking his sweet time in doling out the sites in order to stretch it out over the years into his retirement. He made sure that as well as the homes the entire development of hotel, shopping village, condominiums and commercial recreation down at the Marina level was the highest quality and left an incredible legacy for Dana Point.

### Alameda Marina Village, Alameda, California (1980)

I had worked with Mick Humphreys of Vintage Properties on several smaller plans when he and another client of ours formed Alameda Marina Village Associates and acquired the old shipyard properties on the estuary in the City of Alameda. This hundred-acre waterfront property was quite different from the pristine coastal sites we had worked on with the Coastal Commission: it was derelict from long-term neglect and its large piers and waterfront facilities were beyond repair. To address these facilities, the client paired us together with Fisher Friedman, Architects, with whom we had done a number of successful residential projects.

The City of Alameda and the relatively new Bay Conservation and Development Commission (BCDC) were anxious to remediate the conditions

**Above** The plan for redevelopment of the old shipyard in Alameda, California into residential, marina, and commercial uses.

**Opposite Page** Aerial view of the lagoon homes on the marina with commercial areas beyond at Alameda Marina Village.

124

and put the property to productive use. We took the lead in analyzing and planning the property in a city known for solid residential neighborhoods that had direct access to San Francisco Bay and the Alameda Estuary.

Located right off the tunnel that connected Alameda to Oakland and the East Bay, the property had commercial and industrial potential, and if properly configured, it could also house a water-oriented residential neighborhood. I remembered how well Fisher Friedman designed water-oriented housing with us in Foster City, and how they were able to take advantage of even small lagoons. My work in Florida with Arvida also had us designing manmade lakes, so on the plane back from Florida I sketched out a series of manmade freshwater lagoons that would connect a central residential neighborhood visually but not directly to the Estuary.

BCDC mandated that public access to the estuary would be a requirement. Most commercial uses would be deemed by BCDC to have acceptable access by their very nature of being open to the public, but in residential areas public facilities would be required to ensure access. With SWA GROUP Principals Mike Sardina and Jim Lee, we designed a public linear shoreline park as a connector between the commercial and residential uses and the estuary. Conveniently, this park would also serve as a transition band between the shallow fresh water lagoons and the brackish waters of the estuary. This had another advantage: since the homes could be sited directly on the controlled water levels of the lagoons, we did not have to worry about the effect of a six foot tidal range on the appearance of the shoreline at the homes. This was actually a significant design issue, since the most economical way to treat the estuary shoreline was with stone riprap, which created a rough and rocky edge down to the water eight feet below at low tide allowing for seasonal super high tides. By putting the linear shoreline park between the lagoons and the estuary it made an attractive green transition from the lagoons and homes to the estuary and marina beyond.

The form of the shoreline park created a crescent-shaped harbor in the center of the site, and we wanted an attractive sailboat marina for the harbor to buffer the industrial uses that lie across the narrow Alameda Estuary in Oakland and take advantage of the deep water access to the bay and ocean. According to the BCDC, any new marinas or structures were considered bay fill and any new bay fill was prohibited. So, we turned to the large areas of derelict pilings, piers and structures left over from the old shipyard. By removing them, we were allowed to replace the same overall area with new marine structures, so in a double benefit, the derelict structures were removed and a large new marina was built out in front of the residential area. To the east of the Shoreline Park and marina, we retained an existing restaurant and a commercial boat harbor that later became the Oakland Yacht Club.

The western edge of the property was adjacent to Webster Street, which connected central Alameda to the Oakland Tunnel. We designated this area for commercial and business parks on the inland portions, and marine-oriented and recreational uses along the waterfront. There were substantial shipyard structures along this end of the shoreline, and we planned for the adaptive reuse of these in the commercial areas to lend a special waterfront character. A large concrete building from the shipyard and a brick utility substation from the 1920's were easy candidates for reuse. The shipways and head houses were robust concrete structures that would be prohibitively expensive to remove, but could be effectively used for marine services and shops.

The most interesting candidate for a mixed-use residential and commercial redevelopment was a large, beautiful cathedral-like brick building from the late 1800's. However, we ran into a unique provision of Alameda zoning: the city did not allow any more than two residential structures to share a common wall. Strangely, apartments and residential condominiums were not allowed at all in the city, which meant that our lagoon homes in the center of the site were all limited to duplexes, but also that the brick building could not be converted to residences.

We thought this very special and historic building could be an exception. The city staff were excited about our plans and this was not just a multifamily building, but a unique mixed-use building. But a vote of the people was required, and they did not agree. Their fear that Alameda would lose its identity vis a vis Oakland and the East Bay was too ingrained and unfortunately, their bias against density had social factors too strong for any exceptions. The saddest part was that the building did not configure well for commercial use only, so when we could not move forward with our mixed-use intensions, the building had to be demolished. The city changed this onerous rule in 2012 after many years of misguided policy.

With this issue resolved, we received the first ever unanimous approval by the BCDC and a quick approval of the plan by the City of Alameda. Alameda Marina Village was then built out over the years following our plans and design criteria. In addition to master planning, we designed the landscape development for the first phase of the project, which included the entry, the entry boulevard, the linear Shoreline Park, the lagoons, and the water-oriented

**Opposite Page** A detail of the homes on the Alameda Marina Village lagoon. **Bottom** Riding bikes along the Alameda Marina Village shoreline park.

homes in the residential neighborhood and the large boat marina. Later phases were designed by others, but they followed our plan for the Oakland Yacht Club and Marina to the east along the waterfront as well as retail, marine, recreational and office uses to the west along the estuary. The inland areas of the site became retail and office uses near Webster Street, with a light industrial technology center in the middle.

Alameda Marina Village received the Urban Land Institute Award of Excellence in 1991. A few years later, in 1997, the adjacent Alameda Naval Base was closed. Today the base is being redeveloped as a community that connects to Alameda Marina Village, rounding out the west end of the Island of Alameda.

**5**

# Growing nationally the group practice matures, new offices, and teaching in the East

1980s

In the late 1970's, Pete Walker accepted a teaching position at the Harvard Graduate School of Design and soon after was named Chair of the Landscape Architecture Department. When he left the Sausalito Office, we set up a special SWA East Office that he and the firm jointly owned, and this office gave Pete the flexibility to pursue his teaching as well as some personal art projects. By the end of the 70's, Pete had made great strides at the GSD, and had totally revitalized its Landscape Architecture program. He also had generated more consulting work than he could handle, and he needed help. We discussed turning SWA East into a full-fledged SWA Office, and I agreed to come to Boston to get the office off the ground as well as to teach a Development Studio that had recently begun in the Landscape Department.

The SWA GROUP work shown here demonstrates this period as a maturing of the group practice as Pete goes on to teaching. Dick Law plays a transitional mentor role as the firm's senior designer and a number of the principals find their distinctive voices in design, planning and construction projects, creating new ideas and iconic projects.

The timing to go east worked well for me and our family, as our youngest child David had just finished high school and was accepted at Oberlin in Ohio. Janne had begun a Learning Disability Clinic a few years earlier in California, but she agreed to leave the clinic in the hands of her associates so that we could go to Boston and then two years later to Florida. We had met in Florida and had many friends and family there, and Boston was not far from New Jersey and her family. And so, in 1980 we moved to Boston. Since the office was in the Back Bay, we took advantage of the depressed Boston real estate market and rented a penthouse on Commonwealth Avenue, a beautiful part of Frederick Law Olmsted's "Emerald Necklace" of landscape spaces in the city. Boston was a remarkable place to live.

The Boston Office had interesting projects, in part due to Pete's interest in art and his connections to Harvard. While there I worked on the Prudential Center Redevelopment in the Back Bay with Eduardo Santaella, the fan pier on the Boston waterfront and The New Seabury Master Planned Recreational Community on Cape Cod with Martha Schwartz. The office at that time was also overseeing the construction of the Tanner Fountain, one of the most iconic landscape works on the Harvard Campus.

Illustrated on pages 128-139 are projects that show the diversity of the work of the principals in a true group practice.

**Opposite Page** The Williams Square bronze horses race across an abstract version of a West Texas stream.

**Above** The plaza and its horses at Williams Square are one of the best loved attractions in the state. **Middle** The granite steps, waterfalls and horses crossing the streambed have made Williams Square a people place. **Bottom** Sculptures of Texas Mustangs form the centerpiece of the Williams Square Plaza commercial uses at Las Colinas.

Being on the east coast also helped me to continue my work with Arvida in Florida, as sharing the same time zone and the shorter air trip from Boston and help from Rick Lamb made it much easier to schedule my consulting work around my teaching commitments. At the same time, two colleagues helped make my job as President much simpler. Mike Gilbert had by that time been brought on as our firm wide business consultant and Wendy Simon, our Controller, had established regular business procedures that allowed me to be out of the Sausalito Office and still have quick and efficient communication. Following our tradition of establishing new offices with experienced Principals from the Sausalito office, Tom Adams and Mike Sardina came out and took over the Boston office in 1981, and then Roy Imamura from Sausalito joined Eduardo Santaella in taking over the Florida office when I returned to California in 1984.

In late 1983, before I returned to Sausalito, Pete Walker decided that as he finished his teaching at Harvard, he wanted to begin a practice with his new wife, Martha Schwartz. He wanted to establish this office in New York so that he could also pursue his interests in art, and though he felt the larger multi-office group practice was doing well, he missed the days when he ran the firm as his studio. Given these differences, we agreed to phase out his involvement on SWA GROUP projects and wished him success in his new venture, family and personal projects. Years later, after he and Martha divorced, this passion for studio culture led him to form Peter Walker Partners, where he could finally create such a studio to attract the select clients and projects that allowed him to fully realize his unique gifts as a landscape architect and an artist. Martha went on to form a truly international practice. Though Pete is no longer with the firm, we at SWA GROUP and I personally have always held him in the highest esteem, for I know firsthand that in his search to achieve his dream he never shortchanged us, but did what he could to help us also achieve our dreams of a group practice of which we and he could be justly proud.

**Above** A gathering place for families under the palm groves at the Hyatt Regency Scottsdale. **Bottom** A series of gardens, pools and a sandy beach embrace the luxury Hyatt Regency Hotel in Scottsdale, Arizona.

**Opposite Page** The Hyatt Regency is set in the golf courses and valley of the Gainey Ranch in Scottsdale, Arizona. **Bottom** People at the pools and terraces in the Arizona sun at the Hyatt Regency Scottsdale.

**Pages 132-133** The large Citicorp Plaza and garden on the backside of the office building is focused on the domed trellis that covers a multilevel shopping mall below.

In the mid 1980's I returned to Sausalito and resumed my work with clients in the West as well as continuing with those in Florida. I was again working in close proximity to the firmwide business and support people. With both our children gone from home, Janne and I sold our large shingle home in the hills of Mill Valley and became part of the houseboat community just a few blocks from the Sausalito office. It was a most diverse community with one neighbor owning one of the largest non-corporate wineries in California in a beautiful custom made boat on a sturdy concrete barge, and another with a helicopter pad. Stewart Brand, author of the "Whole Earth Catalog," lived in a well-restored tugboat down the dock, and Gordy Nash lived across the dock in a shack on Styrofoam floats that gradually sank until he added more pieces of foam. Gordy was an "old timer" in the community who had the benefit of subsidized rentals and other perks, and he built me a beautiful New York Whitehall rowboat with which I plied the bay each morning looking out for harbor seals and seabirds.

Our own houseboat was built by a friend from an 1889 railroad coach that had been retired from the rail system than ran through Sausalito in the 19th century. The coach was split in two, and the mail and freight section became our bedroom while the paneled passenger section became our dining room. These two sections were placed at right angles over a large concrete barge that housed below a multipurpose room, bedroom and bath where you could look up at the beautiful all-wood construction of the coaches and the equally interesting floor structure of the two-story living room that enveloped the coaches above. Our boat had decks overlooking the sailboat marinas and San Francisco in the distance. We could also see across Richardson Bay to the mansions of Belvedere, and the few remaining homemade houseboats "anchored out." illegally in the bay. I did say this was a diverse community!

After completing the restoration of the boat for its 100th anniversary in 1989 and holding a waterfront event to celebrate, we sold the boat in 1992. In 2003, the houseboat now fondly called the "Train Wreck" appeared on the cover of Barbara Flanagan's "The Houseboat Book," which was and remains the most comprehensive guide to North American houseboats. With our houseboat adventure in the past, Janne and I returned to Mill Valley to live in a shingled cottage downtown, and we bought a larger farmhouse with a small vineyard in the Sonoma Valley wine country for weekends with friends and grandchildren.

**Above** The major office building entry at Citicorp Plaza in downtown Los Angeles. **Bottom** Night time in the retail center under the domed trellis at Citicorp Plaza.

**Opposite Page** Dallas Alley is a popular nighttime entertainment zone in the West End.

**Opposite Page** With new offices, restaurants and entertainment uses, the Dallas West End Historic District attracts tourists as well as downtown workers. **Bottom** The Dallas West End Historic District was transformed from obsolete industrial uses to a place for people to enjoy.

**Above** The stark abstractions of Harlequin Plaza in this business center at Englewood, Colorado.
**Bottom left** The loading docks of the historic Curtis Publishing Center in Philadelphia have become an atrium for the new office uses.
**Bottom right** People are drawn to the "quilt" of marble pavements, columns and oversized planters of this new interior courtyard at Curtis Center.

**Above** The community includes apartments and condominiums set in the new landscape of First Colony. **Middle** A "reforestation" approach to the entire open site of First Colony made the community an attractive place for outdoor activities.

**Above Right** The First Colony New Town in Sugarland, Texas has a variety of residential neighborhoods, a Town Center and employment areas.

## The Development Studio Case Studies at Harvard (1980-82)

The Development Studio in the Landscape Department of the Harvard Graduate School of Design (GSD) was an interesting combination of things. The goal was to introduce designers to an area of practice that was coming into prominence. Private developers were beginning to make large-scale decisions about building cities, and they needed design talent that understood the process that these entrepreneurs used: obtaining property, studying markets and financial trends, planning for their chosen development, getting approvals, financing and then finally building, marketing and operating these complex works. To convey this process, we embraced a truly interdisciplinary approach with GSD students from Landscape Architecture, Architecture and Urban Design, along with students with interest in real estate development from the Kennedy School of Government and the Harvard Business School (HBS).

Miller Blue, who had a joint appointment at the GSD and HBS, taught a course in real estate economics and finance at the time that was a prerequisite to the Studio. We also brought him in to consult on the studio from time to time. The studio itself was organized on a project basis, or case basis as termed in the Business School, using real projects brought in by developers, who also participated in the project and provided funds for the students to travel to the project sites. With this format, the students were thoroughly exposed not only to interesting development projects, but also to developer representatives, who gave them a first hand exposure to how the process really worked and how they thought about the role of planning and design.

I knew that if we allowed the students to team up from the beginning of the Studio, the designers would design, the planners would address planning issues, and the business students would do the financial pro formas. So instead, at the beginning of each semester we would have at least one individual project that required each student to do all of those essential components themselves. I also knew there would be lots of trading behind the scenes, designers showing business students how to draw a site plan, planners showing designers how to read a zoning ordinance and business students showing the others how you could translate markets and physical development into numbers and a rudimentary business plan. But this was really a desired kind of information trading, so in the subsequent projects we would have them team up in well balanced teams, allowing each team member to share their own area of expertise but also to draw on the general knowledge they gained from the first project. That would be as important a learning experience as any in this kind of complex real estate development, fraught as it is with uncertainty and risk.

We kicked off the studio with remarkable results in my first year. The developers were enthusiastic about working with the GSD students and appreciated the results of their work. The students learned a lot from each other, and from us. The word got around about how the course was conducted and the following year I was inundated by students during the "shopping frenzy week" at the start of the term. Running SWA as its CEO and setting up the firm's Boston office made my schedule difficult, but I never missed a class. But the students also needed help when the studio was not in session, so I was fortunate in the first year to have Don Cameron, a great planner and designer who had worked with the Irvine Company in California, volunteer to come to Boston on his own tab and work intensively with the students for the entire

**Opposite Page Left** The interior of Gund Hall had the different design studios on a series of stepped "trays". **Right** Gund Hall was the home of the Harvard Graduate School of Design when I taught the Development Studio in the 1980's.

term of the studio. They quickly recognized all he had to offer, and he really made all the difference in my ability to focus them intensely when I was available, while having someone there who could hang out with them when they needed support.

In the second year of the studio, I quickly accepted a proposal by a Mike Horst, a Harvard Loeb Fellow whom I knew before as an economic consultant, to come to help in the studio. Mike was excellent with the students and was so taken with the concept of the Development Studio that he was instrumental in having it continue at the GSD with Chuck Harris taking over my role after 1982. Mike went on to Berkeley and established a similar course there, and finally ended up at the ULI as a senior executive. I greatly enjoyed the experience of teaching the studio and met many bright students along the way that made it all worthwhile. As an added benefit, we were able to bring a number of these students to the SWA GROUP where they carried what they learned in the Studio on into their work.

Pete asked that, in addition to the Studio, I take on a Professional Practice course that had gone by the wayside at the GSD. I did not need another duty at that time, but agreed to do it since I had seen how unprepared graduates from the GSD were in assuming the responsibilities of clients, running an office, and the legal and ethical challenges of a professional in a market-driven society. So for several days I sat in the Loeb Library and put together a reading list that included everything from writings of the Olmstead Brothers on the landscape profession to AIA documents and astute essays by economists on why the "bottom line is not the bottom line" in professional business practice.

The students who were required to take the course got together and with the librarian's consent, made copies of all the reserved readings in sequence, and so a "Syllabus on Professional Practice" was born. I used this syllabus many times over the years, and it was also used by SWA Principal Tom Adams and subsequent teachers. In teaching this course I also took advantage of our firm's outstanding legal and business advisors, John Taylor and Mike Gilbert, asking each of them to attend for one week to give a lecture on their area of expertise. We also managed to schedule them for informal seminars during their time in town—the students wisely and widely attended these. After I left Boston and Harvard for Florida, I was very happy to learn that the Professional Practice course had been made a requirement. Moreover, this new course built upon my syllabus and John's, Mike's, and my efforts, and ultimately played an important role in setting up some of our future landscape firms, while making other established firms run much better.

**Opposite Page** A place to sit or play on the carefully set stones in the wet or dry at the Tanner Fountain at Harvard. **Bottom** The lighted mist and the stone circles of Harvard's Tanner Fountain are mystical at night.

**Above** Stone circles, grass and asphalt panels combined with a mist fountain creates a abstract but delightful people place at Harvard's Tanner Fountain.

## University of Miami Campus Planning, Coral Gables, Florida (1983)

In early 1982, when I was still in the Boston office, we were asked to work on a campus plan for the University of Miami in Coral Gables, Florida—which I have described before as a city that perfectly fits its motto, "The City Beautiful." I was just about to move to Florida to start a new office in Boca Raton so the timing was good, and the fact that I had been a student there over 30 years before made this a particularly appealing project for me. We were recommended to the university by Chuck Cobb, our Arvida client, in his capacity as the Chairman of the Master Planning and Construction Committee of the University of Miami Board of Trustees. The university, under the direction of a new president, Edward T. Foote II, had the desire and will to finally bring the physical as well as the academic environment of the Coral Gables campus up to its full potential, to truly reflect the university's impressive growth and excellence. For the planning effort, we joined Walter Taft Bradshaw, a local landscape architect, to prepare a Master Landscape Plan for the campus.

The University of Miami was founded in 1925 in Coral Gables with a donation of 160 acres by George Merrick, the city's visionary developer, and a goal "to establish Coral Gables as the educational center of the South and the natural meeting place of the culture of North America, Central America and South America." The first students arrived in 1926, but it was a long and rocky road from then on, taking over 60 years to be able to fulfill that lofty founding vision. By the time we were hired, the university had become the largest private educational institution in the Southeastern United States, with Schools of Law, Medicine, Engineering, Education, Architecture, Music, Nursing, Marine Science, Business and Arts and Sciences. President Foote realized the potential jewel he had in his hands, with a university set in the exotic sub-tropics in a region fast becoming the center of Inter-American learning and culture.

The Coral Gables Main Campus encompassed two hundred and fifty acres in 1982, and showed the results of its discontinuous yet rapid growth over the past six decades. In addition to the disorganization and discontinuity, the campus was lacking in overall identity, cohesiveness and quality except in a few special areas. Luckily, the campus had a good basic structure, being bound on all sides by public roads with access to mostly peripheral parking areas, an academic core, supporting special uses, student residential areas, athletic fields, and a student center on the seven acre Lake Osceola. Most parts of the campus were within a 10-minute walking distance, and early campus plans determined there would be no vehicles or parking lots in the core so it could be a pedestrian precinct. However, this was most notoriously violated by a faculty parking area in the center of the academic core between the library, administration building and Memorial classroom building.

Another big problem was that the major entry for visitors came from the south of campus at Stanford Drive near Dixie Highway, and this route did not provide a direct and easily understood access to the administration building, academic core or library. Lastly, there was very little other than Lake Osceola and the student center that gave the campus any common areas of distinction or connection to its unique climate, or relationship to its setting in the sylvan neighborhoods of Coral Gables.

**Opposite Page** The University of Miami is located in the garden city of Coral Gables, south of the City of Miami. **Bottom** Highway One and the University of Miami Metrorail station provide easy access to South Miami, Coral Gables and the university hospitals in central Miami.

**Pages 146-147** A new image and identity for the University of Miami was created by the fountain and plaza with its grove of majestic Royal Palms at the academic core, administration building and library.

President Foote had a vision of "a campus in a tropical garden." This became the primary goal of the first element of a new University Plan, a *Landscape and Urban Design Plan* prepared by SWA Group Principal John Wong and me with Walter Taft Bradshaw. This plan was quickly implemented, with the first phase beginning construction in 1983 to set the new President's vision in motion. New academic buildings and campus facilities quickly followed. The first phase construction transformed Memorial Drive, a small road that provided access from the northwest peripheral roadway into a memorable major entry statement to befit its role as a major gateway to the academic core, library and administration building. The entry, with its Taft Bradshaw designed Coral Rock walls with lush tropical plantings, special stone pavements, and pedestrian-oriented lighting, was easily located by visitors.

The faculty parking lot at the center of campus had to be removed, as it violated the long-planned central green mall. We had full support from the president to remove the lot, and so the large area was transformed into a continuous open space that connected the University Arboretum on the north edge of the academic core to the Student Center and Lake Osceola on the south. The shortened Memorial Drive ended on a large fountain and a multifunctional plaza connecting to the central greenway designed by John Wong. Within this plaza, a loop of special pavement served as a turnaround for the University shuttle buses at the end of the drive.

**Above** The central part of the University of Miami campus is a car free greenway with pedestrian walks and a sculpture garden.

148

The plaza was set within a large grove of majestic Royal Palms that we planted to frame the fountain and provide shade for benches and pedestrian ways. After our plan was implemented, the Royal Palm became a signature tree for the University of Miami, as it cannot flourish anywhere in the mainland U.S. outside of South Florida, and its striking form and height make it an unique image for the subtropical educational institution. Very quickly, the Royal Palms and Fountain in the center of the expanded academic core became the symbol of the University of Miami on television and in print.

To replace the removed faculty parking, the underutilized peripheral parking lots were transformed by heavy shade tree plantings and connected to the core by wide walkways lined with rows of Royal Palms that branched out from the plaza. In building this signature image for the University, President Foote knew he had violated one of University of California President Clark Kerr's three ingredients of a great university president—providing for sufficient sex and parties for the students, a winning football team for the alumni, and close-in convenient parking for the faculty—but he realized that providing a close community and strong identity were far more important legacies. The faculty did not go down without a fight, however. Even though they were told before the summer break of the plan to replace the parking, they revolted over having to walk this small additional distance. They angrily interrogated Taft Bradshaw and me about why we did this, but we held our ground and refused to repent from a design that was not only quite appropriate for the university but also had quickly become its defining identity. Their unhappiness led to our removal from the next phases of implementation which Taft and I assured President Foote was a small price to pay for such a beneficent result.

Faculty dissent notwithstanding, President Foote saw to it that later phases followed our guidelines. These phases included the extension of a broad walk lined with Royal Palms that connected the library to the student center and included cafes and outdoor seating, as well as a forty foot high fountain in Lake Osceola given to the university by Chuck Cobb to provide a focal point for the south campus and to help in providing oxygen to the deep lake waters. The "campus in a tropical garden" had taken a permanent hold.

Ten years later I was asked back by President Foote to look at potential redevelopment opportunities in a sixty-acre area on the south side of the campus, where a series of 1950's era residence halls had become physically and functionally obsolete. The desire was to keep the academic core at the north end of campus as compact as possible, so this redeveloped area would only have a few academic components, and these would be limited to sites adjacent to the edge of the core. Other uses in the middle of the redeveloped area would be reserved for residential colleges and university support facilities. Finally, more public oriented uses would be located toward the southern edge of the site, which faced the Miami Metrorail station and Dixie Highway. We saw the site offering the university a 21st century opportunity to create a Transit Oriented Development (TOD) on the campus that would serve all of Metropolitan Dade County. This plan revision was presented to Coral Gables and approved.

The first site to be redeveloped was for a large Convocation Center that the university needed for public functions or athletic events. The public access nature of the Convocation Center made the south campus location a good choice. To further enhance access, a parking and shuttle bus garage followed as well on the southwest periphery near the Convocation Center and close to the Metrorail station, offering easy train, bus and parking connections. The land directly across from the Metrorail Station meanwhile was designated for a major health care facility for the South Miami and Coral Gables areas. The health facility was sponsored by the University of Miami Medical School, which is located a distance away from campus at Jackson Memorial Hospital in central Miami. Since the Metrorail station at the Coral Gables campus connects directly to a station at Jackson Memorial, this will facilitate not only quick transit connections for doctors and medical students, but will also open easy Metrorail access to healthcare for the public in the greater Miami region.

Policies by the new university president Donna Shalala and her staff continue to move the campus toward the visionary education goals aspired to in the 1925 plan as well as the Smart Growth principles we instilled in our plan, which range from increased transit use and transportation choice, to easy pedestrian access to the compact academic core and supporting facilities, a protected open space and greenway system throughout the campus, a mix of university and public serving uses, and a distinctive sense of place. The University of Miami now has more than 15,000 students from around the world spread across five campuses with celebrated theater, music, art museums and intercollegiate athletics. Moreover, the school has been ranked number 47 in *U.S News and World Report* putting it among the top-tier of national universities.

## Walt Disney World Resort, Florida (1984)

I returned to our Sausalito headquarters in 1984 after several years away starting new offices in Boston and Florida. During this time, I learned of a merger between our client Arvida and the Walt Disney Company. Together they formed Disney Development Company (DDC), with Chuck Cobb as its head which was charged with managing and developing all of Disney's real estate assets. The first major task for DDC was a master plan for the 28,000-acre Walt Disney World near Orlando.

Opened in 1971, Disney World had developed the Magic Kingdom and in 1982 added the EPCOT attraction. As the park experienced tremendous success and stratospheric numbers of visitors, Disney had also developed five thousand hotel rooms on its own, with another fifty thousand rooms in the Lake Buena Vista complex by an array of established hotel brands. The task of Disney Development was to further shape the world-class attractions and the supporting recreation functions into a true resort experience and by doing so to also increase the company's economic yields from these properties.

The Disney Development team included Peter Rummel and Roger Hall, who brought with them extensive experience in resort development at Arvida, along with Wing Chao from Disney's in-house staff, who had extensive experience in planning and building Disney attractions and facilities. Pete Walker and I at SWA GROUP were hired along with economic, engineering and other consultants with resort and recreation experience to assist in preparing a strategic plan for Disney World that would take the next critical steps in achieving the goal of a complete and cohesive Walt Disney World Resort.

The original approvals for Walt Disney World in 1967 involved a special district set up by the State of Florida, the Reedy Creek Improvement District

**Opposite Page** The Royal Palm walk at the University of Miami library café continues on to the student center.

150

(RCID). The District and its Comprehensive General Plan had the same status as any Florida city or county had in regulating development under state law. Our master plan was intended as a strategy document for Disney Development Company, and as new policies were established through this plan, the official RCID plan would be modified as required by law.

For this working level plan, we called on Doug Way, an SWA GROUP Consulting Principal, to further the land analysis in the RCID plan by utilizing the then new *Landsat* satellite-based imaging technologies. Doug had adapted Landsat to identify areas suitable for future development based upon soil types and capacities, depth of muck, drainage, depth to water table and vegetation. Engineering consultants used this research to add water management, utilities and transportation components, including roads, bus, monorail and water travel modes. Economic consultants meanwhile provided projections of market trends—both nationally and in the Orlando recreation complex; and the Disney members of the planning team contributed information on visitation issues as well as projections and opportunities for new venues, accommodations and needed support facilities, and infrastructure.

The challenge for the new plan was to better utilize and build upon the incredible entertainment resources and investments represented by the Magic Kingdom and EPCOT. The newly opened EPCOT was off by itself, not near any visitor accommodations, and was not attracting enough visitation. With this in mind, our plan considered not just what new attractions or uses would bring visitors to the resort as a whole, but especially those that would bring

people to EPCOT. To help facilitate this, the locations of the themed attractions, visitor entries, transportation corridors and accommodations needed to better connected and coordinated in a way that made it less time consuming and stressful for guests to move about the property. We wanted to make sure that the great joy and magic that the attractions could produce was not being overridden by the frustration of traffic and delays in getting from the hotels to the attractions and other activities.

It has long been evident that no one in the world does controlled entertainment attractions better than Disney. But that level of quality and entertainment needed to be expanded to include all parts of the resort experience, not just the attractions for which Disney had become world famous. A small beginning had been made early on in 1971 with the construction of the Contemporary and Polynesian Hotels on the lakes next to the Magic Kingdom. These hotels, for which SWA provided the landscape design, were the first in a series of themed hotels, a revolution at the time for they provided not just standard resort accommodations and amenities, but also an attraction-like quality that extended the Disney brand into a 24-7 experience. The continuous themed experience was further amplified by the addition of the iconic Monorail and several options for water transportation that added unique and fun ways to arrive or move about the Magic Kingdom, EPCOT and hotels—the Contemporary Hotel even had the monorail whisking through the lobby! Because these two hotels brought the theme park experience into the visitor accommodations, they remained the most popular with visitors. Unfortunately, the hotels built after 1971 were built not by Disney but by national franchises and did not do enough to incorporate the immersive quality of the theme parks.

We felt that our plan needed to remedy these issues, and so to expand the resort experience, we proposed that a number of new Disney-themed visitor accommodations would be built in the areas directly adjacent to EPCOT, the Magic Kingdom and the newly designated attractions in the plan. These could be hotels, timeshares, or new "Vacation Club" villages, which were designed to be walkable and environmentally conscious, but no matter the type, the goal was to move accommodations away from the bland environment at Lake Buena Vista. Building a large number of rooms inside the resort went along with Disney's desire to immerse visitors in the Disney experience, but this was also a strategic competitive move for Disney as it would draw visitors away from the standard corporate-branded hotels in Lake Buena Vista, which were not adding to the Disney experience and did not include the same variety of recreation experiences that the Disney hotels offered. Disney also knew early on that when visitors spent twenty-four hours a day in the resort, they also spent money on hotel rooms, meals and nighttime activities in addition to the park passes.

With the expansion of the park, transportation became critical, so a major component of our plan involved how people moved around Walt Disney World. The monorail was an enchanting mover of people between EPCOT and the Magic Kingdom, and was unique to Disney in the U.S. It was a great image maker but was not able to effectively move large numbers of visitors; moreover, it would have been prohibitively expensive to extend the Monorail to the Lake Buena Vista hotels, even considering Disney-scale budgets! We noted that the use of water transportation, begun earlier at the Magic Kingdom, was very successful in moving large numbers of people in addition to being a

**Opposite Page** The monorail connecting EPCOT to the Magic Kingdom at Disneyworld at Orlando, Florida. **Bottom** Walking through the Caribbean Beach Club, and to the close by attractions at Disneyworld.

**Pages 152-153** The new resort areas at Disneyworld were placed next to EPCOT with new entertainment venues, themed accommodations and water access.

fun experience in itself thereby. Part of the reason our plan proposed that the new themed accommodations be located next to EPCOT was so they could be served by waterways and boat transportation systems, as well as by pedestrian or bicycle access and small people movers. Automobile parking and buses served each accommodation or attraction, but the fun nature of the new types of public transportation encouraged was meant to encourage people to use their cars as little as possible once they arrived, keeping the special Disney feeling alive.

Our Disney Development team began to sketch out a phased roadmap of essential steps to fulfill the goal of making the property into a multi-faceted destination resort, the "Walt Disney World Resort." Experience showed that the most successful resorts create, control, and deliver a highly amenitized environment to the guests from the moment they arrive on the property until the moment they depart. This became the overarching goal, and all elements of the plan and phasing were designed to further the idea of an immersive "entertainment environment" that was consistent across the entire property. The entertainment environment began with "entertainment architecture"— the creation of themed hotels, golf villas or condominium villages—and continued with the "entertainment environment" between the various components of the resort—in other words the special landscape, streetscape and signage treatments that helped to create a seamless resort fabric.

While our plan was primarily focused on the idea of a cohesive entertainment, many of its features had added economic benefits. Making transportation around the resort a fun experience was also cost effective, utilizing a mix of pedestrian, people mover, bus, bicycle, waterway and boat transportation. We made more efficient use of the existing Monorail rather than opting for costly expansion. In addition to cost savings, revenue was generated and new markets were targeted through an expanded variety of visitor accommodations including timeshares and vacation club ownership developed and marketed under the Disney brand according to proven resort real estate principles. By blending Disney's outstanding entertainment capabilities with Arvida's resort operations and real estate know-how, Disney Development Company was positioned for success with the Walt Disney World Resort.

When Disney sold Arvida , implementation of the plan was transferred to Walt Disney Imagineering and DDC. We did not continue further at Walt Disney World after this point, but were invited to take on the task of expanding and rehabilitating Disneyland and the area around it in Anaheim, California under our Principal Bob Jacob and our close by Laguna Beach office. Peter Rummell, a key Arvida executive with whom I had worked at Sawgrass, stayed on to run Imagineering and in the following years successfully carried out many of the ideas and plans formulated by the Arvida/Disney Development master plan.

First priority was to complement the Contemporary and Polynesian Hotels with more resort accommodations in the area next to the Magic Kingdom around the Seven Seas Lagoon and Bay Lake. These new hotels became the Grand Floridian and the Wilderness Lodge, next to which several Wilderness Villas were later built. To diversify the resort's offerings, the existing Palm and Magnolia Golf Courses to the west of the Magic Kingdom, were to be complemented later by a timeshare village and extensive club facilities.

The next priority was ambitious, and involved creating an expansive destination resort area directly adjacent to EPCOT. This would include new Disney hotels and villas from which visitors could walk or take a quick tram or boat ride to EPCOT. The resort would be structured around a landscaped waterway and series of lakes running through the parks and accommodations, beginning at the World Showcase Lagoon in the center of EPCOT and ending on a new attraction added in 1989, Disney's Hollywood Studios. Along these waterways, sleek, low slung river boats similar to those in Paris or Amsterdam could take visitors directly to and from EPCOT and The Boardwalk, Yacht Club and Beach Club resorts, or to the iconic 1500-room Dolphin and 750-room Swan Hotel designed by architect Michael Graves, and finally down the waterway to the Hollywood Studios attraction.

In addition to the hotels, theme parks, and golf courses for which Disney World is known, our plan introduced new uses that expanded the market for the resort. The idea of Vacation Clubs, where one could own a timeshare or fractional interest on the Walt Disney World property under Disney management, was carried out with great success in the Caribbean Beach Resort, Port Orleans and Old Key West, each balancing privacy and seclusion with close proximity to the various resort attractions. Downtown Disney later added shopping and new daytime and nighttime entertainment in a highly walkable "downtown" format to energize the Lake Buena Vista area and bring that area's amenities into line with the new resort areas. And finally, we allocated space for a large planned community located south of I-4 that later became Celebration, one of the first and most successful New Urbanist communities. This range of options allowed people from all walks of life to enjoy the resort, whether for a once-in-a-lifetime experience, a seasonal stay, a second home, or even a primary home. All in all, our plan was extremely successful in setting the structure that formed the identity of the resort now renowned for: an entertaining, unique, and cohesive experience that is firmly representative of the Disney brand.

**Opposite Page** Cruising from EPCOT to the Yacht Club, Beach Club and Boardwalk resorts, and then to the Dolphin and Swan hotels at Disneyworld.

### Kezar Corner, Golden Gate Park, San Francisco, California (1987)

SWA Group had been working with ED2 International, Architects in San Francisco on a number of projects when they were asked by the City of San Francisco to make a proposal for the planning of the extreme southeast corner of Golden Gate Park. John Wong, Elizabeth Shreeve and I joined them in their successful proposal to plan for the removal of the obsolete Kezar Stadium from that area of the park and its replacement with a use that would be more in harmony with the adjacent neighborhoods and the rest of Golden Gate Park, the famous greensward that was so highly valued by the people of the city.

Kezar Stadium was built in the early 1920's as a multi- purpose venue in the park. The stadium and the adjacent Kezar Pavilion, built in 1924 as an attractive enclosed sports and entertainment arena, were both funded by the Kezar family, who envisioned that the facilities would serve as a memorial in honor of the family's Pioneer roots. The pavilion made for a fitting "edge' to the green park, sitting as it did along Stanyan Street, a busy commercial corridor. However, while the city and its citizens supported the continuance of the pavilion, the stadium was a different story. The original small stadium became much larger and all the more formidable when in 1946 it became the home of professional football teams. The San Francisco 49ers used Kezar for twenty-five seasons, and the Oakland Raiders used it for their opening season after the 49ers left in 1971 for Candlestick Park. After that, the 60,000-seat facility was used for famous concerts and events, all of which exacerbated its functional and physical incompatibility with the adjacent neighborhoods and the park.

The stadium sat along Frederick Street, the southern edge of the park, and was adjacent to a residential neighborhood. The vast difference in scale between the large stadium and the residential blocks yielded an unattractive blank wall of some forty to fifty feet in height along the street that blocked views and access to the green park beyond. This of course had a negative impact on the adjacent community, but was also a hindrance to a potential redevelopment on the other side of Frederick that was being planned and supported by the city.

For this redevelopment of the park's corner we launched into an intensive effort that involved working closely with local citizen and park interest groups as well as the city's Recreation and Parks and Public Works agencies. Our plan was to remove the unsightly walls and bleachers, and take advantage of the fact that the Kezar playing field was depressed into the earth. In the space this opened up, we could accommodate both a new grass multipurpose sports field surrounded by a track as well as limited 10,000-person bleacher seating within the depressed area, without the need for any walls. The effect would be a stadium that harmonized with the sylvan park and could provide a green edge along Frederick Street. It would open new and extensive views from the residential neighborhoods into the new "green" stadium and the larger park, and would enhance the redevelopment of the adjacent neighborhood. The smaller stadium and track would be used by local high schools, soccer clubs or for other events that would have a positive, rather than detrimental impact on the neighborhood. The new stadium would share school bus and car parking areas with the adjacent 4000-seat Kezar Pavilion, but was also easily accessible by transit.

With citizen support, our plan was approved in 1988 and the stadium was closed. Destiny was with our plan as in 1989 the Loma Prieta earthquake seriously damaged the old structures of Kezar stadium and it needed to be demolished as soon as possible. The implementation of the plan by the City Public Works and Parks staffs was swift and satisfying to all, and today a much needed and utilized community recreation facility in close harmony with Golden Gate Park has been created at Kezar Corner and a mature, residential-scale green edge has been restored to the park along a redeveloped Frederick Street.

**Above** The sketch shows how the dramatically reduced Kezar stadium and the adjacent Kezar basketball and swim pavilions fit well in Golden Gate Park and the neighborhoods of San Francisco.

159

## Greenway Communities for South Florida, Palm Beach and Martin Counties, Florida (1988)

In 1988, the John D. and Catherine T. MacArthur Foundation set up a study for a 180,000-acre planning area that included their extensive properties and the surrounding developable areas in Palm Beach County and adjacent Martin County in South Florida. This was an unusual and challenging effort for many reasons. First, the Foundation was not able to develop their lands due to their status as a non-profit charitable entity. Secondly, when they periodically sold parcels of their 40,000-acre land holdings near Palm Beach Gardens to developers to raise funds for their charitable work, they could not participate in setting any standards for the developments in those sales. This left them quite concerned about how their lands would be used and what the impact would be on their future sales and entire holdings. The law did however allow them to provide funding for a study that offered general ideas about improving the quality of new growth, though this study was not allowed to include any specific development plans.

The area of Northern Palm Beach County and Southern Martin County that surrounded their properties was relatively undeveloped and growth was rapidly approaching, so this was an opportunity to raise the bar for the development of their lands, so to speak. We were hired along with William J. Johnson Associates as Urban Designers and Planners backed by a team that included economic, transportation, and public policy consultants. Our task was to raise the awareness of better ways to develop and create community and to communicate these concepts to the Treasure Coast Regional Planning Commission, a state agency with purview over large developments in this region, along with several city and county jurisdictions and citizen planning groups in the study area.

**Opposite Page** The Kezar Pavilion forms the edge of the park on busy Stanyan Stereet with its commercial uses and adjacent public transit. **Bottom** A historic remnant arch of the old Kezar stadium in Golden Gate Park was preserved as a remembrance of its long history.

**Above** The low profile stadium is used for school and community activities and allows views into Golden Gate Park from the surrounding neighborhood.

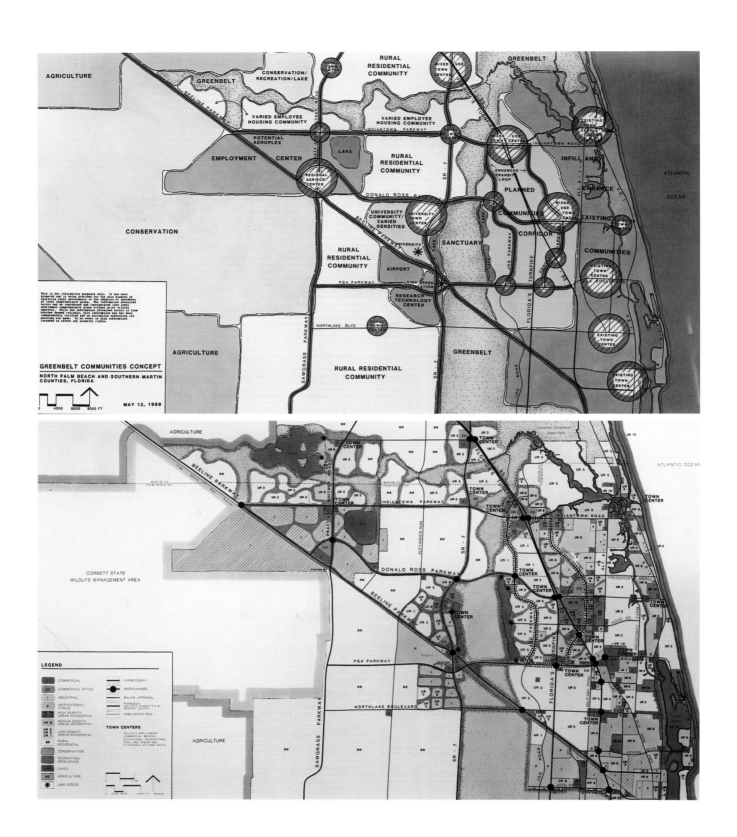

162

The team from SWA GROUP, which included Principal Elizabeth Shreeve and myself, as well as our Consulting Principal Doug Way, began by putting together a satellite based computerized geographic information system (GIS) that aided us in defining land characteristics, wetlands and water management areas, soils, land uses, transportation facilities and traffic analysis zones. We also studied population and economic development and made projections related to densities and to utility and transportation infrastructure needs, development and funding. Our concepts were presented to the various stakeholder groups through meetings, reports, maps, diagrams, and magazine and newspaper coverage. The large planning area had some weaknesses—small areas of sprawl where it was difficult to create a sense of community—but there also were some good examples of small community town centers that our concepts built upon.

We started in the huge study area with proposed guidelines for better regional public infrastructure based on a system of greenways around the critical waterways that traversed the area. This thirty-mile long regional structure of greenways could provide environmental protection and open space and include environmental mitigation, conservation and recreation uses. These corridors would also be integrated with the regional infrastructure of utilities, roadways, transit and high-speed rail. The typological roadway sections we proposed included seventy-five miles of innovative linear parkways that accommodated autos, transit, bicycles, and pedestrians, and also fostered recreation and amenity to adjacent land uses. This green infrastructure could involve the donation of Foundation Land according to a public greenway corridor plan.

Future commercial, employment, civic and residential land uses and densities were derived in aggregate from growth projections from demographic and economic activity research. Our recommendations could not be site specific, but we emphasized how the major growth would be in higher density mixed use town centers that would anchor each community and relate strongly to the greenway corridors and their multi-modal transportation, open space and park networks. Broad architectural and landscape guidelines were set to create unique and cohesive community character.

The materials were well received by the Treasure Coast Regional Planning Commission, as they did not have the resources to perform such a complete study for this high growth area. As the agency that reviewed all Developments of Regional Impact as mandated by Florida Law, the TCRPC was required to consider infrastructure capabilities and sufficiency in their formal review. Our study of desirable kinds of infrastructure and urban forms—including distinct communities with strong Town Centers—provided highly useful information and ended up being an important reference not just for the MacArthur Foundation's lands, but also for the review of other proposed development projects.

**Opposite Page** The Greenway Communities concept relies upon a system of environmental greenbelts, multi modal transportation systems in dark green and new high density town centers graded by size of red circle. **Bottom** A more detailed land use plan for the 180,000 acre planning study blending new growth areas with existing communities along the coast and preserving the large water conservation and agricultural preserve areas toward the everglades.

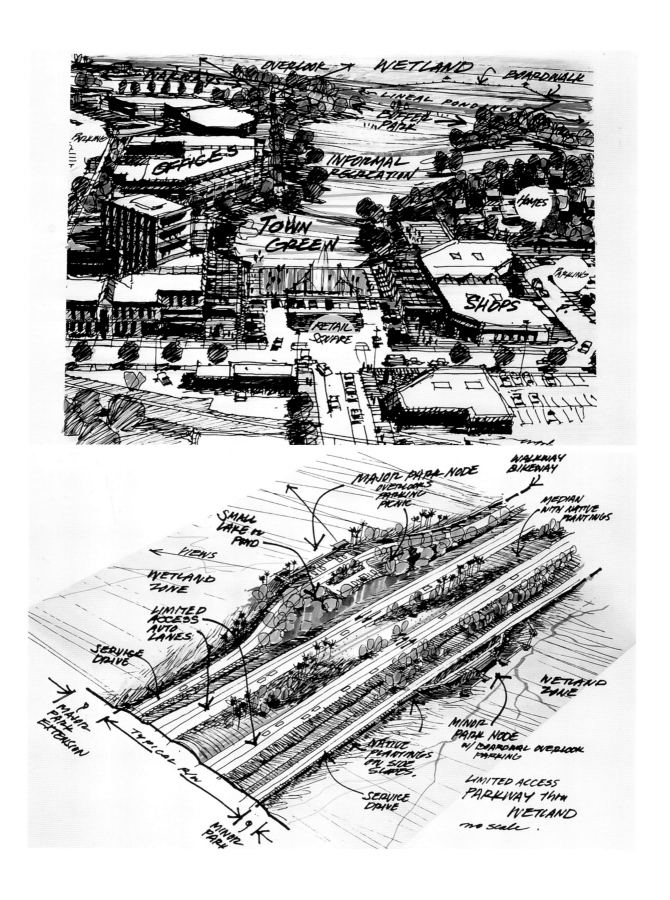

## Mountain House New Town, San Joaquin County, California (1988-2008)

The San Francisco Bay Area, a ninety-mile stretch running from Santa Rosa to San Jose, is blessed with a unique geography that pairs the Pacific Ocean and San Francisco Bay with the foothills and mountains of the California Coastal Range. The linear nature of the bay and the mountains, however, make easterly travel difficult due to the need for bridges and mountain passes, and as such, there are only two freeway corridors running eastward toward the San Joaquin Valley. One corridor heads northeast on I-80 along the bays and the Sacramento River Delta to Sacramento and then across the country. The other, I-580, stretches from Berkeley and east Oakland through the San Ramon Valley and then over the steep Diablo Range via the Altamount Pass. It was this point, where I-580 emerges from the Altamount Pass to connect to I-5 and the San Joaquin Valley, where Southern California developer Bill Johnson, having been impressed by our work on the Irvine Ranch, asked me to assist him in creating a new town, Mountain House.

Located fifty miles east of San Francisco in the San Joaquin Valley, the site for Mountain House could not have been better located for accessibility and land suitability. It fronted on I-205 where it connects with I-580 from the Bay Area and shortly thereafter with Interstate 5, the great north-south interstate that heads south towards Los Angeles and north toward Stockton and Sacramento.. With the eastward growth of the Bay Area threatening development of the fertile agricultural land in the heart of the San Joaquin Valley, the 7.5-square-mile Mountain House site was made all the more ideal for development given that it was on relatively poor agricultural land on the western margin of the valley. This put Mountain House in a key position to intercept growth before it spread into prime agricultural land.

In 1988 Johnson formed Trimark Communities to plan and develop the site, and we began an exhaustive series of studies and public meetings that went above and beyond the typical public participation process, as the area's largely rural and agricultural population had little understanding of or experience with planned communities. To extoll the virtues of these communities, we worked with local interest groups to bring community members on site visits to nearby communities in order to show them the advantages a coordinated and planned new community would have over the incipient sprawl. We argued that a full service "New Town" with higher densities offered the county an alternative to the lower density subdivisions being planned in many different locations, which were consuming too much of the region's valuable arable land. Unlike the homogenous, single-use subdivisions, a planned community could absorb a large portion of the county's growth and, if developed properly, could provide jobs, economic growth and efficient infrastructure.

I provided the public interface on the project, while SWA GROUP Principal Elizabeth Shreeve took on the task of working with the county to prepare a Master Plan Amendment and Specific Plan. The 4,748-acre plan we devised called for 44,000 people and 16,000 dwelling units in twelve neighborhoods, with residential densities that ranged from 4.5 to 20 units per acre—this was low by urban standards, of course, but was far more dense than the area was used to. Each of the twelve neighborhoods would be anchored by a central core consisting of a school, park and small retail, while pedestrian and bicycle

Opposite Page Town Center sketch -Sketch of a prototypical town center development in the Greenway Communities plan. **Bottom** Infrastructure sketch-Sketch of a prototype Greenway Communities infrastructure corridor with multimodal transportation and water management functions.

**Above** A lighted bicycle path on the greenway in
Mountain House. **Bottom** One form of cluster
homes that make up the diverse neighborhoods of
Mountain House.

**Opposite Page** The School-Park center of a
Mountain House neighborhood.

trails running through the neighborhoods would connect to a ninety-five acre linear park traversing the entire community along Mountain House Creek. To ensure a good balance between housing and jobs, there would also be 13,000 jobs located on 12.5 million square feet of industrial, office and retail space in business centers and the 120-acre Mountain House Town Center. Most of these commercially viable sites had frontage on I-205 or Mountain House Road, the main road heading north from I-205, making them accessible to the larger region as well.

Because this was a new town, one of the first tasks was to provide sufficient infrastructure and services. Special state legislation allowed the Mountain House Community Services District (CSD) to provide the full range of urban services that would be provided by a city. These included building and maintaining roads, water, sewer, and parks, and providing police and fire services, animal control, flood control and enforcement of covenants and restrictions. Land Use, Zoning and Building Codes would be under the jurisdiction of San Joaquin County and would fall under the approved Master Plan and Specific Plans adopted in 1994. The community would have its own public schools, and San Joaquin Delta College opened a campus in central Mountain House. Affordable housing would be under the nonprofit Housing Trust Fund, which would collect affordable housing fees and provide for affordable housing development. And last but certainly not least in our book, green infrastructure

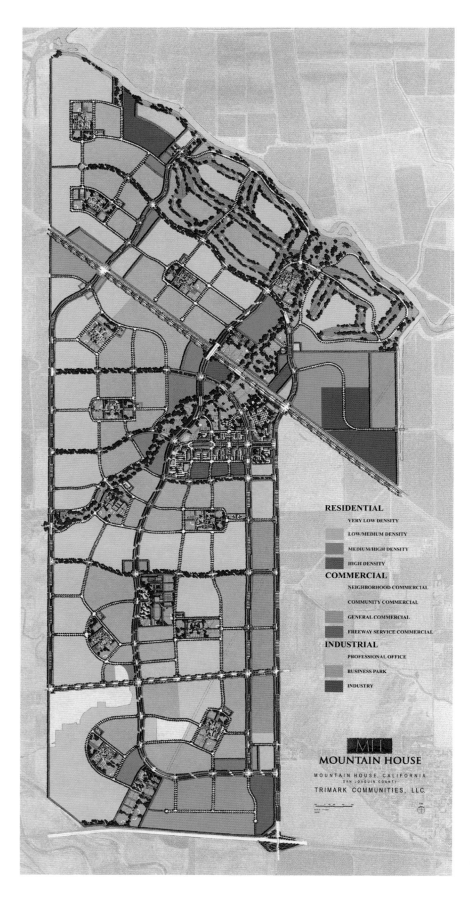

**RESIDENTIAL**

VERY LOW DENSITY

LOW/MEDIUM DENSITY

MEDIUM/HIGH DENSITY

HIGH DENSITY

**COMMERCIAL**

NEIGHBORHOOD COMMERCIAL

COMMUNITY COMMERCIAL

GENERAL COMMERCIAL

FREEWAY SERVICE COMMERCIAL

**INDUSTRIAL**

PROFESSIONAL OFFICE

BUSINESS PARK

INDUSTRY

MH
**MOUNTAIN HOUSE**

MOUNTAIN HOUSE, CALIFORNIA
SAN JOAQUIN COUNTY

TRIMARK COMMUNITIES, LLC.

**Left** The overall plan for Mountain House shows the structure of the neighborhoods around their school-park centers, and the greenway connections to the Town Center and employment uses.

**Opposite Page** The greenway along Mountain House Creek provides water conservation and connects the neighborhoods with bicycle and pedestrian ways.

including water quality control lakes and wetlands and an 82-acre linear park along the Old San Joaquin River in the northern portion of the town would provide both conservation and recreation, with overall open space and water quality treatment areas in the town comprising 626 acres.

In the next few years, forty million dollars of infrastructure would be built at Mountain House by the CSD and Trimark with SWA GROUP and Principal Joe Runco providing detailed design guidelines and landscape design and development. The first New Town in California in twenty years, Mountain House opened its first neighborhood in 2003 and it quickly became fully occupied, averaging 600 units per year. It was well received and there were even lotteries on some of the units. The opening of the I-680 freeway added a direct connection from I-580 to the South Bay and Silicon Valley, and so Mountain House soon became a magnet for engineers who were looking for family housing in the very expensive Silicon Valley housing market. Demand pushed the second and then third neighborhoods into development in rapid succession, and Mountain House received an award from the American Society of Civil Engineers as the best project of 2004.

However, building a new town in America is always risky, as it is difficult to predict the ups and downs of the economy across the twenty or more years it takes to fully complete the community. And so, despite its early success, Mountain House became a victim when the housing bubble burst in 2008 with a magnitude no one expected. Housing prices had soared considerably above the affordable 1994 levels thanks to irresponsible bank and mortgage lending during the 2003-2008 bubble—the period of Mountain House's nascent growth—so housing prices were depressed but have seen a great resurgence as of 2013. With its well planned and built neighborhoods, Mountain House remains popular with the residents, and its strong Community Services District has survived this difficult downturn.

This resurgence has been the experience of master planned communities throughout America after previous real estate market crashes, and Mountain House is following suit. Developers like Bill Johnson and all the people at Trimark, like Jim Rouse and Chuck Cobb before them had visions of a better way to build suburban America, and they built great new towns and communities. The public value these solid communities create still offer a better way to build a significant part of America's future growth.

**Opposite Page** The natural plantings and trail at the Mountain House greenway.

**Above** The parks at the schools are open for neighborhood use at Mountain House.

## Marin City USA, Marin County, California (1987-1995)

Between our office in Sausalito and my home in Mill Valley (a distance of only 4 miles), lies Marin City, an unincorporated city that has a unique history. In 1942 just after President Roosevelt called the country to war with Japan, the Bechtel Company of San Francisco contracted with the government to build thirty-four Liberty Ships and, using emergency powers granted during wartime, built in several months time a shipyard in Marin County, just north of the Town of Sausalito. Marinship, as it was called, desperately needed thousands of workers to build the ships and so reached to the rural South to bring black and white workers to live next to the shipyard. This unincorporated city, created virtually overnight, soon grew into the second largest city in small, affluent Marin County.

After the war, the shipyard closed and many workers left to find employment elsewhere in the booming postwar economy. Black workers found it much more difficult to find work and housing as Marin became increasingly affluent and white, and to help address this population, the Marin Community Services District (CDS) was formed in 1950 to build attractive public housing apartments and "pole houses" on the hillsides around Marin City. Some residents stayed on in the public housing and pole houses, but eventually the region's land became too valuable to continue being used as public housing, and the surrounding areas were developed with private housing that priced out the poorer population of Marin City. Marin City became an anomaly: a small, predominantly black and poor enclave of 2500 people in one of the country's most affluent and Caucasian counties.

172

The vast inequality between Marin City and the rest of Marin was in desperate need of a fair solution that was suitable to all of the area's residents, and so in 1956, the Marin County Redevelopment Agency was formed and tasked with building a permanent community in Marin City. However, the agency was unable to realize its goals, a planned high school was not built, and the central "bowl" area of Marin City became a vacant and neglected area. A very popular flea market took over the site for temporary use for a few years, but it raised many concerns of just *what* was being bought and sold at the market.

The county created the Marin City Community Development Corporation (CDC) in 1980, which decided to take a new approach when in launching the Marin City USA project. Under the leadership of Al Fleming, the CDS formed a partnership in 1982 with the Marin Community Services District and Bridge Housing Corporation, a local affordable housing nonprofit. Bridge, led by former California Director of Housing and Community Development Don Terner, had built over six thousand units of affordable housing throughout the Bay Area. This dynamic duo of Al and Don could not have been more qualified, and with major Marin Community Foundation support, they were able to buy the vacant school site, assemble the fifty-acre bowl area, and begin a process of creating a mixed-use project that would end the neglect of this central part of the community.

In 1987, SWA GROUP in conjunction with well-regarded architect Peter Calthorpe was asked to prepare a master plan for the mixed-use project and to work with the county to prepare the required specific plan that would provide the details. As part of this process, SWA GROUP Principal Elizabeth

**Opposite Page** A sketch of the Marin City USA commercial and residential redevelopment in Marin County, California.

**Above** Marin City in the foreground next to the City of Sausalito with the City of San Francisco and the bay in the distance.

Shreeve and I conducted two years of intense workshops with a very skeptical community, which were painful at times but necessary to gain community support. We took the time to explain the complexity of the partnership, in which Marin City CDC owned the land and Bridge acted as housing developers, bringing in the Martin Group to develop the commercial portions.

This was not to be a "get rich" scheme for the current residents. Rather, the residual value of a successful project would go back into the community in the form of jobs, community facilities and a sustainable revenue source for community maintenance and social projects. A ninety-nine-year land lease for the apartments and shopping center meant the community would continue to own that land, and fifty percent of the tax revenue from the shopping center would go directly to the community. We were glad we explained the process completely, as the reality did involve many economic ups and downs before the full buildout was accomplished ten years later. Patience was needed by all!

In the final plan for Marin City USA, SWA GROUP Principals Dan Tuttle and Cinda Gilliland,  designed overall landscape development as well as the landscape for the 340 housing units—255 rental apartments and 85 for-sale townhouses—with a full forty percent of the development reserved for low-income residents. In addition, the freeway interchange was remodeled to better serve Marin City, a new 8500-square foot church and day care rebuilt the old St. Andrews, and the Gateway Town Center was added to provide 186,000 square feet of retail space, a bus transit terminal, and a county branch library. Other community facilities include the Martin Luther King Academy, Manzanita Recreation Center, several parks, and a business enterprise incubator facility with job training capabilities.

Marin City USA is a great example of a public private partnership, and it received an award from the American Planning Association in 1998. The project has finally delivered the viable and attractive community that has been sorely lacking for so long, and the result has been satisfying to all of its residents and continues to be a positive asset for Marin County. Most importantly, the long but satisfying process proved to Elizabeth and me that the work you do in your own backyard can be just as interesting and important as the work you do around the world.

**Opposite Page** A family oriented neighborhood in Marin City. **Bottom** This street is a direct connection between the new multi family neighborhood in Marin City and the Gateway Town Center at its far end.

**Above** Shops in the Gateway Town Center in Marin City.

# 6

# A global practice

## 1990s

In the beginning of the 1990's, another significant recession hit our major American markets, and SWA GROUP again faced challenging times. We had opened new offices in in the boom times of the 1980's: Boston in 1980, Florida in 1982, Dallas in 1984, and Los Angeles and Alexandria in 1988, bringing our total number of offices to eight. However, just as in 1974, we had expanded too quickly, and when this major recession hit in 1991, we were forced to downsize. We had weathered several real estate cycles, but the U.S. real estate market was becoming more severely cyclical and a good portion of our work dried up very quickly and unexpectedly. The Irvine Company, our largest client at the time had their financing abruptly shut off and canceled all of our projects within a week. We took action to close the Los Angeles and Alexandria offices immediately, since they had not yet established their local markets. Following that, since the U.S. national market continued to remain weak for several years, we then closed our Boston office in 1992 and Florida in 1995 when our Arvida client was sold. Our four surviving offices—Sausalito, a much reduced Laguna Beach office, Houston, and Dallas—were set up to weather the storm, but our Principals needed additional work.

I saw an interesting opportunity arise in 1992, when Harumasa Kudoh, an experienced architect from Tokyo, visited the SWA GROUP to discuss our two firms working in the then booming Japanese market. We had long been discussing how to project our capabilities to international markets in a significant way, and Kudoh-san had an astute understanding of what we could bring to the Japanese market. He had lined up some significant clients who he felt could use our skills to their advantage in Japan as part of a new company he was starting, Landscape International, Ltd (LIL). It was to be structured as a loose joint venture formed specifically to work with SWA GROUP, where we could each stay independent while working together closely. This format allowed us to combine our planning and design skills and his knowledge of the culture, language and methods of doing business in Japan.

**Opposite Page** The view down to World Wide plaza which provides access to restaurant and theater pavilions as well as to the residential and office towers.

**Bottom** The view into World Wide plaza from 49th Street and the theater district.

**Pages 178-179** Looking north in Manhattan with World Wide Center in the foreground comprising the light colored office tower with the pyramid top, the plaza and the residential tower and mid rises reaching to Ninth Avenue.

Illustrated on pages 176-188 are SWA Group projects that demonstrate the global practice of the firm.

Our first project with LIL was a small hotel project on Kyushu, which was a kind of trial run to prove that we could effectively work together to achieve a better overall result by combining our very complementary skills with Kudoh-san's genuine desire to better the Japanese landscape. Bill Callaway and I began an intensive ten-year joint operation working with LIL on Japanese projects that exposed many of our undersubscribed Principals to working abroad, and proved without hesitation that when properly organized and supported, we could export our skills on exciting and relevant projects in other cultures while achieving results that were as high-quality as our domestic projects. This experience led me to conclude that foreign work was going to be necessary if we wanted to keep all of our experienced people working on good projects. We would have to reach beyond America if we were to have enough of the high quality work that the firm was dedicated to produce.

The 1990's saw SWA GROUP projects not just in Japan, but all over the world. In China we built on the lessons learned from our not-so-successful 1994 project in Beijing, and on our successes in Japan. When Kevin Shanley led the Houston Office in the late 1990's on a China initiative, he brought together Chinese Mandarin speakers as SWA GROUP employees, Chinese consultants with local contacts, and a business-like approach to fees and expenses to begin what has become a very successful process. Meanwhile, the Houston Office was also running projects in the Middle East, where Ed Kagi had gone twenty years earlier when we needed that work to even out downtimes in the U.S. economy during the 1971-74 recession. Latin America also began to come on the scene, as I broke new ground with the Lagoa dos Ingleses New Town outside Belo Horizonte in Brazil.

**Opposite Page** Night time is prime time at Centro in Oberhausen, Germany. **Bottom** The canal that forms a focal point for the redeveloped industrial district that was transformed into Centro Oberhausen, a Shopping, Entertainment and Sports center in Oberhausen, Germany.

**Above** The water garden next to the retail building at Arizona Center attracts families and community events in downtown Phoenix. **Center** The nighttime uses at Arizona Center add to downtown Phoenix activities and viability. **Bottom** Looking down on the gardens and retail center from the hotel and office buildings of Arizona Center.

**Opposite Page** The plan for the Newport Coast of the Irvine Ranch in Orange County, California with public beaches and parks along the Pacific coast and residential clusters and hotels along the golf course and the major hillside open spaces.

**Above** The spectacular views from the Newport Coast to the Pacific Ocean and the sailing season at adjacent Newport Beach. **Center** A sketch of the location of a new Universal Studios attraction in a larger entertainment and media district in the redeveloped Port of Osaka, Japan. **Bottom** A sketch of the use of piers for the entertainment functions at Universal Studios at the Port of Osaka.

**Above** The Nasu Highlands Resort Golf Club rounds out the resort activities. **Center** Hot rods and a giant Juke box set the jazzy tone for this part of Fantasy Pointe. **Bottom** The Fantasy Pointe amusement park at the Nasu Highlands Resort, north of Tokyo.

**Opposite Page** Sunset at the winding infinity pool edge toward the ocean at Las Ventanas al Paraiso is unforgettable. **Bottom** The winding pool and cabanas are set in against the ocean and rugged landscape of Cabo San Lucas in Baja California, Mexico.

**Page 186 Above** The Central court at the Fashion Island Renaissance in the mixed use Newport Center in Newport Beach, California. **Bottom** Shopping is a family affair at Fashion Island in Newport Beach.

**Page 187 Above** Outdoor dining near the Atrium Court at Fashion Island. **Bottom** Walking through the pedestrian streets of Fashion Island with the office buildings of Newport Center in the background.

## The Landscape Design Training Program and Work in Japan with the Fujita Corporation, Tokyo (1992-5)

In addition to the project collaborations we had with Harumasa Kudoh's company Landscape International (LIL), we began a four-year program with one of his major clients, Fujita Corporation, a large Japanese construction company with many infrastructure and development projects all around Japan. Fujita wanted to use current American technology in landscape and urban design to better compete with other Japanese construction companies that were even larger. When we first became involved, Fujita had built up strong expertise in engineering and architecture, but had little capacity for landscape design. This was partially a product of the Japanese design education system, which, like the engineer-dominated company, did not focus on landscape design. Ironically enough, though the Japanese were world-renowned for their gardens and sensitivity to nature, they had somehow not adapted these skills to the needs of modern cities.

Japan's economy was booming around this time, but many of its cities suffered from weak urban design and the rapid development did not help. Fujita wisely realized that urban planning and large-scale landscape design experience was critical to Japan's future, and so they asked us and Landscape International if we could help by teaching landscape design to a new group of young and talented engineers and architects. We agreed under the condition that the training would occur in an internship-style format at a collaborative landscape office in Tokyo: SWA GROUP's most experienced principals would work on multiple real Fujita projects, while Fujita's young trainees would assist—thereby learning by doing. We would also ask each SWA Principal to present illustrated lectures of their particular approach when they came to Tokyo so the students could better understand how the design process worked.

Over the first year of the program, which was broken into one-week-per-month segments, I provided illustrated lectures on the overall structure of urban design and planning, and my partner Roy Imamura did the same for landscape design. This process, which had excellent LIL support, proved to work well for all of us, and so over the next two years we rotated the monthly teach/work visits among our Principals. In addition to the project work and our monthly lectures on landscape topics, we gave presentations on our work in America and hosted the student group for a cross-country tour of those projects and other significant North American landscapes. This tour proved very successful, and so we also helped Fujita schedule a European tour and visits to significant Japanese landscapes—both site visits to projects we were working on and trips to historic Japanese gardens and scenic landscapes. Lastly, we wanted to make sure we covered all phases of landscape design, from conception to implementation, and so we scheduled workshops on landscape drawing and field construction as well as planning and design.

Over the three years we ran the training program, Fujita gradually gave the students more responsibility on projects, and we finally turned the program over to Fujita in 1995. After that, the students continued their progress without our formal involvement for two more years until Fujita established a formal Landscape Division within the company. We did some work with Fujita after that, but Japan was headed into a very long slowdown that

**Opposite Page** The perspective shows the winning plan in the competition for a new government center in Shanghai, China, with the civic center complex and its adjacent residential and commercial blocks and a large new city lake. **Bottom** A sketch of the central civic plaza at the Shanghai Government Center.

**Above** The students of the Fujita Landscape Training Program in Tokyo with SWA Principals Roy Imamura and Jim Reeves.

saw Fujita experience significant restructuring, and our work diminished. Landscape International also had restructuring problems when Kudoh-san retired. I was delighted to receive a photograph of a reunion of the Fujita trainees in 2013 at Fujita where they still are working on projects.

In total, eight of our Principals participated in the training program on a wide range of projects. We not only gained good projects that took us through the 90's, all of these Principals gained confidence and skills in working globally. Below is a selection of the diverse landscape projects we did in Japan from 1992 to 1997, the period of our most intense work on the Fujita Program.

*Projects with Landscape International:*

**THE UZUMINE GOLF CLUB, GUEST HOUSE AND THE CENTER FOR CONTEMPORARY GRAPHIC ARTS:** a Dai Nippon Printing Company-owned golf resort for employees and guests, to which we and LIL, working with ED2 Architects of San Francisco, added a world-class museum and center for graphic arts.

**DAI NIPPON HEADQUARTERS AND G PROJECT OFFICE TOWER:** redevelopment of the printing plant site in central Tokyo. This major complex mixed use urban project continues with our involvement in 2013.

**THE KARUIZAWA RESORT:** a famous resort area in mountainous Nagano Prefecture, to which we added a master plan and landscape design for a resort community, with hillside villas, condos and a sports center. Native stone and wood materials were specified for all structures and open space was dedicated around the mountain streams.

**THE ISLAMABAD NEW CITY:** a master plan for a satellite city of the capital of Pakistan.

**THE SUGINOI HOTEL, BEPPU CITY, KYUSHU:** a revitalization plan for a historic hot springs hotel in the volcanic region of Japan's major south island.

**THE SHANGHAI GOVERNMENT CENTER, CHINA:** the winning submittal to the Shanghai government for a new civic center and supporting town in suburban Shanghai.

**TOKYO UNIVERSITY OF FOREIGN STUDIES:** a new campus of this historic university built upon and conserving many open spaces and trees planted in 1945, when this was a major U.S. Military base in Fuchu, Japan near Tokyo. The Tokyo University of Foreign Studies received awards from the American Society of Landscape Architects in 2003 and 2005.

**ANGEL NO MORI RESORT (ANGEL KINGDOM):** a master plan and urban design for a large 2500-acre resort community in Ueno City, Mie Prefecture, including entertainment facilities to celebrate the 100th anniversary of Morinaga Company, a milk product and confectionary provider with a well recognized angel logo. The resort community included forest preserves, a town center, an amusement area, a candy manufacturing display area, a resort center, a golf course, residences and a botanic garden.

*Projects with Other Clients:*

**UNIVERSAL STUDIOS AND AJIKAWA INNER PORT DEVELOPMENT, OSAKA:** a plan prepared for the US-based MCA Recreation Services Company to provide a Universal Studios theme park as part of the redevelopment of older parts of the port of Osaka, which also included multi-media and technology industries, a marketplace, a civic promenade, and residences.

**NASU HIGHLAND FANTASY POINT PARK:** master planning and complete landscape architectural services for a 142-acre, year-round family theme park adjacent to the Nasu Highlands National Park located one hour north of Tokyo via shinkansen bullet train. The project, prepared for the Towa Nasu Real Estate Company, included hotels, resort residences and a golf course and club.

**SUN CITY COMMUNITIES:** a series of life care communities patterned after American life care communities, designed for Health Care Japan and their operating company, Half Century More. New projects continue to the present.

Today, due in part to the deep recession of 2007-2012, more than half of our work is international, with most of that coming from China where we now have a Shanghai office. In addition to China projects, we continue working with a few longtime clients in Japan and have expanded into the Middle East, Brazil, Russia and Eastern Europe. I believe this transformation into a truly international firm owes tremendous credit to our work with Landscape International in Japan in the 1990's, as we learned that our core

**Above** The Karuizawa Resort is in one of Japan's most famous mountain resort regions and native stone is used throughout for landscape walls and other structures. **Bottom** The sports center at the Karuizawa resort community in Japan.

**Opposite Page** Sketch of the center of the Angel No Mori Resort in Mie Prefecture, Japan. **Bottom Left** A sketch of the Angel No Mori resort village center. **Bottom Right** A sketch of a canal in the Angel No Mori village.

skills translated no matter where the sites were located and to the later work in China led by Kevin Shanley.. Any cultural differences could be mitigated by emphasizing relationships, training, hiring native speakers who met our professional requirements, and creatively adapting our successful business model through leadership and administration. With the right balance of hard work and cultural sensitivity, the challenges of working with foreign cultures in far away places were far outweighed by the professional and business rewards that foreign projects yielded—often matching and even exceeding those we gained on American projects.

ITRY TO OLD DAYS PARK AND THEME PARK

## The Tejon Ranch Vision Plan, Kern & Los Angeles Counties (1992-7)

Tejon Ranch is one of the premier cattle and horse ranches in the country, with huge agricultural operations spread across 274,000 acres—the largest privately owned contiguous property in California. The sprawling ranch, along with historic Fort Tejon, form the key entry into Los Angeles County, as the I-5 Freeway abruptly exits the fertile agricultural plain of the California Valley in Kern County and enters the mountainous Tejon Pass. Aside from the "Grapevine" commercial center along the pass, this scenic entryway gave no sign of urban Southern California or downtown Los Angeles located just sixty-five miles to the south, but the remoteness of the Ranch was changing rapidly as the growth of the Los Angeles metropolitan area approached its boundaries.

In 1992, Ray Watson, president of the Irvine Ranch in Orange County, was asked to become involved with the Tejon Ranch. He organized a Vision Conference to determine the possibilities and development issues facing the ranch management, and to address what was to become of this strategic, historic and beautiful property located at the nexus of three California regions: the Tehachapi Mountains of the Sierra Nevada Range, the San Joaquin Valley, and the Antelope Valley, an extension of the Mojave Desert. Since I had worked with Ray for many years on the Irvine Ranch, he asked me, along with Bob Jacob and Jim Culver of SWA GROUP to participate in the conference..

Recognizing that development was occurring rapidly in the region, the conference results stressed the need to immediately create a Vision Plan for the entire ranch that would guide the Tejon Board in making critical decisions about the property's future use. Understanding that development of some parts of the property was a desirable outcome for the future of the Ranch, the conference members recommended strategies that would help strike the right balance and preserve the property's environmental and historic legacy. Fortunately, the immensity of the Tejon Ranch property would provide ample space for development, agriculture and conservation.

The first of the conference's recommendations was unanimously agreed upon: entitlements for any development of the ranchlands should consider Tejon Ranch as a whole. We knew there would be keen environmental scrutiny of any major proposals particularly on the federal and state as well as the two counties at the local level. A piecemeal approach would just exacerbate and unify the opposition. The plan for the ranch as a whole would enable complementary proposals of development, agriculture, and open space areas: for instance, the Ranch's designation of critical environmental resources as permanent agricultural and conservation areas could serve as mitigation and buffer zones for developed areas. As such, conference attendees agreed that the protection of the environmental resources should be focused upon up front as a significant aspect of the Vision Plan.

Foremost among the environmental resources of the ranch were the vast expanses of mountains and canyons in the middle of the property—the "crown jewel" of Tejon Ranch. These features could significantly increase the value of the overall property if they were protected and could also increase the chances for entitlements if done through proactive rather than reactive environmental strategies. This was an appropriate strategy since the Tejon Ranch management company had a longstanding commitment to environmental stewardship, and many parts of the Ranch had land and environmental management practices that won it acclaim from environmental groups. Continuity of this commitment through the transition into entitlement and marketing would greatly enhance the image of the Ranch and promote it as a leader in sustainable development. In addition to sustainable development and overall land management, the conference recommendations also focused on other issues, such as marketing potentials and economic cycles, transportation potentials, utilities and infrastructure, water and environmental sensitivities.

All of the recommendations of the Vision Conference were well received by the Tejon Board. They immediately set up a Land Planning Committee of the Board, asked Ray Watson to head up a special Real Estate Advisory Group, and asked SWA GROUP to head up their consulting team to prepare a Vision Plan for the entire Ranch and the I-5 Corridor—the conference established that the planning should put special attention on the role of the sixteen-mile freeway frontage of the Ranch.

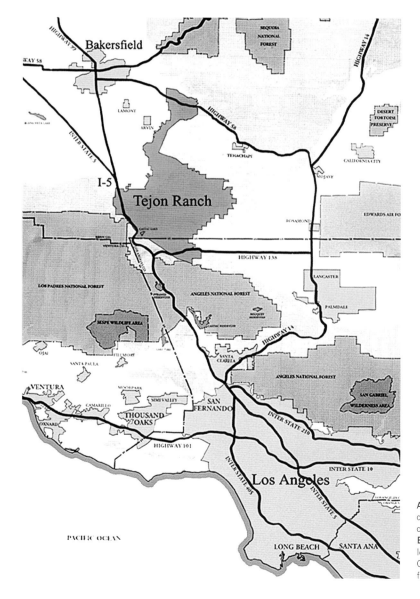

**Above** A sketch of a guest ranch illustrating the character of rural open land uses in the central canyons of the ranch near Castaic Lake. **Bottom** The 274,000 acre Tejon Ranch is located at the border of Los Angeles and Kern Counties on I-5 at the mountainous Tejon Pass from the Central Valley to Los Angeles.

During 1993, a team of consultants led by me and Monica Simpson from our Laguna Beach office worked closely with Ray and the Land Planning Committee. We intensely studied markets for different kinds of development along with environmental constraints, transportation issues, and planning alternatives. Paired with our research, environmental and legal consultants for the Ranch began to develop an endangered species assessment and strategy for mitigation that fed into the plan alternatives. We merged this information into a comprehensive environmental atlas for the Ranch, and settled on planning units based upon watersheds as the best way to relate land use issues to environmental and infrastructure issues. By the end of 1993, we came up with an outline for the strategic Vision Plan for the Ranch.

We knew that, given the size and uniqueness of the ranch, our plan would receive attention from all of the major state and national environmental groups, as well as the federal government, which already had a presence on the Ranch with the protection of the endangered California Condor. We were mindful of the importance of the project and its environmental implications, and closely followed the Vision Conference recommendations of providing a plan for the entire Ranch and not just parts of it to ensure the mitigation necessary for the major development projects.

We wanted the plan to lead with a big idea that would highlight the special nature of the Ranch, and to determine what this would be, we delved into the history of the property. Again and again, the quality of the Tejon Ranch management and stewardship practices surfaced—practices that equaled or in many cases exceeded those of the best-run major parks and conservancies. I put together a white paper for the Board that described this long tradition of integrity over 150 years, called simply "The Tradition Continues". The paper encapsulated the notion that in this next stage of development, this tradition of stewardship would be the basis of the plan, whether for urban development or preservation of the existing rural and agricultural uses.

All our studies showed that even looking fifty years ahead, only a small part of the ranch—about fifteen percent—would be used for urban development, though this still comprised over forty thousand acres. This development would take the form of several master planned communities, business parks and commercial centers, and would be concentrated on the less sensitive flatlands and foothills along the northern and southern edges of the Ranch and along the I-5 corridor.

Thirty-five percent of the ranch would be reserved for the "Crown Jewel" cited in the vision conference—the mountains and canyons in the center of the Ranch. This large area, which contained the existing Ranch Equestrian Center, Castac Lake, and the areas around and including Bear Trap Canyon, would be permanently designated for a rural open land character with extensive open space and ranchlands surrounding carefully-sited guest ranches or resorts, as well as a small number of large-lot, rural "second home" preserves. Barring this land from intensive development would permanently maintain the classic ranch character where it was most visible from I-5: right up front in the center of the Ranch.

The final fifty percent of the ranch, The "Ranch Core" would encompass the most unique and environmentally sensitive lands, including the most mountainous, inaccessible portions of the property that would remain permanently out of development in carefully designated environmental preserves, ranching and other open land uses. Thus living in or visiting the Tejon Ranch

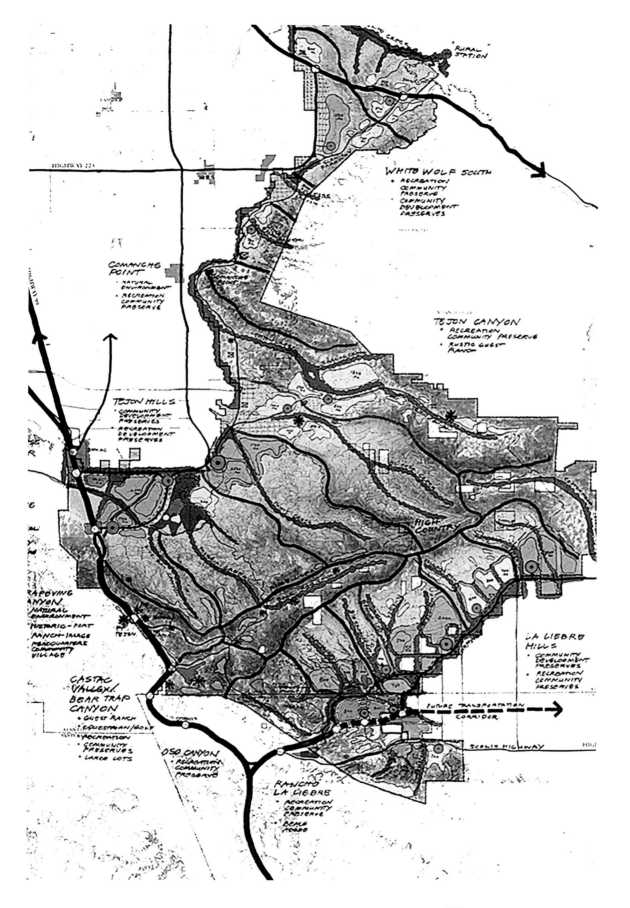

in the future would benefit from the protection of the property's greatest environmental resources: since a major part of the center of the Ranch would be permanently protected as greenbelts and rural ranchland, and would have their views, stormwater mitigation, and other features preserved in perpetuity.

The Tejon Board adopted our Vision Plan in 1994, and in the subsequent years we outlined how a Ranch Resort and a custom lot community could be carefully sited in Bear Trap Canyon near Campo Teresa, and how it related to the Ranch "window" at Castac Lake and the central canyons. We then carried forth development guidelines for the resort, the I-5 corridor and for the major development use areas through 1997. We also began the process of considering alternative ways to permanently preserve the major Ranch Core and crown jewel area. However, at that time there was a major ownership and management change on the Ranch, and we unfortunately did not continue with the new owners.

To our dismay, the new management changed the basic strategy in the Vision Plan and began extensive development studies, going against the primary recommendation of the vision conference by not tackling the critical resources of the ranch as a whole. In 2002 they proposed major developments

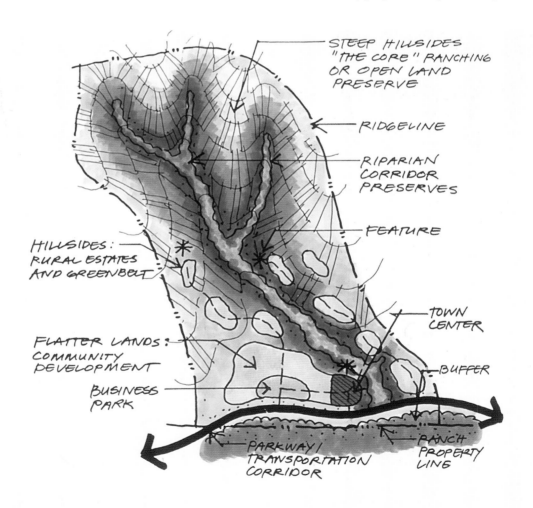

PROTOTYPE WATERSHED PLANNING AREA

to Kern and Los Angeles Counties in the form of a 1400-acre industrial park at I-5 and Highway 99 in Kern County, and a Master Planned Community with 23,000 housing units on 11,700 acres in Los Angeles County. These developments did follow the general guidelines we laid out in the Vision Plan, but left out any consideration of the Ranch Core or a plan for the remainder of the Ranch as mitigating factors. This became a fatal flaw as we had earlier understood. Kern County approved the industrial park, but soon after was sued by environmentalists who demanded a plan for the entire Ranch. Meanwhile, Los Angeles County delayed any considerations of the plan, sensing the battle that was coming. After this backlash, the management company went back to the drawing boards and working with the Trust for Public Land, proposed in 2003 the sale and protection of a 100,000-acre preserve in the Ranch Core. This was a step in the right direction to be sure, but as it only protected about thirty-five percent of the property, still fell short of getting the entitlement process back on track.

Thus, it did not take me by surprise that in a grandiose public relations release in 2008—six years after their original development proposals—the Ranch management established the Tejon Ranch Conservancy in a belated attempt to gain the support of the government and environmental groups. This move formally dedicated 100,000 acres of the Ranch Core's most valuable environmental resources, and over time they would dedicate or put in open space or conservation easements another 78,000 acres, also in the Ranch Core. In addition, the management put an additional 62,000 acres up for sale to the state using state conservation bond money. When all was said and done, a total of 240,000 acres would be permanently designated for conservation, agriculture, or open space, which was even more than the 226,000 acres we had allocated in the original Vision Plan (the 130,000-acre Ranch Core and the 96,000-acre Crown Jewel).

It took the action of powerful environmental groups, but the new ranch management finally came back to our original strategy of holistic planning and using the sale and protection of precious environmental resources to entitle development elsewhere on the ranch. With this concession secured, the environmental groups agreed not to oppose the planned community in Los Angeles County and to remove their opposition to the large industrial park in Kern County. They also agreed to not oppose two other developments: an 11,700-acre planned community in Kern County and the 5,000-acre Tejon Mountain Village, a high-end resort with hotels and five thousand homes and condominiums. These developments, totaling about 30,000 acres, were all located where our Vision Plan proposed such developments ten years earlier.

The fact that our visionary plan was eventually implemented in full was quite satisfying to me. The fact that it happened even though they did not keep us on as planners was particularly satisfying, since we avoided spending a frustrating decade following a circuitous path and working against our primary strategy. Though the planning experienced some pitfalls along the way, the original Vision Plan and the eventual implementation were able to give the Ranch economic vitality through its huge development areas, not by developing freely, but by abiding by the "Tradition Continues" strategy based on the ranch's historical land stewardship values. Because of this, the Tejon Ranch will continue to build upon its legacy into the 21st century, providing both sustainable communities and precious permanent open space at the gateway to the Southern California metropolitan area.

**Opposite Page** The Vision Plan for the Tejon Ranch used a watershed unit approach to planning the natural and developmental resources of the historic ranch.

## Heron Bay, San Leandro, California (1993-9)

Having worked with public planners in California for many years, it was not unusual for me to run into them in the many different cities where SWA GROUP had projects and to be listed by them for prospective planning work. It was unusual though for them to ask a prospective development applicant on a project in their city to directly involve us in the project. Heron Bay in San Leandro was such a case.

The site for Heron Bay sits on the edge of San Francisco Bay. The site was originally called Robert's Landing for the boat launching area that was on the site in 1851—Alameda County's first shipping port. Once a marshy bay, the site changed dramatically between 1900 and 1963, as the marshes were filled to make way for an industrial plant producing explosive powders and munitions. By the time Citation Homes purchased the 478-acre site in 1980, the plant had become vacant and degraded. However, though the scattered remaining marsh areas were in poor condition, they still provided habitat for the Salt Marsh Harvest Mouse, a federally protected endangered species.

After purchasing the land, Citation Homes formed a partnership with the City of San Leandro to revitalize the large bayfront site and its natural resources. 178 acres directly along the bay were given to the state for a Harvest Mouse wildlife refuge, 116 acres were set aside for open space, and a hundred-acre site was reserved for permanent dredge disposal for the maintenance of the San Leandro Marina. Along with these uses was a comprehensive strategy to restore those lands to their idyllic original state: by breaching the dikes that were built in the last century, the plan would restore much of the site's marshland, and a vegetative restoration program would be put in place for the open space and wildlife habitat refuge areas. To allow people to benefit from these naturalization efforts, the plan also included a segment of the Bay Trail that was to extend all around San Francisco Bay.

Where we became involved was that the remaining land, approximately one hundred acres, would be designated for home development. Though we were often brought on by developers who had heard of or seen our work, in this case, the City Planning Department of San Leandro asked Citation in 1993 to retain SWA GROUP for this sensitive development. Citation had gifted home designers, but their subdivisions were very standardized, and the city wanted more urban and landscape design capability on the team. Also, because the developed area was so limited and the agreement called for 730 units of single-family homes, or 7.3 units per acre—an exceptionally high density for a development that consisted exclusively of single family homes—the interface between the developed area and the shoreline trail and the wildlife refuges required careful transitions. We could help ensure that the density of the development did not pose a risk to the sensitive preservation areas. The overall design challenges lay in making the homeowners feel they were a bayfront development even though the bay waters were far separated from the development by the marshes, and by making shoreline trail hikers feel they were in a restored marsh environment, and in preventing both the housing development and the trail from intruding on the refuge.

Citation agreed to retain us, and we worked closely together to get the necessary public approvals. They quickly recognized that we could be instrumental in helping the project get approved, as the public was sensitive to the location and character of the proposed homes and the marsh restoration.

Our overall plan included three residential villages where the 4000- and 3500-square foot lots were designed as "wide and shallow" or in a "Z" configuration. The wide and shallow lots had the advantage of maximizing the attractive street frontage on the small lots, with the long, street-facing elevations of the homes' architecture being articulated with front doors and windows to scale down the effect of the garage doors. This configuration also allowed for more street trees and landscape. The Z lots, on the other hand, had varied setbacks and some garages were turned ninety degrees from the street. Finally, a courtyard configuration was used in the northernmost village, with groups of up to eight attractive, small detached homes built around specially paved and landscaped courtyards.

Working with Principals Jim Lee, Cinda Gilliland and Corazon Unana, we were able to use these layouts along with extensive architectural and landscape guidelines to provide complete landscape services to translate a dense residential neighborhood into an attractive series of streets and villages that were appropriate for the naturalistic character of the site. All of the streets were landscaped and narrow in width, and the small, well-designed homes fit nicely into the villages. To cap it off, the development brought the people together with several small parks and a recreation center with plenty of community facilities.

We felt that it was important to accentuate the gateway of the property and give it a unique identity, and so the last section of Lewelling Boulevard, from which the Heron Bay community was accessed, was given an extensive parkway treatment starting with a landscaped gateway and street trees. Upon entering the property, a specially paved and landscaped traffic circle and small park completed the gateway landscape. Within the development, the entry road ended on a larger park at the edge of the development facing the restored marsh. This park included a pavilion overlooking the marsh that explained its restoration, and a pedestrian trail extended from the pavilion directly out along a linear park to the edge of the bay, leading pedestrians to a small waterfront park and the Bay Trail. The Heron Bay trail acted as a subtle yet effective buffer between the sensitive refuge and the development, with landscaped mounds and swales on both sides and additional continuous fencing along the habitat refuge edge to prevent unsanctioned access.

Following our plans, Citation quickly and successfully built out the Heron Bay community. Our efforts to ensure that the marsh restoration and development would work symbiotically, and the residential community's direct connection to the Bay Trail were much heralded, as they gave the community the feeling of having direct access to nature, a very special kind of neighborhood on the San Francisco Bay indeed. Based upon Heron Bay's success, Citation later asked us to join them in planning and complete landscape development for another community in San Leandro, Cherrywood, located on an infill parcel along San Leandro Creek near the Downtown station of the Bay Area Rapid Transit (BART). This development was also well received by the residents and the city.

**Opposite Page** Heron Bay has a park and a walk that leads to the Bay Trail with a protective fence along the edge of the marsh preservation areas. **Bottom** One of the residential neighborhoods of Heron Bay.

## Alphaville Lagoa dos Ingleses New Town, Nova Lima, Brazil (1994-9)

In 1994, I received a cold call from an architectural firm in Rio de Janeiro about a New Town Master Plan in Brazil that they had been asked to submit a proposal for planning. This firm, Coutinho, Diegues and Cordeiro (CDC), knew quite a lot about us, but we did not know much about them, so I wasn't sure what to think. So I looked them up, and they seemed well qualified in architecture but with little experience in planning large communities. Despite my reservations about the firm, this seemed like it could be a good opportunity for growth, as I had long been interested in expanding our work to Latin America and particularly Brazil due to its size and its common use of English as a business language. We had difficulty in the Spanish-speaking countries due to our deficiency in Spanish speakers, who were really necessary to win significant projects, as I had learned after an unsuccessful proposal for a project in Buenos Aires.

I learned that the client for this project was Caemi, one of the largest mining companies in the world, with extraction activities predominantly in iron ore, and the Japanese at that time being their largest clients. Caemi had major landholdings in the mineral rich state of Minas Gerais (General Mines), and the 3182 hectare (7868 acre) site for the new town was located outside that state's capital and largest city, Belo Horizonte, which is also the third largest city in Brazil.

Caemi seemed willing to pay our way down for an interview after CDC explained our interest and capabilities, and so I set off for Rio and the wonder of nature that was Brazil.

Caemi's office in Rio was a beautiful building with gardens by Roberto Burle Marx. Their executive in charge, Augusto Martinez de Almeida, was efficient, highly educated and from an old Brazilian family. I could see this was a great opportunity to begin work in Brazil and was delighted when Augusto asked CDC and SWA to make a proposal to do the planning for the site, known then as Lagoa Grande, for the large lake that was in the center of the property.

After that initial visit, we went down to Belo Horizonte to begin our studies. The city was well planned, but lacked the chaos and dynamism of Rio—it had an almost "Midwestern" feel, with solid businesses and a family-oriented atmosphere. Geographically, the city was circled by high mountains and the basin was intensely developed, meaning that there was little land left for expansion, unless you went over the mountain chain. What was incredible from the air was that the backside of the mountains were hollowed out by the mining that still went on at a strong pace, even though this was not visible from the city. The Belo Horizonte Metropolitan Authority (PLANBEL) had wisely designated a principal axis for expansion along the major highway to Rio de Janeiro through the mountains to the south toward Nova Lima, a nearby small town where our site was located.

We were able to ascertain that the site was suitable for building a satellite new town, as there was enough developable land to accommodate the whole range of land uses for a true new town, and the site had good access to and frontage on the main highway between Belo Horizonte and Rio. Commute time into the Belo Horizonte city center was reasonable, with Lagoa Grande being just a twenty-minute ride back into the outlying high-end commercial

**Opposite Page** An illustrative plan concept for the first phase residential villages, university, town center commercial and Minas Club on the lake at Alphaville Lagoa dos Ingleses. **Bottom** View of a lakeside residential village with the Minas Club and Town Center in the distance.

AERIAL VIEW OF PHASE 1

areas of the city. Moreover, the site benefited from its location at the interchange with the highway to Ouro Preto, a United Nations Cultural Landmark Site with a historic mining town and university. Finally, the site had a wonderful attraction: the lake in the center of the property, which was indeed grande at 222 hectares (550 acres), and had beautiful clear water and a striking blue color that contrasted with the tawny red color of the iron-rich soil.

Another key element we discovered was that the prestigious Minas Tênis Clube, which had extensive recreational and social facilities in two locations in Belo Horizonte, was looking to expand to a third site as the growth of the city was straining their capacity. Augusto had been in talks with them, and found that the site's lake had some attraction to them. I immediately told Augusto of our experience with the Villages of Arvida in Boca Raton, where we had used the hotel and club as the key to setting the character and quality of the entire 5000-acre community. The prospect of attracting this club made me aware of several cultural phenomena that would give us an advantage in planning the new town. Unlike Rio, Belo was an inland city with no beaches to act as natural social meeting places for young people. Moreover, the more conservative and status-conscious local culture made it imperative that the middle classes had appropriate places for families to expose their children to the children of the right social status. Local clubs like the Minas Tênis Clube became the center of the citizens' social lives, and since Minas was the premier club, we were especially eager to have it as a central piece of the new town and knew how to set the plan so the club would be interested in building its newest location on our site!

We planned for the club site to be a major focus of the New Town and located it on the shores of the beautiful manmade lake, near the main entrance to the community. The lake had been built by a British gold and silver mining company in the1930's, but since it was only used as a reservoir that stored water for the mills that were downstream, it remained uncontaminated and pristine. This was in contrast to the unattractive manmade lakes I had visited at Pampulha, the famous Burle Marx new community in Belo Horizonte. There, I was struck by the lakes' murky brown water, a product of soil erosion and the lack of erosion control or properly landscaped edges. I knew that the key to Lagoa remaining a blue lake would be construction techniques and engineering design that would protect the lake from erosion, and the use of shoreline parks around the lake to catch surface drainage in swales. I was delighted when Augusto recognized this and brought in a highly qualified engineer who understood the issue and who designed good water catchment systems. Augusto also enacted construction practices to stop soil excavation work around the lake during the rainy season. Viewing the lake in 2012 from photos, it is still strikingly blue even after 18 years of development.

We prepared an ambitious twenty- to thirty-year master plan for the site, with an anticipated population at full build-out of over 100,000 people. They would be housed in a series of distinct residential villages with a variety of primary and second homes ranging from ten to sixty units per hectare (four to twenty-four units per acre), each with its own schools, parks, and neighborhood services. The plan also included a twenty-two hectare (fifty-acre) town center, a private university, a golf course, hotels, seven hundred hectares (1759 acres) of parks and open space, and 288 hectares (720 acres) of environmental preserves. Across the Ouro Preto highway from the town center, a 153-hectare (382 acre) business park was planned to capture technology or

Opposite Page View of a hillside residential village with bicyclists in the foreground. **Bottom** An overall view of the center of the New Town of Alphaville Lagoa dos Ingleses with the Town Center, residential and commercial buildings built surrounding the lake, lakeside park and Minas Club.

office uses that might find the new town, with its premier club and high-quality executive housing, an attractive place to establish themselves. Finally, seventy-two hectares (180 acres) of commercial uses were planned with direct access to the Rio highway.

Our plan included significant landscape design in addition to the planned development. This consisted of parks around the lake for trails and water quality protection as well as landscaping for the major entry to the community, a boulevard running through the town center and ending on the main lakeside park, with good views of the lake along the way. Next to the lakeside park, The Minas Tênis Náutico Clube added sailing and small craft boating to their extensive social and recreational facilities. Further increasing access to the lake, an eight-mile long bicycle and pedestrian pathway was planned to circumnavigate the lake and connect the residential villages to the town center.

Our plan was well received by Caemi, and in 1995 we began the process of establishing comprehensive development and design guidelines for the community. CDC bought in Vicente Del Rio, a planner with whom they had worked on several projects, and he did a great job of translating all of our plans and documents into a development entitlement document with the City of Nova Lima. By this time, Augusto had changed the name of the new town to Lagoa dos Ingleses (English Lake), as he felt that Lagoa Grande was too generic and not distinctive enough.

It was around this time that Augusto moved Lagoa to a separate company, Lagoa dos Ingleses Urbanismo, which would ultimately begin implementing the town's development. Caemi had other major priorities in the global economy and realized this was outside their main business, so they offered Augusto a chance to form his own company to buy Lagoa and develop the new Town. Realizing the potential of the development, Augusto was happy to take the reins on an entity that would place the town's growth as its top priority.

As his first move, Augusto turned to Alphaville Urbanismo, a successful and unique Brazilian company that specialized in planned developments. Founded by Renato de Albuquerque, an architect, the company was a good choice for its emphasis on high quality and careful planning in its smaller, more residential communities. They also had experience with American and global companies in Brazil—who desired suburban, controlled environments having worked on a planned community at the 1500-hectare (3700 acre) Alphaville Sao Paolo, which included good housing and a town center. Alphaville saw that their scope of work in Brazil could grow with Lagoa, and so they made a deal with Augusto to partner on developing the New Town. Soon after, Augusto and the Alphaville executives came on a tour of SWA projects in California and Florida to get ideas on how to implement our plans.

SWA Group was retained by the new joint venture to plan and implement Phase 1 of Alphaville Lagoa dos Ingleses. Development of the basic landscape infrastructure soon started under the direction of SWA Group Principal David Thompson of our Dallas office. After a well coordinated construction effort, in 2000 we celebrated the formal opening of the new town upon the completion of the Minas Club's lakeside facility, as the Town Center, several villages, a small university and a private school were under construction along the lakeside parks. Home sales were extraordinarily robust and the first village sold out in record time. In partnership with the City of Nova Lima, a General Community Association and multiple neighborhood and commercial associations were established to govern the approvals of new homes and the maintenance of the town facilities.

Recognizing the success of this type of development, in 2001 President Fernando Henrique Cardoso gave Alphaville Lagoa dos Ingleses the master award for large-scale real estate development in Brazil. With the Lagoa dos Ingleses successfully underway, the Alphaville Company asked us to plan several of their new communities in Salvador and Goiana. There were major downturns in the Brazilian economy in the early 2000's and we have not stayed involved in the projects. However, a Brazil-based American landscape contractor whom we brought in to implement the plan has continued on, and in 2012 Lagoa is growing into new phases as Brazil experiences a robust upturn in its economy. In a country not accustomed to master planned, large-scale development, Alphaville Lagoa dos Ingleses provides a new model for development throughout Brazil and the region.

## Beijing Wellbond International Golf Club, China (1994)

Up until the mid-1990's, we had not done any significant work in China, though we were active in Japan and did win a competition with the Fujita Corporation for the Shanghai Civic Center. With China at the beginning of what would turn out to be an astounding growth spurt that continues to this

**Opposite Page Left** People at the lakeside park at Alphaville Lagoa dos Ingleses with the Minas Club behind and condominiums on the surrounding hills. **Right** People on the path through the lakeside park approaching the Town Center at Alphaville Lagoa dos Ingleses. **Bottom Left** Some of the shops, arcades and covered walks in the Alphaville Lagoa dos Ingleses Town Center. **Bottom Right** Joggers on the main entry road to the Town Center and lake at Alphaville Lagoa dos Ingleses.

day, we were looking for more opportunities to get into the China market when we were contacted in 1994 by a Chinese-Thai pharmaceutical company that had gotten an option on an 800-hectare (2000 acre) site on the outskirts of Beijing. The site, located a suitable distance from central Beijing, consisted of relatively flat farmland that the local community wanted to use for generating revenue. SWA Principal John Wong and I met with representatives of the company, including its president who was the daughter of the company founder, at our office in Sausalito.

We went to Beijing and visited the site of the ambitious development, for which the client had recently retained Jack Nicklaus and his company to design golf courses. At that time, there were very few golf courses in China, but what better way to introduce the sport to the country than with two world-class championship golf courses and a golf academy? We proceeded to work with Nicklaus in siting these facilities on the plan, which also included a hotel and convention center, commercial and entertainment centers, different types of residential villages on the golf course, several lakes, a school, a hospital and an equestrian area—also something quite unique in China at the time.

The client had rented a villa at the grounds of the old Daiotai Palace and each meeting we attended for the project included a banquet that was simply remarkable. These meetings at the villa, where we presented to representatives of the local government and the communist party, were always encouraging. We prepared the plan for submittal, but at that time we had no Mandarin speakers at SWA, so we had to rely on the client's translators. I spent one week at the villa working with Nicklaus' golf designer and writing the plan, which fortunately was efficiently and immediately translated.

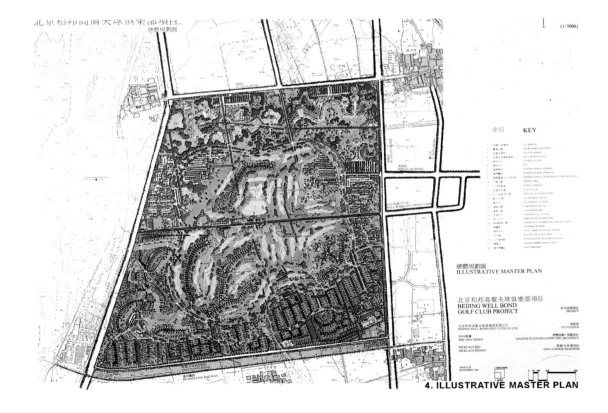

**4. ILLUSTRATIVE MASTER PLAN**

We submitted the plan, and the project seemed to be going very well, but it suddenly met some kind of political resistance, which we never fully understood. To our dismay, the project did not go ahead, and to make matters worse we were owed fees that were never paid. We learned a lot from this episode about what did and did not work well in China, which came in handy several years later when Kevin Shanley and our Houston office began a concerted effort to expand in China. This time, Kevin made sure that we had ample assistance from in-office Mandarin speakers, native Chinese employees, and consultants knowledgeable about doing business in China.

One of the factors that has made SWA GROUP a successful company over the decades is our ability to learn from our mistakes, and we certainly learned from this poor experience in China, as well as from our successful efforts in Japan and other Asian countries. Each experience, whether successful or not, taught us how essential it is to really understand the uniqueness of each culture, and how culture played a strong role in winning important work and doing it well. Armed with this knowledge, Kevin's leadership of our efforts in China this time around have been very successful, and work in the country has proven to be a mainstay of our practice in the 21st century.

**Opposite Page** The plan for a Jack Nicklaus golf club community near Beijing with residential, hotel, commercial and office uses.

**Above Left** A sketch of the golf course and adjacent residential in the Beijing Wellbond community. **Above Right** A sketch of one of the waterways throughout the Beijing Wellbond community. **Bottom** A sketch of a typical residential street in the Beijing Wellbond community.

# 7

# A transition to new leadership

## 1996 to present

In 1996 I was 65 and the firm after a rough patch in the early 90's was doing well. It seemed a good time for me to step aside and after 23 years provide for new leadership for SWA GROUP.

This opened up the opportunity for Bill Callaway, who was President while I was CEO, to take over as CEO in 1996 while I would remain Chairman. Bill then named Kevin as the new President. This smooth transition process was utilized again after Bill's twelve year tenure as CEO, when in 2008 Kevin Shanley as President could take over as CEO and Bill took the role of Chairman as I then retired from that role. In the future this orderly transition process will occur between Kevin Shanley as our current CEO and our new President Gerdo Aquino.

While the primary intent of making SWA GROUP an employee stock ownership (ESOP) company was to share ownership and retain the best professionals, a secondary but very important benefit was the ability to smoothly transition leadership from generation to generation. In a profession where leadership transitions have always been a problem due to the fact that buying out a CEO, President, or senior Principal was typically beyond the means of the next generation of potential leaders, the ESOP offered a straightforward way to buy out the current leadership. As a retirement program, the ESOP is set for payout of any employee at age 65. The buyout of these larger accounts by the ESOP was facilitated by federal regulations that required all participants 55 years or older, including firm leadership, to have the option to diversify their account from company stock to public securities in steps up to 50% of the account. In addition to making participants less vulnerable to fluctuations in company stock value, this greatly eases the process of buying out of the company stock upon retirement.

Because of the way the ESOP was structured, when I retired in 1996 at age 65 I was able to roll over my diversified portfolio and the proceeds from my thusly-reduced company stock account into a tax-deferred Individual Retirement Account (IRA).

After my retirement as CEO and then Chairman I continued as a "Consulting Principal," a category that Mike Gilbert and I established in the 1970's to act as a bridge between a active role as a full time Principal and a different role, whether prompted by retirement, part-time involvement, or other reasons. I operate upon a mutually agreed upon billing rate, receive no ESOP or other employee benefits as any outside consultant to the company would not, pay rent for my workspace and am paid only for any company approved services that I provide. Today, my work as a Consulting Principal includes serving on the SWA GROUP Board of Directors and ESOP Committee, promoting my previous clients, assisting other Principals with getting new clients, and helping document the history and legacy of the company. But as I have always done, I continue to greatly enjoy working with SWA GROUP people on planning and design projects, some of which follow below.

Illustrated on pages 212-217 are SWA Group projects as new leadership takes over the firm.

**Opposite Page** The Park and residential and commercial buildings in the Victory Projects in Downtown Dallas.

**Opposite Page** A street event at the Victory Projects in downtown Dallas. **Left** Looking down on the landscape framework of the Lewis Avenue Civic Corridor in downtown Las Vegas. **Right** People at an event at the three block long Lewis Avenue Corridor in downtown Las Vegas. **Bottom Right** Removal of a traffic lane, sidewalk widening and dense tree cover in the Lewis Avenue Corridor in downtown Las Vegas makes it attractive to walk to downtown activities.

**Above** The complete renovation of the Beverly Hills Hotel included the preservation of or reuse of the heritage landscape elements with any new landscape was to retain the overall historic character. **Center** The pool area of the Beverly Hills Hotel was modernized but retained its period character. **Bottom** The walk to the bungalows retained the iconic garden qualities of the famous Beverly Hills Hotel.

215

**Above** The pond forms a focus of the Dreamworks Animation Studio in Burbank. **Bottom** The Dreamworks Animation Studio outdoor dining for its employees.

**Opposite Page** Walking through the gardens and stream at the Sun City life care community in Yokohama, Japan. **Bottom Left** The gardens of the Sun City life care community in Chofu, Japan. **Bottom Right** The granite fountain and stream at the Sun City life care community in the Ginza district of Tokyo.

## Foundry Square, First and Howard Streets, San Francisco, California (1998)

Throughout our long history, SWA Group has worked on many urban projects with truly creative architects, but one of the most unique is Foundry Square, with Studios Architects and the developers Wilson Meany Sullivan. Rarely in a large American city do you work with one developer who controls four parcels on each of the four corners of a major downtown intersection. At Foundry Square we faced such an opportunity for a unified design at First and Howard Streets, in Downtown San Francisco. This unique prospect allowed me to tap into all of my training and experience as an architect, planner, urban designer, and landscape architect.

Wilson Meany Sullivan saw the need for buildings with large floor plates that could serve San Francisco's ever-growing technology sector. These SoMa (South of Market) properties were set for a maximum of 1.2 million square feet and a height of ten stories in the City's plan, which meant that floor plates in the four buildings suitable for these flexible uses would range from 17,000 to 30,000 square feet, with some going up to the largest at 65,000 square feet. Each of these would have raised floors with energy conserving features.

This midrise enclave was surrounded by the bus ramps of the Transbay Terminal, which is today being redeveloped into a modern rail, bus and commuter facility with adjacent high rises oriented toward Market Street. Thus, Foundry Square would serve as a transition from the huge terminal and high rises toward and north of Market Street, and the midrise mixed residential and commercial developments in the newly redeveloping South Beach and Rincon Hill areas.

Working with SWA Group Principal Dan Tuttle and Jim Lee with Jerry Goldberg as a consultant, and Studios Architects, we looked at several alternatives but ultimately decided that the uniqueness of the parcel locations called for an urban design of coordinated open plazas at each of the four corners, designed to create a larger square around the intersection. The developer brought in Jim Jennings as a consulting architect, and to strongly define each plaza, he added a second façade layer of full-height glass walls set on slender columns and separated from each building by four feet of air. At the street edges of each of the four plazas, SWA Group Principals Jim Lee and Ross Nadeau designed and placed a grid of mature tulip trees packed in a tight square and placed in low granite planters that also served as seating. To further enhance the unity of the square, each plaza had black granite paving, a water feature, artwork by celebrated sculptors, and ground-level cafes.

The buildings combine the glass curtain walls at the corners with brick faced and glass curtain walls that relate to the older brick buildings along Howard Street. This transition is also achieved through massing, as each ten-story building has a seven-story base and a three-story "penthouse" set back to create landscaped roof terraces. The penthouse floors have uniquely shaped folded roofs that create a dynamic composition to top off the four-building complex. Though the fourth and final building at the southwest corner of the site will be completed in early 2014 Foundry Square was awarded the Urban Land Institute Award of Excellence as well as an award from the American Society of Landscape Architects in 2007.

**Opposite Page Above Left** The plan is for technology oriented uses in buildings at each of the four corners at First and Howard Street in downtown San Francisco, with the four corner plazas creating Foundry Square, a unique urban space. **Above Right** Space for people to enjoy the winter sun under the deciduous trees in the corner plazas of Foundry Square. **Center Left** Foundry Square corner plazas are popular for lunchtime or sunshine breaks. **Bottom Left** View of one building's penthouse roof garden looking across the street to a second building's penthouse at Foundry Square. **Bottom Right** A sculpture at one of the four Foundry Square plazas.

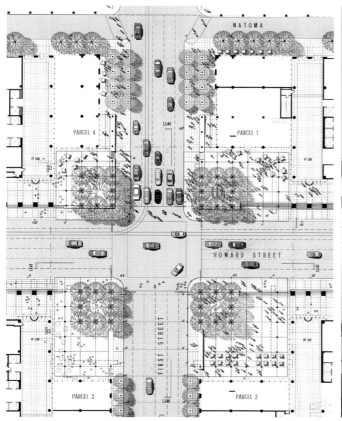

## Courthouse Square Competition, Santa Rosa, California (2007)

We usually shy away from public competitions, since they typically take up significant chunks of time and money, and wins are far from guaranteed—and in some even a win did not ensure continued work. However, we saw that the City of Santa Rosa set up their process to avoid this problem, ensuring the winner would continue to do the implementation so we decided to enter when they announced a competition for Courthouse Square.

In the early 20th century, Santa Rosa became the county seat of Sonoma County, which is located along the California coast 50 miles north of San Francisco. At that time, a stone courthouse was built on a square block in the center of the city to house the courts and administration. Santa Rosa Avenue, the main highway from the south, ended on the square and the main highway north, Mendocino Avenue, began on the other side of the square. After an earthquake damaged the old courthouse in 1906, it was rebuilt, but in the late 1960's all of the expanded courthouse functions were moved to the new County Administrative Center north of the city center. Rather than keeping the square intact as a park, as would have been preferable from an urban design standpoint, the city ran a major road through its center to connect Santa Rosa and Mendocino Avenues. The two parcels that resulted from the square's split were enlarged somewhat by closing the two side streets—Exchange and Hinton—and the split square then became small parks and plazas.

In the mid-2000's, the city debated whether these open spaces could better serve downtown by becoming one large square again. The 20th century was the era of the automobile—should the 21st century usher in a more pedestrian friendly attitude? If so, decreasing the role of the fast-moving main avenues that bisected the square would certainly go a long way to help. Moreover, downtown Santa Rose remained an attractive center of Sonoma activities, but it was teetering on the edge of decline and needed a revitalizing boost. Thus, in 2007 the city put out a call for a professionally managed design competition with a modest stipend, with the winner receiving the commission to build the selected plan. We sent in our qualifications and were selected as one of five finalists to propose a renewal of Courthouse Square. Having worked together so well on Foundry Square, we again joined forces with Studios Architects and began an intensive effort that would produce interim studies and a final plan and model.

Led by SWA Group Principals Cinda Gilliland and Jim Lee, our plan reinstated the two side streets but made them narrow with special paving and limited curbside parking to encourage pedestrian activity. Looking to the great squares of European capitals, the sidewalks in front of the buildings were widened to encourage sidewalk cafes in the salubrious climate. We called the large square in the center Santa Rosa's "living room," a place for all kinds of activities, from festivals to just sitting and talking. Over the large central space, paved in decomposed granite like the great plazas in Paris, a light arbor would glow at night through the many trees we had preserved or newly planted. For major events, this arbor would come alive with festive lighting and sound capabilities, and at each corner of the lighted arbor structure, we located four glass pavilions with surrounding gardens, terraces and outdoor seating areas. These pavilions further enlivened the corners of the square with exhibits, cafes, sheltered activities, childcare and restrooms. At the south end of the plaza near traffic-heavy Third Street was a glass "waterwall" fountain that would help to buffer the traffic noise and headlights and would double as a backdrop for a performance stage. The north side of the plaza opened onto the main shopping street, Fourth Street, completing the transformation of the square.

Our submittal was well received and was selected by the highly qualified jury as the winning plan. The jury thought it was an exciting scheme with a powerful big idea—the new "Heart of the City." However, as in many planning ventures, all was going well except the timing in the world around us. The city was quick to give us a contract and to set us off on preparing development plans in early 2008. But then the recession came down upon us, and the city was hard hit by budget cuts and hard up on funding. Despite a plan to finance the square renewal through private and foundation funding, everything dried up at once. The city employees faced severe cuts or reduced pay and benefits, and the City Council had to bring a vibrant ten-year program for the square's renovation to a screeching halt.

In 2013, five years later, the city is finally taking steps towards beginning the renewal of the square. Using stimulus money and special infrastructure funds, they are putting in the new utility infrastructure, and they can take the first step for basic rebuilding of the side streets and the permanent closure of the wide street though the center. However, there is no budget for building the new square according to our plan, unfortunately. This is a dilemma, as in the next few years they will only be able to install a small number of the experimental temporary spaces currently being used in street closings in New York and San Francisco. These could be fun, certainly, but as the economy improves there needs to be a concerted effort to build Downtown Santa Rosa as a great civic place. These temporary programs are temporary fixes, and they will not have the desired renewal effect. Without greater investment, downtown Santa Rosa may continue to decline.

That said, I remain optimistic about Santa Rosa's future. The city of 170,000 people is very livable and attractive, and in my experience, the city has followed through in the past on plans to shape its development. For example, in 1978 SWA Principal Jim Lee and I prepared a Subdivision Design Guide for the city to shape the then fast-growing new parts of the city. They followed that guide with diligence and great effect for over thirty years, transforming the new growth areas into distinct neighborhoods. This kind of dedication bodes well for their ability to meet the challenge now being faced by their downtown district.

**Opposite Page** A model of Courthouse Square showing the light arbor, glass performance wall, pavilions and major trees.

**Above** Nightime under the light arbor watching a performance at the glass wall from the large decomposed granite square and pavilions.
**Bottom** Preserved and newly planted trees would provide much of the character of Courthouse Square.

### Consulting on Coastal Properties, Sonoma and Mendocino Counties, California (1970-2009)

This last project is not one project, but a series of projects for coastal properties in Sonoma and Mendocino counties over a series of thirty-nine years. Together, these Northern California projects show the different but extremely valuable roles that a planner can play in trying to find the best use of land.

*Sonoma County*

In 1970, SWA was retained by a real estate group that had acquired an option on thousands of acres of coastal land in Sonoma County on both sides of the Russian River around the town of Jenner, which is ideally located where the river meets the Pacific Ocean. This spectacular property partially belonged to a sand and gravel company that periodically mined the mouth of the river for the deposits that were the result of wave and tidal action interacting with the flow of the river. The remainder belonged to a redwood harvesting company. We were to plan for recreational homes as a more sensitive use that would take the place of mining and timber operations, which would cease and phase out, respectively, once the development proceeded.

The success of a different coastal development located further north in Sonoma County, the well-known Sea Ranch designed by Lawrence Halprin in the 1970's, indicated that coastal properties could become resort or second home attractions to Bay Area residents. In this regard, Jenner had a considerable advantage over Sea Ranch as it was a good forty minutes closer by car, and being located on the same main route from the Bay Area, avoided the tortuous coastal highway that ran from Jenner to Sea Ranch.

The 1970's were a turbulent era for the beautiful California coast, and people up and down the state were concerned that rapid private development was closing off this great thousand-mile long resource. We had just come off helping a grass roots effort to protect the Town of Mendocino from such development and were sensitive to the issues of public access, use and views of the coast. When we began environmental and planning studies for the 1800-acre property on the south side of the river along with some preliminary work on the 4000 acres on the north side, we strived to ensure that our plan recognized these concerns.

To begin with, our plan for the relatively flat coastal terrace portion of the southern property between Highway One and the ocean recognized the sensitivities of views from the scenic highway. We adopted the use of condominium villages like those at Sea Ranch that worked so well in this kind of condition. But unlike Sea Ranch, we did not place the second home lots on the ocean side of the highway, as this would interfere with views of the coast. Instead, we only sited several condominium villages with large areas of open space between them, allowing for unimpeded views and trail access to the coast and the nearby Goat Rock State Park. Continuing in this manner, on the hillside lands east of Highway One we placed lots in two villages built on the higher ground with views toward the coast, leaving the lower slopes adjacent to the highway as natural open space. Each of these diverse villages had a small commercial center and a range of housing types within easy walking distances, and the villages were all connected by walking trails.

We began our entitlement process with Sonoma County in 1971 and soon after gained preliminary approval for this example of responsible planning on the coast. This approval occurred just before two major historic events took place. First, the citizens of California in 1972 passed the Coastal Act, which controlled all development of the coast. Second, within a year a drastic real estate recession began that put any recreational developments on hold for the next five years. The combination proved deadly for the Jenner Bay project as any financing for infrastructure dried up right alongside the market for recreational properties, while the new Coastal Act allowed anyone to appeal a development with just a simple postcard to the regional Coastal Commission. With multiple appeals looming and the economic incentives for development gone, the owners of the southern property sold a beautiful, environmentally valuable inland portion of the property along Willow Creek to the State. Eventually the remainder was also sold as a substantial addition to Goat Rock State Park. Fortunately, though indirectly, the highest and best uses for some of these properties were realized.

To create some cash flow for the owners, we turned to 750 acres at the northern edge of the 4000-acre properties north of the river. That property was located some distance from the coast and was out of the Coastal Commission jurisdiction. Muniz Ranches, as this large ranch community was called, was located along one carefully contoured road. Seventeen ranches, each more than 40 acres in size, were governed under a community association to maintain the entry and access road, and control the design of the buildings to ensure they blended in with the landscape. The sale of these ranches allowed the owner of the northern properties to continue grazing and redwood timber harvest operations on the remaining 3300 acres.

Some twenty years later in 1994, the owner of the 3300-acre Jenner properties, Dr. Ollie Edmunds of Sonoma Coast Associates and the Gualala Redwoods Company, contacted us about his properties. However, after taking a new look at the Jenner properties in the late 1990's, it was apparent that any thought of planning for development on that property was fraught with difficulties. In the long period since our initial work, policies and positions by the citizens, Sonoma County and the Coastal Commission had solidified against any form of development on these lands. At Dr. Edmund's insistence, a market study and sketch plan were done that showed economically viable uses for this relatively accessible and beautiful coastal property including homes, golf, and a lodge. Still, water remained a potential problem since the town of Jenner was dependent on the limited water resources of the properties.

Economically, the development was justifiable, but we found out quickly that politically it was a non-starter. My advice was to talk to the Trust for Public Land to see if they could advise him as to a way to come up with some practical forms of resolution for his sensitive land, since the Trust had much experience in this kind of land use issue for coastal properties. We met with them in the late 90's, but he was not ready to take any definitive steps in this direction: Dr. Edmunds, a prominent orthopedic Surgeon in New Orleans whose family had owned land on the California coast for a generation, could not easily accept that there was no viable development use for his land.

As his family was eager for some resolution, he prepared offerings of his properties to a wide audience of real estate investors through his real estate arm, Delta Pacific. The reaction or lack of interest in the following years was

223

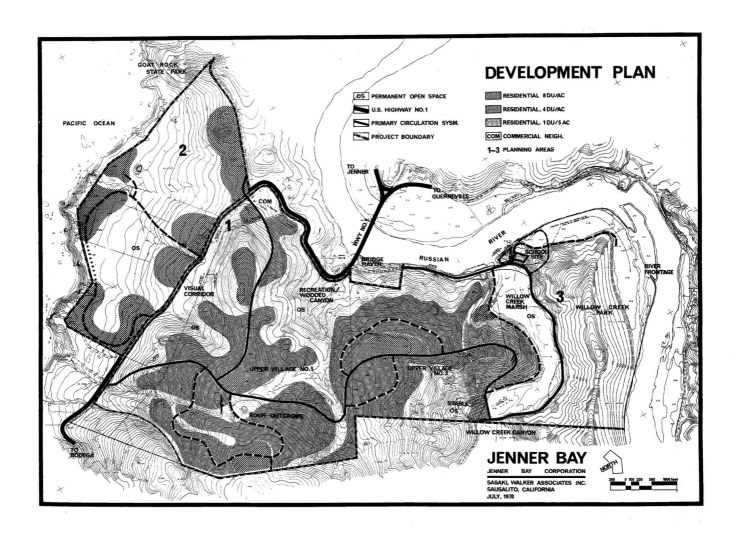

sobering, and he started to move toward our suggested direction. Meanwhile in 2003, the Trust for Public Land worked out a deal to preserve 3400 acres of the Willow Creek Ranch on the south side of the Russian River, adding it to the lands we had worked on that had already been acquired by the state and significantly enlarging the highly popular Sonoma Coast State Beach.

Seeing this, in 2004 Dr. Edmunds began a five-year negotiation with the Sonoma Land Trust for the Trust to acquire the entire 3300-acre Jenner property along with adjacent inland ranches from other owners, adding up to a total of 5400 acres. Calling the property the Jenner Headlands, the Sonoma Land Trust led a group including the Sonoma County Open Space District and garnered funds allocated from approved California open space bonds for the land acquisition. With the negotiations down to the last stage in 2009 and with yet another major real estate and recession looming, I urged Dr. Edmunds not to delay as the bond money was finite and would not soon be replenished. As I was also a member of the Sonoma Land Trust, I also encouraged Ralph Benson, the Trust's Executive Director, to keep pursuing the deal as I knew of the longstanding philanthropic activities of the Edmunds family and their commitment to the communities along the coast.

Finally, in December, 2009 the Sonoma Land Trust announced the purchase of the entire Jenner headlands, including Dr. Edmund's 3300 acres, for 36 million dollars. Though it took 39 years to permanently secure the protection of this precious coastal property, including both sides of the Russian River where it meets the Pacific Coast of California, it was worth the wait to be able to preserve the land for future generations.

*Mendocino County*

As a footnote to the long Jenner process in Sonoma County, we also worked in the late 1990's and early 2000's to plan for the best use of two important coastal properties in Mendocino County. Unlike the more affluent Sonoma County to its south, Mendocino County was cash strapped and needed to use its coastal land for economic and tax base growth and to increase employment opportunities. Dr. Edmunds of the Gualala Redwoods Company, owner of the Jenner property, also owned properties with development potential in the Town of Gualala, just over the Sonoma County border from Sea Ranch. By this time Sea Ranch was close to full build-out and the attractive little town of Gualala had much to offer to residents of Sea Ranch and the other coastal communities.

I started working closely with a citizen based group, the Gualala Municipal Advisory Council, to prepare the Gualala Town Plan, which included the 82-acre Lower Mill Site where the Gualala River met the coast, as well as the Gualala Arts Center, which Dr. Edmond's family had dedicated and built for the community ten years earlier. The plan that Larry Pearson and I prepared for the relatively flat Lower Mill Site was for a walkable village of art galleries, commercial space, restaurants and a hotel directly connected to the Gualala Town Center. In addition, the plan would include small cottages and apartments, a community/senior center, and a library. The land between Highway One and the coast would remain untouched as open space, as would the land along the Gualala River. We had far fewer issues with this plan than with the plan for the Jenner property, and the plan was adopted by the community and county. However, due to the issue of difficult access from

**Opposite Page** A study of placing development in a complete system of open space along the California Coast and along the Russian River near the town of Jenner in Sonoma County. **Bottom** The model shows the use of tight condominium clusters on the ocean terrace as a way to create major open spaces along the coast and to protect views from Highway One in Sonoma County.

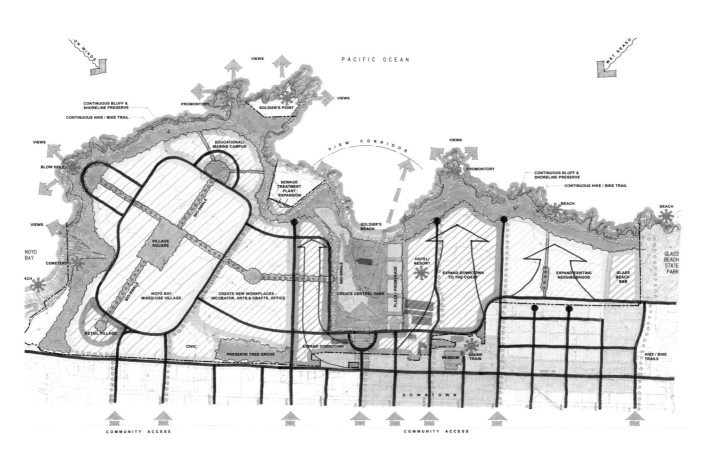

the Bay Area and a continued real estate recession, development has been very slow in this remote part of the coast.

The other property in Mendocino County was the much larger Georgia Pacific lumber mill site in Fort Bragg, one hundred miles north of Jenner. The 450-acre mill Georgia Pacific (GP) mill closed permanently in 2002, and a year later we were part of a GP-sponsored team that studied the potential reuse and replacement of the town's major employer. It would be difficult to attract significant new employment to this remote site, and the potential for second homes was limited not only by the four-hour drive from San Francisco along twisting narrow roads, but also by the region's wet winter and cool summer.

After learning that the Coastal Commission considered Ft. Bragg an urban service center on the north coast, Nancy Fleming and I developed a plan that revitalized that role. The key purpose of the plan was to reunite the city with its coastline and to provide permanent public access and public use of this long denied resource, which had been fenced off by the mill site. Our plan extended the downtown Fort Bragg shops, tourist facilities and the small-lot downtown residential neighborhood several blocks into the mill site toward the coast, where it met with a three-mile long linear park and coastal trail we designed along the ocean bluffs of the entire mill site. The larger portion of the site south of downtown meanwhile was planned to accommodate employment uses, parks and cultural facilities or possibly a neighborhood of vacation homes.

After we finished our plan and presented it to the community, Georgia Pacific tried to sell the site to developers, but no one was interested in buying unless the entitlements from the city and Coastal Commission were fully in place. This could take many years since a Specific Plan and a Local Coastal Plan and all the environmental studies would have to be done and approved beforehand. As Georgia Pacific looked to beginning this long entitlement process and the required environmental remediation of the site, our planning team and the city jointly prepared a strategy to open the site to early public access. This was done as a goodwill gesture to the local citizens so they would not have to wait for the entitlement process to slowly unfold before gaining access to their city's coastline. This interim plan was for GP to donate fifty-seven acres along the entire coast for a hundred-foot wide coastal trail. In addition, the City would utilize available California Coastal Conservancy funds to build the trail and to purchase twenty-five additional acres from GP for a coastal park.

After Georgia Pacific was sold and new management took over, they went through a process to re-evaluate all their properties, and we did not continue in any active role with the new management. In 2013, the planning process still grinding away, with the Specific Plan just beginning its long environmental report and review, and the Coastal Commission yet to consider the plan. However this year the coastal trail will open, bringing to an end the many generations of lost access by the citizens of Fort Bragg and by all Californians to this wonderful coastline.

Opposite Page The lower mill site village green, library and commercial adjacent to downtown Gualala in Mendocino County. **Bottom** The concept plan for the Georgia Pacific 450 acre mill site in Fort Bragg, California that allows for the expansion of the city toward the Pacific Ocean shoreline with a three mile coastal trail and park.

Above A residential street scene in the lower mill site village at Gualala. **Middle** A plan perspective of the lower mill site village along the Pacific Coast adjacent to the town of Gualala in Mendocino County, and protected open space at the mouth of the Gualala River.

# 8 Shaping the SWA Group: lessons from 55 years of practice

This chapter focuses on the unique approach to structuring the business of design firms that was fostered for twenty-three years of incredible change and transformation as I became the first president of the SWA Group in 1974 when it emerged from the Sasaki, Walker firms. I mentioned some of the key issues we faced in the preceding chapters that covered both my professional work as well as my leadership role, but I hope to give a more coherent view here of how WE shaped the firm and dealt with this great transformation of our practice and the profession of landscape architecture in general during the last half of the twentieth century. I would suggest that, while as a group practice we were not obvious as "stars" to the media, the firm always remained on the cutting edge of the landscape architecture profession, moving it to a larger role in addressing the key issues that are now framing the twenty-first century: an increasingly urban world with great concerns for sustainable ways for people to live a better life.

This longer historical chapter covers the 40 year history of shaping the SWA Group from 1974 on. The illustrations here however follow the overall book timeline format by showing iconic SWA Group projects at the end of the 20th century and into the beginning of the 21st.

*Landscapes are places for people* **AND** *nature*

The basic work of the firm is the design of the cultural and natural environment. To do this we brought together the key economic, social and environmental issues of finite locations, whether they are a large city, a small school, a section of a river, or a bustling commercial center. Each site is put within its human and natural context. The plans, designs and built places aimed to balance and resolve these complex issues in an elegant and beautiful way. The work was with cities, communities, and public and private developers as clients, and in collaboration with architects, engineers and natural and social scientists. We have proven to generations of clients, whether public or private profit-making enterprises, that this work added to the lasting value and desirability of the cities, communities, homes, business places, institutions and green spaces they fostered or developed, and in the long run was in better harmony with the land and its resources.

*Creating high quality projects is the bottom line,* **NOT** *profit*

The issue I deal with here is how to structure a firm as a continuing business where the practice of our profession to the standards mentioned above was our bottom line, not purely the profit motive that is the classic definition of the bottom line. We needed to pay our bills, meet our payrolls and provide a secure future for our employees, but as a group we wanted to be able to do that in a firm that proudly put the excellence and success of our work as our prime goal. We believed that a professional group practice that focused on planning, designing and guiding the building of great projects could meet those key business needs where "the bottom line was not the bottom line." We would rely on maintaining the highest level of performance in our professional work and in demonstrating the value of our ideas to our clients. As it turned out a profession first firm was also good business. Clients demanded services that produced quality.

*Time and budget constraints put* **DISCIPLINE** *into the design process*

I believed that running a design-oriented firm as a successful business did not have to mean that the quality of the work would suffer. Quite to the contrary,

**Opposite Page** The promenade at the Luohu transportation center in Shenzhen, China with the long glass median providing light down to the multiple levels of train and bus terminals below

my experience over my first seven years at Sasaki, Walker Associates (before it became SWAGroup) convinced me that meeting time and cost budgets put a discipline into the design process. These constraints could add to the effectiveness of our design decisions by making them timely in the process. Our experienced designers avoided blind alleys, knew when to take an early lead, and when to wait for our client or architects to resolve issues that might have us redesigning our work. Our charettes led quickly to deep inspiration and "big ideas" that could be practically translated into built realities. When an unavoidable problem occurred, we would work hard to resolve it, and the resultant overrun could be contained by the design, drawing and field people working together. With the quality and training of our people, we would have much more of our work come in within our and our client's budgets.

*Whatever we do* **TOGETHER** *will make us different*

I also believed that a collaborative group practice could do great design work. The modern composer Philip Glass put this best when he said in an interview with the New York Times, "When I talk to young composers, I tell them, I know that you're all worried about finding your voice. Actually you're going to find your voice. By the time you're thirty you'll find it. But that's not the problem. The problem is getting rid of it. You have to find an engine for change. And that's what collaborative work does. Whatever we do together will make us different."

How I was able to do this is simply the story of how WE were able to make this happen. Each section below carries a tribute to those in our group who were most involved in making our firm's successful transformation into a "World Leader in Landscape Architecture."

## History: A Tribute to Hideo Sasaki and Peter Walker

*"Landscape Architects can make a significant contribution to bringing the ecological point of view to the planning process for cities."* —HIDEO SASAKI, 1953

*Making Landscape Architecture* **CENTRAL** *to building America*

When Hideo Sasaki hung out his shingle as Sasaki Associates in 1953, and then when Peter Walker joined him and formed Sasaki, Walker Associates in 1957, they represented optimism and ambition for the field of landscape architecture. They were determined to bring the profession of landscape architecture out of the doldrums of the depression and the war and to make it central to the building of a new post-war America. Those characteristics continue today in the three firms that evolved from this partnership, Sasaki Associates, The SWAGroup, and Peter Walker Partners..

*Carrying on the* **OLMSTED** *tradition*

Hideo, who became Chairman of Landscape Architecture at the Harvard Graduate School of Design, believed that landscape architects were too willing to just make something of spaces created by others. He wanted to shape spaces from the beginning and reinvigorate city and site planning by landscape architects, carrying on the profession as practiced by its founder Frederick Law Olmsted.

Olmsted's practice, from Central Park in 1857 to the Columbian Exposition and the Biltmore Estate at the end of the nineteenth century when he retired, left an incredible legacy of work. He had a major role designing everything from the grounds of the United States Capitol to universities, city and community plans, communities, park systems and work all across America. Best known for his work on Central Park as designer and superintendent, he first used the term "Landscape Architect" in 1860 when he laid out the remainder of Manhattan Island from 155th Street north.

His sons continued their father's work after he retired, and gained three thousand more commissions as Olmsted Brothers until the firm shut its doors in 1950, leaving completion of many large projects going until the 1970's.. Frederick Junior helped establish the American Society of Landscape Architects in 1899, and in 1900 at the request of Charles W. Eliot, President of Harvard University, created the first curriculum in the country for Landscape Architecture. This curriculum included City Planning and Urban Design as a natural outgrowth of the scope of work of the hundred-year practice of the Senior Olmsted and the Olmsted Brothers' firms.

Before coming to Harvard, both Hideo and Pete had studied at the University of Illinois under Stanley White, who had worked with the Olmsted Brothers. White fostered a landscape profession that espoused a broad view and was critical of any kind of poor physical development of cities or places. He stressed formulating ideas that created, restored and enriched the overall environment of places for people that had social and economic as well as environmental relevance.

*Hideo and Pete form* **SASAKI, WALKER** *Associates in 1957*

*"Pete was always so full of bright ideas—he and I put out our projects in the fastest time possible"* —Hideo Sasaki, 1958

Hideo found a partner in Peter Walker, who White had sent to Harvard to study under him. Pete was a powerful designer who went after big ideas in his work and did not limit his view of his profession. They both saw the spaces between buildings and the urban infrastructure not as leftovers or as negatives, but as positive design elements that could be more significant than the buildings themselves in making the city more livable. They added Site Planning and Urban Design to their letterhead along with Landscape Architecture. Both men were natives of California, both studied at Berkeley where Hideo had briefly taken City Planning, and both wound up at Harvard where they were influenced by Gropius' teaching of the use of both the arts and sciences in collaboration with the other design disciplines to bring about a better society. At different times both also headed up Landscape Architecture at Harvard and contributed to the advance of the profession by teaching while continuing to practice.

After Pete graduated from Harvard, they formed Sasaki Walker Associates in Watertown, Massachusetts, where the new firm's masthead specifically listed site planning and urban design as well as landscape architecture. The two men had shared strong views about the continuum of planning and design in creating places, and about a land-based approach that included an

"ecological point of view"—and this was a decade before the environmental movement began in the larger society. They preferred ideas to style and went with timelessness and problem solving as their hallmarks. They wanted their ideas to shape the betterment of the human condition, not be superficial embellishments. The quality of their planning and design work and the final built product was their paramount goal. They would hire only the best people and were comfortable doing things they had never done before.

*Two founders, two very related but distinct points of view produce* **TWO SEPARATE FIRMS**

When Pete moved to San Francisco to work on the construction of Foothill College, the two Sasaki, Walker Associates offices on the East and West Coasts continued to practice with all these shared values. As Pete stayed on in California to take advantage of the robust growth along the west coast, differences evolved from each partner's approach to how the firm should be composed. Hideo fostered an in-house collaborative approach and added principals in architecture, engineering and environmental studies as well as landscape architecture. He formed Sasaki, Dawson, DeMay Associates from the east coast office.

Pete meanwhile preferred a design studio of planners, designers and field specialists, and he cultivated an outstanding group of architects as clients and collaborators, along with fine engineering, economic and environmental consultants. He was intensely interested in a multidisciplinary approach and was constantly finding incredibly exotic consultant talent. The two different but

**Above** The new overall streetscape in the commercial district around Disneyland in Anaheim, California.

**Opposite Page Above** The new landscape treatment at the major vehicular entry to Disneyland, Anaheim. **Bottom Right** The new shuttle transportation entry plaza for Disneyland, Anaheim.

still related offices had different principals specific to one office, a different structure, and an emerging national practice that produced conflicts in going after work, not to mention being confusing to clients. After discussing these issues in 1973 and 1974, the two partners decided it was best for both if they created two completely separate firms. Hideo transformed his firm to Sasaki Associates. Pete, conferring with our principals, agreed to go back to focus on our basic strengths of planning, urban design, and landscape architecture. Asking me to become President of the new firm, we established SWA Group as a group practice to reflect our changed conditions.

### A LEGACY for the SWAGroup

Today SWA Group purposefully carries forth this legacy from its founders, for it still has great relevance for the work. The founders were teachers and practitioners, and those roles remain key. Following Hideo the continuum of planning at SWA Group (deciding what should occur on the land) and design (deciding what form and character that should be) is as seamless as possible, so that what is finally built upon the land meets both human and environmental needs in a sustainable way. Pete focused on being a design studio and looked for the big idea in the work as he carried through the transition into the SWAGroup. In this way the new firm and its Principal group continued to establish prototypical plans and designs that both served and inspired people.

**Above Right** Lunchtime at the Fidelity
Investments Regional Campus in Westlake, Texas.
**Middle** A building entry at the layered stone edge
of the lake on the Fidelity Investments Regional
Campus in Westlake, Texas.

**Pages 234-235** The overall indigenous plantings
and stone terraces at the Fidelity Investments
Regional Campus in Westlake, Texas.

Opposite Page Above The campus center and lake at the new Soka University in Aliso Viejo, California. Bottom Left Students taking a break on the campus of Soka University in Aliso Viejo, California. Bottom Right An overview of campus academic and residential buildings at Soka University in Aliso Viejo, California.

## The SWA Group Structure: A Tribute to Mike Gilbert

*"He was quite simply the author of the institution that is today* SWA, *spiritually, economically and socially." —*Pete Walker, of Mike Gilbert

*Paul Michael* **"MIKE"** *Gilbert*

During 1974 and 1975 we went through a fundamental and remarkable transformation into the SWAGROUP. I became the first president of the new firm and along with Pete and Mike Gilbert, our business principal, set out to create a firm structure that would carry on the professional goals of our founders. This was all happening as the economy crashed and our workloads declined. How we did all this in that kind of turmoil is a fitting tribute to Mike Gilbert's clear understanding of how a consulting business worked and how professional organizations could achieve their largely professional goals and still be successful as businesses.

Mike Gilbert was trained as a geologist and mining engineer at Stanford, and worked as a civil engineer and then a project manager for one of our important development clients, Cabot, Cabot and Forbes. He had experience in business, managing and developing real estate, contracts and deal making. He met Pete when he was our client, and in Pete's words, "We were from the first kindred spirits...we loved the game of business and the high purpose of the environment and its design."

Thus, Mike joined Sasaki Walker Associates in 1970 as a business consultant and later became a principal. He established a program to build personal estates for the Principals by buying or developing our own office buildings and other ventures. He had set up EMIC, the Environmental Management and Investment Company, as a separate entity. Becoming CEO of EMIC, he moved to a separate office in a nearby EMIC building. This separate entity, which he and the principals owned jointly, gave him not only freedom to do real estate development and management away from our professional firm, but also to continue to work as our business advisor as a consulting principal and to be a member of the board of directors. In this role he continued to play a vital part in our business and people programs.

Reflecting Peter Walker's desire to further our environmental planning and design work in 1973, Mike was asked to set up a merger with an environmental firm to form Sasaki, Walker Roberts (SWR) to add environmental scientists, engineers and graphics specialists (but not architects) to our staff of planners and landscape architects. The idea was great, but not the timing, as the extreme mid 1970's national recession hit several years later, and generating work and administrating the expanded group and the different disciplines became difficult. Having multidisciplinary divisions in the firm caused a lot of introspection about internal organization and finding projects that used all the divisions. We realized the previous organization as Sasaki, Walker Associates gave us much more flexibility in joining or forming teams while still effectively collaborating with outside environmental scientists, architect/ clients, engineers, graphic designers, or economists. We found we missed the prime design focus of the firm.

So in 1974, coming after Pete's agreement with Sasaki to end the seventeen-year partnership and form two completely separate firms (to take Sasaki's name off our firm and to begin under a new name) we decided it would be best for all if we would completely dissolve Sasaki Walker Roberts Associates to form the new SWAGROUP. This new firm would shift focus back to our design and planning services, though we helped the environmental and graphics groups become separate firms so they could meet their professional goals. Mike quickly worked with the large environmental group to set up a new firm, as they had solid professionals and some good clients. The firm changed over time to become LSA, today a very successful multiple-office company with Mike continuing on the board of directors for years. He did the same with the smaller graphics group, and they in turn became the GNU Group, also a successful firm today thanks to Mike's help.

Thus, through this restructuring Sasaki, Walker Roberts split into three much more efficient firms that could focus on what each knew best with an enhanced ability to move instantly in order to respond to the difficult times. We continued to work very effectively with our previous environmental and graphic employees and Principals as outside collaborators, as we did with the other top consultants we had worked with for decades. It was truly a tribute to Mike Gilbert that he was able—in a very difficult economic time—to help us all forge simultaneously the foundation of three highly successful professional practices.

During these bad times, the SWA GROUP did have some good clients that continued working toward the time when the recession would end. There were a few, like the Irvine Company and Arvida, who could maintain a limited but reliable cash flow and did in fact benefit enormously when the recession ended. They were able to respectively open Woodbridge at Irvine and the Arvida Villages at Boca Raton to incredible success, without any lag time. With Mike Gilbert's acumen, whether handling a very nervous bank that we had borrowed from or his clear view of what needed to be done swiftly and without hesitation to survive while we reorganized, we quickly went from ninety design professionals, environmental scientists, graphic artists and support staff of the previous Sasaki Walker Roberts to the thirty design professionals and a skeleton support staff that made up the new SWAGroup. Under Mike's watchful guidance, we emerged leaner but wiser, and began to prosper and grow again as the national economy recovered rapidly.

*Managing the design firm:* **BUSINESS IN SUPPORT OF DESIGN** *culture and not the other way around*

I had built a relationship with Mike, and I knew with Pete's continued participation we could together do what I alone would be hard pressed to do with complete success. A key ingredient that Mike agreed upon completely was keeping the firm in the hands of experienced professionals and absolutely maintaining the same standard and culture that Pete and Hideo had begun. Among the Principals, Ed Kagi, Dick Law, Gary Karner and I had all studied at Harvard under Hideo, and Ed and Gary had worked at Sasaki, Walker Associates in Watertown. We designers and planners were not as knowledgeable about these kinds of business dealings, but Mike had our trust from his years running the previous iterations of Sasaki, Walker firms in California. We all agreed that the basic business model was that the business professionals like Mike and Wendy Simon, our Controller, had to be in a support role to the design professionals to continue our culture: to reiterate, the bottom line was not the bottom line, rather design was always put before business.

*The ESOP: a true group practice means* **EVERYONE** *has a stake in the firm's success*

Our goal was to set up a group practice where everyone would gain ownership over time and benefit from the success of the firm. The reason for this was twofold: to retain the best employees and to give them a path toward building a personal estate for retirement. To do this, we needed a way to buy ownership from Pete after he had bought out Hideo and owned the entire company. However, the principals did not have the resources to do that directly. Mike set out to solve these issues by considering an ownership split between Pete, the principals, and our newly established Employee Stock Ownership Program (ESOP), which included all employees of the firm as owners. We had a modest pension plan that Mike was able to convert to the ESOP to buy the original ESOP shares from Pete. Also, due to his desire to have more freedom to do things outside the firm like teach and paint, Pete made me, as president of the new company, and senior principals Ed Kagi and Dick Law a very generous offer of a good portion of his stock at attractive terms and price. In turn we would provide a guarantee that did involve some personal risk and a commitment to stay and take a more active role in running the company. In a later section I cover more about the important role of the ESOP in making the firm successful.

*About* **PEOPLE**

This was a basic business structure, but we never forgot that the firm was nothing without its people. It was our job to make sure the individual talents of the Principals were best utilized, that their strengths and weaknesses were reinforced by collaboration, and that we fostered a sense of trust between them. We developed incentives for working together on projects and in working together as an office to mentor the associates and hire and develop the young staff members. Our structure was flexible, so the people had to be flexible. Having been through a tough survival mode, we could demonstrate the value of being able to switch from planning to design and back again as the work required. Likewise, field people should be able to produce documents and train young people to build. Making the group practice work was going to be all about people.

**THE FOUR STEP MODEL:** *Making the group practice work by being involved in all aspects of the work*

*" I always said that SWA is the closest thing to being in practice for yourself without all the headaches that come from your own practice." —Chuck McDaniel, SWA Principal*

Although we were legally a corporation, we thought of the principals as partners in the work and running of the new firm. Mike had set forth a simple but brilliant model of a successful professional firm. He knew design professionals were basically project- and client-oriented people who derived their enthusiasm and challenge from jobs obtained in the marketplace. Professionals did not like just doing one part of a project unless they could feel they were involved in the totality. A Principal or partner gained the most satisfaction when they could do and control four basic tasks:

1) Securing the work, and establishing a relationship with the client
2) Doing the work to a high standard
3) Billing their services at a reasonable rate
4) Collecting their billings in a timely manner

In a true group practice, the principals would be in control of all four steps for their projects, giving them complete quality control of the outcome and thereby achieving the overall goals of the firm for design excellence. But we clearly understood that, while all the Principals could do all or a significant portion of the professional work required, and many could do well in securing work and serving the client, most wanted and needed help in the budgeting, contracting, invoicing and fee collecting roles. The firm would be set up to support all the steps so that all principals could fully function. That was our challenge as we structured the firm.

In theory, if you could do all four steps you could run your own firm. And several principals over time did just that. But most of our principals realized the inherent advantages in marshaling support resources for a group rather than an individual practice. If done right, you could have the advantage of both individual professional freedom and first-rate support services. Chuck McDaniel, our Dallas Managing Principal, put it best in a Land Forum Magazine article where he was quoted: "I always said that SWA is the closest thing to being in practice for yourself without all the headaches that come from having your own practice." That was Mike's and my goal for the firm.

*Securing the work:* **LET THE WORK DO THE TALKING** *for you*

We set out first to help all the principals do better in getting work. We would invest as a group in the major items to provide this assistance. First there was the excellent photography that Gerry Campbell had pioneered and continued as he became a principal and trained our current photographer, Tom Fox, who later also became a principal. This gave us a huge advantage in those days where even mediocre landscape photography was scarce. Gerry, with his magnificent color slides and two projector slide shows, captured the essence of our projects but even more importantly conveyed what landscape design

**Opposite Page Above** Sidewalk dining along the main street in the Santana Row mixed use neighborhood in San Jose, California. **Bottom Left** Overview of the main street in the 42 acre Santana Row mixed use neighborhood in San Jose, California. **Bottom Right** Archway entry into a courtyard at Santana Row mixed use neighborhood in San Jose, California.

**Pages 242-243** View of the Google Headquarters from the public Charleston Park in Mountain View, California.

was and how it could transform a place. Our architect clients saw how our designers understood and took their clues from the architect's concepts to beautifully enhance their buildings. The corporate or developer clients saw how the realistic budgets and our plans and designs for complete landscapes helped them create their identity or community quickly and provide a critical value added marketing tool. Our public clients saw the direct positive response of the public to our work that turned streets, communities, parks and public areas into vibrant places.

Another advantage in assisting principals in gaining new clients was that we had invested in building or buying our offices and in making them into vibrant design studios. Whenever possible, we invited prospective clients to our offices, which we designed as large, light filled spaces with conference rooms that were opened onto gardens and had glass walls that looked out on the swirling activity of a real creative workplace. Our working style was very informal and inclusive, as Principals did not have separate offices but rather worked out in the large space with the associates and staff, where brightly colored drawings filled every wall. The principals' workstations were defined by elbow high partitions that you could easily look over and engage in productive conversation. The clients loved to come to our locations in Sausalito, Laguna Beach, the Houston "atelier" and the historic Dallas "White Swan" building.

One of our advantages was not something we had but something we lacked—marketing principals. Our principals were hands-on in every way and did all the marketing. When it came to the interview, they could honestly say that they would work directly on the project all the way through planning, design and building the landscape. What we did have were a number of highly qualified Principals. Depending on the type of project, one or two principals would sit in on the interview indicating the support they would provide to the project principal and adding to the talent the client would expect to see throughout the project. We had great firm brochures and marketing materials, like tear sheets that the Principals could tailor to their understanding of the client's needs in addition to the slide shows, office tours and introduction to other Principals and Associates who would work on the project.

Another key support item were excellent standard proposals and contracts that could be quickly marked up. These were the exclusive product of one of our principals, Gary Karner, who went on to teach and write many of the official manuals on landscape architectural contracts, insurance and liability. He was backed up by our excellent attorney, Ken Goodin. Our accounting section had information on fees for work of similar scope and our field group had up-to-date per-square-foot and square-meter costs for varying degrees of hard and soft landscape development.

*Doing the work: the* **BEST PEOPLE** *do the best work, period*

Doing the best work possible required investment in a good office, equipment, and later on a computer on every desk, but the essential ingredient followed a simple formula: get the principals the best support associates and staff. We hired from the best schools and trained them in-house, and then assigned them to various principals' projects as required by their schedules. There was no permanent assignment of associates and staff to the principals, so a key process was the allocation of those resources to each project. This was done in weekly "hot list" office meetings, where personnel were assigned to specific projects. In addition, collaboration with other principals that rounded out their capabilities was carefully orchestrated so that each project could reach its full potential.

*Billing the work and collecting the fees: keep the accounting* **SIMPLE AND STREAMLINED**

To make the new firm work for the principals in step three and four of Mike's model (billing and collecting the fees and expenses), we built upon the successful project accounting system that we had used at Sasaki, Walker Associates, which Mike had helped develop with Wendy Simon. We worked diligently on an accounting system that would better support our professionals by providing very accurate and easy to use data that would include simple metrics, which a busy and non business oriented principal or project manager could use to quickly understand where the project was going and what they could do to keep it within budget. They could also directly contact accounting with any questions.

I wanted to keep working on projects myself and understood that if we had the best people, the right structure for the firm was to do everything to let them do their professional work with the least time spent doing administrative tasks. Our rules were simple. First, do a great job for your client: amaze them with your plans, designs and service. If you do that, everything that follows will be easy: set your contract and budget and meet it by following the simple and accurate progress information supplied to you, and if there are problems, ask for help from me, Mike or Wendy. Get your timesheet, and the timesheets of everyone working on the project, handed in promptly so we can accurately let everyone know how we are doing. Review the draft invoices prepared by accounting quickly so we can send out timely and accurate bills to your client. Finally, follow up with your client if they have any questions or have not paid us on time, since you are the one doing the amazing work for them.

We knew the key to this whole process would be the firm's principals. If they followed the rules, everyone would. I set the example by always being one of the first to get in my timesheet, get my billing back to accounting, and let my clients know when they were slow in paying us. By following the simple rules, the principals would have complete control over their project. That is what they and we both wanted, absolute professional control of our work resulting in great projects. If exceeding a budget was necessary for quality control, they could do that if they informed us so we knew how to project overall firm cash flow. We would only ask in return that the project would be of the highest quality so we could regain our losses in fees by the project's public and professional recognition. They could best read their clients so they could give us early warning on any potential payment problems. Our controller also could let them know if she saw any potential problems. We were there to help them.

*Redefining* **PROJECT MANAGEMENT** *for the Group Practice*

Project management at Sasaki, Walker Associates had been originally designed after a system used by Skidmore, Owings and Merrill (SOM), our longtime architectural client and collaborator. They had a project manager and project designer on each project. This system worked for us when Pete was involved in most projects, even though our scope of work was much smaller and less complex than SOM project work. With a group practice this was less important, and in most cases the Principals evolved to both manage and design or plan their projects. Where a planning principal like Ed Kagi or me was involved with a design principal like Dick Law or Bill Callaway on a large project, the planners usually took up the management role. But as the Principal Group grew, the separate project manager role became redundant, except on exceedingly complex projects. By decreasing the time needed for project management, our system allowed each Principal to readily manage their own projects, supported by associates, staff and our specialized principals.

Mike suggested thinking more like a law firm with multiple partners running multiple clients with relatively small support groups, rather than the SOM model of huge projects and large support staffs. He used the example of his experience in the Marine Corps, where a squad leader could effectively communicate day-to-day "face time" with up to a maximum total of seven members including himself. This kind of personal communication was essential to the workings of the kind of firm we were trying to build. We knew we would always have a large proportion of our firm as principals, each of whom would work with several associates and also several staff. The size of the firm would be in direct proportion to the number of principals that made up our group practice.

**BREAKING THE BARRIER:** *fostering mutual respect between design and support Principals*

*"Although SWA is extremely well managed as a business, the financial aims of the company are seen to promote the design and planning aspirations of the Principals, not the other way around." Mike Gilbert, SWA Principal*

The firm structure described above did much to allow our principals and their associates and staff to spend their time and talent on doing the best possible work for our clients, and to spend less time and thought on business matters. It is no surprise that design professionals consider business matters a burden imposed upon them by the accounting department. It is usually thought of as "we designers doing the great things, versus them doing the mundane." One of Mike Gilbert's most valuable insights was how to break down the barrier that most professional firms have between their professional and key business support people. I use the word people here because he saw this as a people problem. The designers felt the controller or billing clerk could never understand the importance of what they were doing in their work. Were these not just number crunchers?

In Wendy Simon, our Controller, and Lori Hjort, who was responsible for billing our clients, we had the formidable capabilities of accuracy, loyalty and hard work. We always knew where we stood financially, and our clients had great difficulty disputing or ignoring our iron-clad invoices. It was not enough to appreciate their work, which was remarkable with their small staff. They needed close cooperation with the principals who would have the final word on any invoice to the client on their projects.

**Opposite Page Above** The light towers on the main promenade with levels of commercial uses above and transportation facilities below at Luohu Station in Shenzhen. **Bottom** Millions of travelers come through the multimodal Luohu Station and commercial complex in Shenzhen, China.

**Above** The Thousand Lantern Lake and Park lights up central Nanhai in Guangdong, China.

**Opposite Page Above** The red trellis connects to old central Nanhai, as part of the Thousand Lantern Lake and Park. **Bottom Left** Walking through the Thousand Lantern Park in Nanhai, Guangdong Province, China. **Bottom Right** Evening activities along the Thousand Lantern Lake in Nanhai, China.

Mike Gilbert's approach was simple, as all great ideas are: find a way to foster mutual respect between the designers and business people. We knew that if the principals bought into this, it would then permeate our culture and the associates and staff would have to follow. Mike's idea of creating that respect was based upon the key business people working together as equals with the principals. All of our key people would share our goals and culture, and this would be based upon efficient communication, knowledge and friendship—not fear or duty. For this he lobbied hard to have Wendy follow him in becoming a principal of the firm. As a principal she would participate in our close-knit meetings, see firsthand the work we were doing, and get to know the other principals—how they thought, what they cared about, etc.

But though we had a culture that from the beginning brought not just designers and planners but also field specialists and photographers into the Principal Group, this election of another numbers person was a hard sell to our group. Luckily, with Mike's clear explanation of the benefits to our new firm structure and my emphatic support, we were eventually able to establish our Controller as a SWA GROUP Principal. This led later on to include information technology (IT) people as Principals, making sure that they operated where they understood that our design work drives the technology, not the other way around.

Now looking back forty years, it was the integration of the business as well as the key support professionals as equals and their acceptance by the Principal Group more than anything we did as a policy that created an unshakable bond between our professional and business functions. Wendy did love our work and it showed. Lori was made a principal at a later date when that was warranted by the Principal Group. Both always put the professional purposes first, even when it was hard to justify the cost or business consequence. In return, the principals at dinner or a principal lunch could express directly, as equal to equal, their concerns or appreciations for things they and their support staff did to make it easier or harder for them to devote their time to the work for our clients. From then on for both the professionals and our business people, it was our clients and our firm, and when we could hardly make payroll in a difficult economic times, we were all in this together.

This has carried on in the firm to our new Controller, Margaret Leonard, who was named principal recently when she took over once Wendy retired. We did revisit the reasons, but this time it was apparent to all why this was an important part of making our "professional first" structure work successfully over time. When Mike retired, Scott Cooper, who was trained by and worked for Mike at EMIC, joined SWA GROUP as an employee and was ultimately named Principal and Chief Financial Officer. Even as an employee he maintained the culture that Mike had begun in which the business person should be in a support position and have outside interests. Scott works four days a week, allowing him time to maintain those interests.

Scott provided critical help to Bill Callaway when Bill took the reins as CEO in 1996 after I retired. Working within the firm, Scott added a marketing function to his responsibilities and was able to put greater organization and emphasis on marketing and public relations as the firm became larger and more international in scope. He continued in the business role, supporting Kevin Shanley when he became CEO in 2006. He has shown real innovation in smoothly and efficiently setting up the business structure for our new office in China.

It is a tribute to Mike Gilbert's vision that he, Wendy and I were each replaced with individuals of such great capability who, with full support of the Principal Group, carry on the business structure he so masterfully created. Mike stepped down as business consultant when Scott took over, but remained on the SWA Group Board and as an advisor. He continued actively at EMIC, the real estate management company that had been completely separated from SWAGroup. There he trained Nancy Conger to take over after his death in 2011, and she has carried on extremely well in that company where I and several Principals and Ken Goodin, our attorney are still actively involved. At Mike's memorial in Sausalito, one after the other of us got up to express what a great friend and advisor he had been. Whether it was personal family issues, financial help, or great ideas about how you can do complicated things at SWA, at LSA, GNU Group, or other professional design firms, whether making movies, music ventures or restaurants, he was unsurpassed as a wise counselor and a true friend. Thanks again, Mike!

## Group Practice: A Tribute to The Principals and Associates

*"SWA is a great place for individual expression, individual growth—a very free and stimulating place where ideas are really what matters." —David Thompson, SWA Principal*

*The Principals and Associates are* **THE CORE** *of the Group Practice*

The SWA GROUP works together toward a common goal founded on the idea that design can shape the environment, but with highly individual points of view. The twenty-five or so Principals of SWA GROUP and around fifty Associates make up the core of the group practice

Each principal can lead a project and have complete professional control, work within another principal's project, or be free to make any project better by question or suggestion. They value each others' opinions and spark off each others' ideas in friendly criticism and competition to make the work better. They work across offices and design studios sometimes when they are shorthanded, or when they need particular skills, but always in a spirit of collaboration and with an eye on the ultimate quality of our work.

The key to a group practice is to attract the best professionals and make them Associates when they show great talent in one or more of the many fields that are necessary to make the firm work. From this highly qualified associate group, principals are found when they show they have proven leadership abilities and ideas that matter, and they stay on when they recognize that their ideas are accepted, nurtured and supported by the group. David Thompson, who was named principal in 1990, puts it well with this quote, "SWA is a great place for individual expression, individual growth—a very free and stimulating place where ideas are really what matters."

**BUILDING** *cities, communities and places is the goal*

I would add to David's comment above that SWA GROUP is not only a firm of ideas, but also is able to translate them very effectively into built places that retain the power of the ideas. The crafts of landscape architecture are built into all the work by every professional. Through building projects, these professionals are mentored and trained to learn basic grading—literally from the ground up—as well as drainage, materials, planting and irrigation, and construction processes. Grading is considered a key design tool as it is critical to producing a varied, three-dimensional result where the buildings, roads, parking and public spaces harmonize with and fit seamlessly into the natural site conditions. The Field Principals and Associates in each office are instrumental in sharing these ideas not only on design concepts but also how to elegantly and efficiently bring them to reality in all these dimensions. John Loomis has spearheaded these efforts along with the other SWA GROUP Field Principals Tim Peterson, David Bickel, Ross Nadeau and David Gal.

The Field people are involved not just during construction but in all phases of the project, from participating in the design, to reviewing the drawings, and working with the contractors and client representatives—all are necessary to accomplish a complete environment. The contractors know the field people are in charge, and that they cannot cut corners. However, if they have legitimate onsite issues, they can count on the field professionals' understanding of materials and processes to help them find the right solution. Seminars with contractors and subcontractors have provided demonstrations on how to procure the right materials and to build to the highest standards. This was done when offices were set up in Houston, Dallas and Florida. A recent firm wide program using all the field people is to raise construction standards in the many building projects in China. The diverse skills of the Principals and Associates serve to reassure clients that SWA GROUP can build their ideas within realistic budgets and get the desired results.

*The Principal Group sets the* **POLICIES** *to guide the firm*

Early on we relied upon all of the principals working together as the Principal Group to guide the firm. Ed Kagi defined the glue that united us as a group early on as: "our dedication to quality in the environment as a powerfully humane and beneficial influence on people who spend their lives acting upon and reacting to their physical surroundings." The overall Principal Group, in their semi-annual meetings, initiates and makes policy decisions for running the company, following this overall mission and then sends appropriate policies to the Board of Directors and the ESOP Committee for their review and action. Principal meetings always start with a presentation and a lively debate and discussion of the current professional work. These discussions and presentations constantly amaze me as to the quality and diversity of the work. Each meeting is a truly inspirational event highlighting what a group of dedicated designers can do when they work closely together. The meetings then move on to topics of interest and discussions of business metrics and financial statements, and always end with personnel issues.

One critical role of the Principal Group is the recruitment, training and mentoring of staff and the selection of Associates and Principals. This is entirely the purview of the Principal Group as a whole, as it is the most critical element in assuring excellence in a group practice. The recruitment of staff occurs through a coordinated, yearlong effort to visit the top landscape architectural schools, teach at some, and gain recommendations from professors and referrals from foreign schools and SWA GROUP employees. The criteria for the selection of Associates from the staff are twofold: professional education and experience and quality of the work produced. Each office offers a slate of potential associates at a principal meeting, and there is discussion with all Principals at that and the next meeting. By the time a vote occurs, the person is well described and the voting can typically be by unanimous accord.

Principals are always, without exception, only nominated from the Associate group, and after nomination one year of discussion is required before action is taken, again typically by unanimous accord. From the beginning there was a commitment to bring in only the absolute best people but not to preclude any skill set that the principals think is required to maintain future excellence in the firm. For this reason there are Principals who are planners, designers, field specialists, controllers, business managers, photographers, and information technologists. This last addition in the 1990's occurred when the use of computers was required by many clients for working drawings and when the graphics and photography people moved to digital media. Computers were first used for business purposes, so to continue the culture that design work drives all the technology,  the head Information Technology

**Opposite Page Above** Filinvest Corporate Center is a planned mixed use development outside Manila, at Alabang, the Philippines. **Bottom** A large shopping mall in the Filinvest Center outside Manila.

persons, Juel Bortolussi, and then Ken Lee were brought into the Principal Group. That way it was made sure the computer platforms served the needs of all the basic work as well as support systems.

*Recognizing the* **INDIVIDUALS** *in the group*

People issues are at the heart of any professional firm. Shared values go a long way toward making the firm work, but there always has to be recognition of the value of individuals to have a successful long-term result. A first order was individual compensation. How to do this fairly without losing the group values? When we set up SWA GROUP my first policy was that, as an employee-owned group practice, we would distribute all profits at the end of each year, retain only enough earnings to cover our mutually agreed upon overhead or investment projects. We would be transparent to all the Principals and keep our books open to them, since after all they were our primary policymakers.

Salaries for principals were based upon our consideration that the firm operates as a partnership even though technically is a corporation. They are based solely on the principal's billing rates, set each year by the CEO upon a multiplier from actual labor costs that are determined by competitive market considerations. All principals were required to be very highly billable. Salaries for associates and staff were set competitively but on the conservative side, as we were looking for people that shared the group practice and long-term compensation approach we pioneered.

Most importantly to the group practice, when the firm later went to multiple offices or design studios we did not make each a profit center, although later they became revenue centers. Only the firm as a whole has all the ingredients to be able to determine the true profits. Each year overall profit for the entire firm after agreed upon investment programs is set by the CEO into benefit programs for all the employees, principals, associates and staff. This includes bonuses, the ESOP contribution, and 401k and Profit Trust contributions which are then approved by the Board of Directors. We accentuate the tax-deferred benefit programs that remain to this date unmatched in the profession.

**Bottom Right** Major renovations for the Lassuen Mall at Stanford University.

**Opposite Page Above** Restoration of the original Olmstead designs at the Stanford University campus in California after the 1989 earthquake. **Bottom Left** The Cantor Museum sculpture garden at Stanford University. **Bottom Right** The Campus Center at Stanford University.

Bonuses for principals were set by the CEO based upon the overall bonus pool allocation in the employee benefits, weighted by the performance of the principal's office and each principal's professional performance and management performance components, since the principals were the key creators and managers of the projects and offices. The administrative principals were tracked with professionals who have similar experience and responsibility. From the beginning, the President and CEO received bonuses according to the group practice concept, that is to say not a multiple of principal bonuses as would be the case in a traditional corporation, but bonuses for their professional and management work on projects —just like the other principals, but with an added component for their firm direction responsibilities.

The bonuses for principals were also influenced by the firm's treatment of them like partners. They knew that they might share risk when the firm had cash flow problems. While SWA GROUP always had a good line of credit from a bank, we never risked using it for operating expenses like payrolls. It was for major planned investment projects or temporary tiding over during year-end tax planning only. When we did at a few critical times have trouble making our entire payroll, the principals would take up the slack. For carrying this risk they would be rewarded handsomely in times of good profits.

SWA Group Principals are leaders in the profession, and many are well known to clients and the profession. They teach and are involved with professional, community and art and environmental organizations. One of the great pleasures of my career has been the opportunity of working with so many of them over 40 years in the firm. Of the current Principal Group, almost one half have been SWA GROUP Principals for thirty or more years. Conversely, as a sign that can assure the future of SWAGroup, more than a third of the current principals have been appointed since 2000, with a large portion of them being women.

## Multiple Offices: A Tribute to the Managing Principals

*"I sought wider responsibilities of a well rounded professional, one who could participate in the whole spectrum of planning, design and business activities of an office." Don Tompkins\**

*"You have to challenge people and make them work beyond their proven abilities....as long as you do that they are excited when they solve the problem." Dick Law\**

*\*Don Tompkins and Dick Law were the Co-Managing Principals of SWAGroup's first regional office, which opened in 1977 in Irvine, California.*

*Why have* **MULTIPLE OFFICES:** *resilience and opportunity*

As the firm grew, we saw a real opportunity to provide more resilience in the structure of the firm through the establishment of multiple offices. First, we wanted our offices not to grow so large that we would have to add a middle management component. We wanted to retain the "design studio" size of fifteen to thirty people per office, with a maximum of fifty. An office could be located in large vibrant markets or near our major clients to serve them better. The first criterion for considering a new office was having the minimum amount of work in that area to carry through the first year, and this usually meant that there were a major client or clients there. Equally important was that there would be at least one or preferably two experienced principals who wanted to go there and become the Managing Principals, to increase their professional or marketing opportunities. As we moved from one office to multiple offices, the management of these offices was defined.

When our first regional offices were set up in the 1970's, I encouraged our two most senior principals, Dick Law and Ed Kagi, to relocate to become the first Managing Principals. Dick went with Don Tompkins to Southern California, and Ed went with Jim Reeves to Houston. Gary Karner and Bill Callaway as senior principals then took over management of the Sausalito office. These early offices had many ups and downs, but they still thrive today, and together the three offices provided a vital "tripod" base for the firm and a pattern for our office management system. Moreover, having all worked together in the Sausalito office, the culture of group practice was carried through to these original three offices. It is particularly satisfying to me that 40 years on I, Ed Kagi, Dick Law and Bill Callaway still are present in these three offices, even if in greatly diminished roles, but not in diminished passion for this extraordinary group.

From these first offices in the 1970's, to the office in Dallas that opened in 1984, to recent offices opened in San Francisco and Los Angeles and Shanghai, the group culture has been kept alive in this way. By always leading with the best, following the example of the first three offices, each has begun with two experienced Managing Principals, appointed by the CEO, who lead the charge for professional excellence in the office. This was demonstrated by SWAGroup's latest office in Shanghai, which opened in 2012 under the direction of two experienced Managing Principals who moved to Shanghai from the two Texas offices. As the offices evolve they can have one Managing Principal depending on size.

**Opposite Page** Arrillaga Plaza is a new addition to the Stanford University Campus.

**Pages 258-259** Gathering along the live oak allee, central mall and fountain at Houston's Hermann Park.

*The Managing Principals as* **PROFESSIONAL LEADERS**

Like the original six, all the Managing Principals of SWA GROUP offices primarily practiced by doing their projects like the other principals in the office, while also providing professional leadership in the office based on their experience. Their business responsibilities were limited so that they can concentrate on professional matters, and did not have to create a layer of middle management between projects and the firm. Since these offices were considered first and foremost as design studios, there was no full profit centering for each office. Rather, projects were individually billed by each principal in every office directly through the firm's accounting department. Like the overall firm, each office was comprised of the sum of its projects.

The Managing Principals were responsible for assisting the principals in their office on their projects by coordinating the allocation of associates and staff to work on these projects in the weekly "hot list" meetings. Working with their office principals, they recruited, hired and fired employees in their office—other than principals, that is. As the CEO and President determined the annual overall bonus pool for associates and staff for each office, the managing principals then set the allocation of this pool to each individual in their office. In addition, they worked with their counterparts in the other offices to bring people to their office or send them out as required. The moving of people was a way to bring the firm together and was supported by the overall firm so the labor budgets were adjusted and costs for travel were borne by the firm, not by the office. People were encouraged to make a move to another office when the need occurs, as it was another way of bringing the firm together.

*Managing Principals run an office and form the* **EXECUTIVE COMMITTEE**
*for firm wide policy*

The Managing Principals also worked with the CEO to make sure that office space and equipment were suitable, working with the business Principals of the firm to help set aside some of the operating and overhead budgets of the offices. SWA GROUP management systems were designed to give the Managing Principals basic information on their office budget and performance that is easy to use and to access. This information came in the form of a compilation of all the projects in the office and concise monthly metrics that enabled them to quickly see how efficiently the key labor component has been utilized, how their total billings met their potentials, and where any problems are occurring in their office. It was designed so they can effectively take action without spending a lot of time gathering this critical data. The experience of the Managing Principals and this concise management data enabled them to operate primarily as professionals and still manage their office with time and freedom to run their own projects and continue a vibrant professional practice.

To coordinate the multiple offices, the Managing Principals established a monthly meeting, which rotated from office to office, in which at least one Managing Principal from each office would meet with the CEO and/or the President as well as the controller and business principal to discuss monthly metrics that show the productivity of the people in each office and the firm, and to deal with any issues that are necessary for running their office. As the Managing Principal group evolved and the firm grew, they became an official Executive Committee, which grew in responsibility and was critical in helping to run the overall firm as well as the individual offices. They would discuss and set up items for firm wide policies, assisting the CEO in setting the agenda for the semi annual Principal Meetings, and implementing firm wide policies approved at those meetings.

## Running the Firm, A Tribute to the Firm Leadership

*"Whatever authority I may have is solely in knowing how little I know." Socrates*

**A TEAM AT THE TOP:** *President and CEO*

When we set up SWAGROUP, firmwide management was also to be lean and efficient, particularly since I wanted to spend eighty percent of my time on professional projects. We would meet semi-annually with the Principal Group to set overall policy, and then with the Board of Directors to review fiduciary matters and provide management advice. We were fortunate to have Mike Gilbert; John Taylor, the attorney who set up Sasaki, Walker Associates; and Paul Shepherd, who was a major development client; as outside Board members. Their insight provided a critical but always helpful look at our suggested policies in those early days. Later on we added Sol Rabin, my Harvard classmate and very successful real estate economist and developer to the Board in 1990 and he in turn served us well for 23 years.

Mike Gilbert, Wendy Simon, the Controller and I met weekly or as needed as a Financial Committee to resolve cash flow, personnel or overhead issues. Our philosophy was that good management means quickly dealing with a crisis and issues as they become evident. Wendy was great at watching the numbers and seeing potential problems before they became crises, and Mike had a deft hand with the bank and kept our line alive and provided overall business advice. I meanwhile kept my eye on the workloads and promotions, and kept the professional energy high. When I traveled, we kept in touch through telephone and later email, and we communicated quickly and efficiently.

As the firm and Principal Group grew larger, and the firm opened more offices in the booming 1980's, it was difficult for me to get around to all eight offices. As such, in 1987 I named Bill Callaway as President and took the role

**Opposite Page Left** Walking along the central reflecting pool in the "heart" of Hermann Park in Houston. **Right** The reconstruction of the central mall and reflecting pool at Houston's flagship Hermann Park.

Bottom The Victoria Gardens town center welcomes all ages.

Opposite Page Above The interior walk at Victoria Gardens town center in Rancho Cucamonga, California. Bottom Left Taking a break from shopping at Victoria Gardens town center in Rancho Cucamonga, California. Bottom Right The main street of the 30 square block Victoria gardens town center in Rancho Cucamonga. California.

of CEO, although I was not keen about that title in our culture. Still, I liked it better than calling Bill a Vice President, as we were to share responsibilities.

*New Leadership: Smooth* **TRANSITIONS** *and new initiatives*

When I retired as CEO in 1996, Bill Callaway, who was President, could take over as CEO and I would remain Chairman. Once he took the reins, Bill did a remarkable job of "upping the ante" for our designers, as he called it, and he oversaw a period of growth and prosperity from 1996 to 2007. He had a very steady hand as CEO and presided over SWA GROUP when it was awarded the 2005 American Society of Landscape Architects Firm Award, the third time this prestigious honor was given in its hundred-year history.

Bill named Kevin Shanley, a Principal in our Houston office as the new President in 2003, and Kevin did a great job introducing forward-thinking ideas for our future. He taught us to always think bigger, for example by pushing the U.S. Army Corps of Engineers into the 21st Century by urging them to move away from planning for hundred-year floods that happen much more frequently as global warming takes effect, instead planning and building Houston's Bayous with a five-hundred year perspective that included not only flood control but community planning and water conservation as well. Also, Kevin spearheaded a large China initiative in the late 90's, which brought us significantly into the huge China market.

Kevin Shanley took over as CEO in 2008, and Bill became Chairman in order to go back to do the design work he loved on a part-time basis with the firm. Kevin, working closely first with Bill and later with John Wong, who became the new Chairman in 2010, faced the very difficult 2008-2012 "great recession" extremely well. Much of that success could be attributed to Kevin and Bill's campaign to create a substantial role for SWA Group in building the new China, and John's leadership in his collaborations with some of the world's best architects on globally significant projects like the world's tallest building in Dubai, the Burj Khalifa.

But above all else, SWA GROUP did so well in the face of this catastrophe in the world real estate markets because of the tireless, impressive work of the entire Principal Group, Associates and staff on major projects in China. A brilliant prospect rotation system distributed the China work to all the offices and continues as Kevin, with the business assistance of Scott Cooper, established a SWA GROUP office in Shanghai in 2012, solidifying our role in that fast growing country. Another mainstay to facing this recession was the extraordinary efforts and leadership of Kinder Baumgardner and the Houston office in the Middle East, and other principals pursuing new work in other countries as well as in back in the U.S.

Gerdo Aquino was then named by Kevin as our new President in 2009. Gerdo is not only our youngest leader but has also pioneered work in landscape infrastructure and landscape urbanism in both academic and practice spheres. With these dual roles, he plays a strong leadership role in both our professional and training pursuits. He is part of a generation of Americans who understand that, in a world that is flattened by technology and opportunity, we compete by the strength of our ideas and ideals. For these reasons and many more, as he takes over in 2014 as CEO, Gerdo is very much a representation of our future.

Scott Cooper, as he became Chief Financial Officer (CFO) and then Chief Operating Officer (COO) provided strong support for Bill when he was CEO, and continued the strong business base in Sausalito with Controller Margaret Leonard and the accounting staff when Kevin became CEO. This base of the Finance Committee, including the CEO, President, CFO and Controller, and the stronger function of the Executive Committee worked well with Kevin operating as CEO from the Houston office and Gerdo as President from the Los Angeles office. I believe this evolution of multi office firm leadership will continue to work well as Gerdo takes over as CEO in 2014 and Kinder Baumgardner takes over as President from Houston.

## On Employee Ownership and Employee Benefit Programs: A Tribute to All Our People

*"When I work with the* SWA *Group people, I always expected and was not surprised when the first person and even the second were exceptional due to the reputation of this fine group of Landscape Architects, but what amazed me is that this exceptional quality was to be found in the third and fourth persons working with us. In my experience this is not just impressive but constituted greatness!" Edward Killingsworth, Architect*

*How we were able to make SWA Group* **EMPLOYEE OWNED:** *The ESOP*

When we were considering setting up a new structure for the firm, as Pete bought out Hideo and we became the SWAGroup, our overriding concern was that we be able to attract and retain the best employees in every aspect of our work. The idea of an employee owned company was not new, but when San Francisco attorney Louis Kelso wrote a book in the 1970's, *The Capitalistic Manifesto*—obviously in contrast to Karl Marx—it solved a critical concern of how employees could earn or gain ownership in a capitalistic system. Kelso used the modern corporate formats and tax-deferred programs familiar to the American system to allow employers to make contributions to an eligible government-approved trust for each employee, which would be made up largely of company stock. In this way, each year the employee would receive stock ownership, without having to come up with funds to purchase company stock. Kelso's ideas were picked up and made by the government into a regulated tax-deferred retirement program called the Employee Stock Ownership Program (ESOP).

Always interested in innovation, whether it was design or business strategies, we were one of the first companies in the country to take up Kelso's ESOP structure. This seemed to us to solve the critical problem of designers who, like many other professionals, did not have the means to buy out owners. And with firm after firm closing or failing when the original owners died or retired, this was important for carrying on our legacy. We were planning a group practice and we wanted everyone to become owners over time. We also needed to have a built-in process of generational succession to keep the good work of the firm going. We knew ownership would be an incentive to do the best work possible, and would also maintain the firm's reputation and keep the work coming in the door. Also, we were somewhat prescient in understanding the need of our people to be able to build an estate for their eventual retirement.

The ESOP worked such that the employer contribution was made out of company profits and would be tax-deductible to the company. The contribution to the employee's trust account meanwhile was tax-deferred in that it was not considered as income at the time of the contribution. The cash or company stock that was contributed each year could increase in value through investment of the cash or by increased valuation of the company by outside specialists, since SWA GROUP stock was to remain private and was not intended to be traded on a public exchange. Therefore, there would be no taxable consequences to the employee as long as their account stayed in the ESOP trust, usually until retirement or separation from the company. Upon retirement or separation, the employee's stock would become eligible to be bought back by the ESOP trust and paid out with taxable consequences or rolled over into a personal Individual Retirement Account. (IRA).

To get the ESOP rolling and assure liquidity for the required buyouts, we originally set a mandatory contribution annually to the ESOP of ten percent of each employee's total compensation, including salary and bonus. The result was that the employees gained ownership of the company over time by increased employer contributions and a vesting schedule that gave them increased ownership of their account until they reached 100%. Also, since the accounts were held in trust for the employees, they did not vote their stock individually but almost all voting was done by the ESOP Committee, which was appointed by the company's Board of Directors. This allowed normal management and decision making to be made for the company by the Principals, CEO, and corporate officers along with the Board of Directors. In its normal responsibility to the company stockholders, the Board selects the company CEO and officers from recommendations of the Principal Group and sets the annual contribution to the employees upon recommendation by the CEO.

The ESOP Committee's primary responsibility is to assure the fair and equitable treatment of the owner employees in accord with the rules of this federally-approved retirement program. First representing a majority ownership and gradually becoming a 100% owner by buying outside stock over a number of years, the ESOP Committee holds the employee stock accounts

in trust for the employees according to the law. The Committee sets the payouts for all employees on retirement or separation, and monitors the liquidity of the trust to assure the payments are met. They vote the stock to select the Board or in major corporate changes, and with the Board and ESOP Committee being composed of an internal majority and external minority, there is not only a strong connection between the required corporate boards and the Principal Group, but also an outside view that is well represented. In recent years SWA GROUP became a S Corp entity allowing for more flexibility as an 100% ESOP company.

*Adding to ownership the wisdom of* **DIVERSE RETIREMENT SAVINGS** *and* **BENEFITS**

The ESOP grew in popularity with our employees, and several years later we then formed a self-directed profit trust involving no company stock in order to diversify their personal estates. After that.we added the new federal tax-deferred 401k program with a matching contribution by the company. Together these three tax deferred programs allowed us to make the full tax-deferred contribution allowed by law of twenty-five percent of salary plus bonus.

This twenty-five percent contribution compares very favorably with the industry-wide standard of only five percent. SWA GROUP has been operating these programs for thirty-seven years, and have been able to pay out millions of dollars to our employees when they retire or leave employment. As a true sign of the success of these programs, most of our employees over sixty-five have not had to continue working unless they choose to do so—though many do choose to do so since they love the work! The programs have been key to attracting and retaining the highest quality professionals.

In addition to these estate-building programs, SWA GROUP has had continuous health care insurance covering 100% of all full time employees' premiums, as well as an optional dependent and child care program paid 50% by the employee on a tax-deductible basis and 50% by SWA GROUP, still another remarkably generous benefit. There is also a limited dental preventative care program. Another benefit are subsidized Commuter Checks for local public transit, especially popular with young people.

## Professional Development; A Tribute to SWA Group Young People

The ESOP and generous benefit programs are one way of attracting and keeping the best people in the profession. By themselves they would not work if the firm did not place doing excellent work and globally significant projects as our top priority. Moreover, in all likelihood a young person is going to weigh satisfaction with their work and working environment as a higher priority than retirement benefits when they are choosing careers. It was made that you can have it both ways: you can do great work and you also can own part of a legacy of fifty-five years of design and environmental excellence. Also important has been the mentoring, training and continuing education of the young professionals.

Because of these commitments, the firm have been able to attract the best young landscape architects in the world. Less than five percent of the many applicants are hired to become part of the team. The SWA GROUP current

**Opposite Page Above** An abandoned rail bed becomes the popular 4.5 mile Katy Trail through the core of Dallas. **Bottom Left** A rest stop on the pedestrian and bicycle Katy Trail through the core of Dallas. **Bottom Right** The popular Katy Trail connects to many of the city parks through the core of Dallas.

landscape design staff and associates number over one hundred fifty and come from the best schools all over the world, from the U.S., China, Korea, Taiwan, Japan, Russia, Iran and the European Union. The support staff and Associates are top notch too, whether in the front office, accounting, information technology or photography.

*The SWA Group* SUMMER INTERN PROGRAM

One significant education and recruitment effort was begun in 1972 as the Summer Intern Program. Noting that the schools were graduating landscape architects without a real knowledge of what the expanded profession involved, particularly on drawing and design skills, Pete began a summer program that is still going strong forty years later. The program is well-known in the landscape schools around the world, and each year SWA GROUP receives up to one-hundred and fifty applications from graduate students and professional bachelor degree students from many countries. While many of these applications show great skill and creativity, only six to ten students each year are selected from the portfolios of their work they submit.

For six weeks, the Summer Internship Program is hosted at one of the offices. It is an educational program that combines real world and academic planning and design projects run by several principals. Juries of principals, associates, staff and people brought in who might be involved in the actual problem serve on critiques during the program, similar to how real projects are critiqued in the office. After the six weeks of hard work on the projects, as well as lectures, field trips and a goodbye party, the students are sent to work in one of SWA GROUP offices for the remainder of the summer—they are of course paid for these efforts.

The success of the program is best shown by the fact that SWA GROUP's current CEO and Chairman were both interns in the program and were recruited quickly when their great skills were first observed. They have clearly proven the potential that was seen in them! More of these long-term relationships have been established with the Summer Interns, and they have created a website where they can stay in touch with the firm and their classmates. Many of them have gone on to work productively in the firm, and in many other fine landscape offices as well. One unexpected but positive side effect of the program is that it gets real interest and attention from the host office employees, whether professional and support staff. They offer places for the interns to stay, bikes for transport or rides to the office. When it was realized they envied the interns for getting all this exciting attention from the principals, the juries and review sessions were opened to all office people and the summer has become a design seminar and great fun for all.

*Support for gaining* ADVANCED DEGREES

Many of the professional staff have advanced degrees in landscape architecture, architecture, planning, urban design, horticulture, environmental planning or ecology. Another popular program has been encouraging our best people to get a graduate degree if they do not already have one, since that advanced training is important to their future career and is helpful in the practice. SWA GROUP assists them in applying to the Harvard Design School or others and provides them with a stipend to help them accomplish an advanced degree. When they return, they are energized and contribute greatly to the practice and their own professional development. A good example of the success of this program is Sean O'Malley who after returning from graduate school saw his capabilities in the firm soar to leading major projects and taking over as Managing Principal of the Laguna Beach office.

*Annual* **FELLOWSHIP COMPETITIONS** *for individual research projects*

Most recently, SWA Group began an incredible program called the Patrick Curran Fellowships, named after one of its most promising Associates who died at a very young age after a severe illness. He was very interested in breaking new ground in the profession, and I had the pleasure of co-authoring a chapter in an Urban Land Institute book on "Sustainable Land Planning" with him. Any staff member or Associate can apply each year for the several Fellowships to do research on any credible professional topic. Even though this is an in-house program, there still are many more applications than can be approved. There is a real sense of excitement for the time allocation and expense reimbursement that each successful applicant gets, not to mention that they get prime airtime with the Principal Group when they present the finished study during the Principal meeting. Recently, the best fellowship projects have also been presented in professional symposiums such as the ASLA Annual Conference. There has been an incredible and creative series of fellowships, including an Urban Agriculture paper published subsequently in professional journals and a 1000-mile bicycle trip from Beijing to our new office in Shanghai by a young woman professional who was tracked by both internet and print magazines.

Ed Killingsworth, a great California architect, put a fine perspective on the people in the firm. When we worked together on many projects he said the first person he met was always exceptional. He was not too surprised given the reputation of our firm when the second person working on the project was also exceptional. But what amazed him was that the third and fourth people were also impressive! That kind of depth to a design firm was, in his experience, not just impressive but was greatness. Ed is right: the third and fourth generations are what make a great firm, for you know it is only going to get better!

## It Doesn't Happen Without Them: A Tribute to SWA Group Families and Clients

*Recognizing the families as a* **VITAL PART** *of the Group Practice*

By the mid 1970's we had moved beyond our early struggles in getting SWA GROUP started and were beginning to see some growth and good results. All the Principals were working very hard with long hours to create the kind of firm we wanted. At a Christmas party for Sausalito office (then the only office), I detected some hostility and unhappiness from the spouses even though it was a good party. I asked my wife Janne to see if she could find out what was going on and Mike Gilbert, who had helped several Principals and their families with some financial and mid life issues, also talked to several of the spouses. Wendy also got some strange questions from spouses about the salary checks that were brought home and given to them without much explanation.

We were all in our thirties and children were coming or had arrived, and these young women (we did have a few male spouses and partners) were struggling to keep their families going. They had married landscape architects, dedicated professionals who traveled frequently and worked late hours, sometimes on weekends. They felt they were being singled out for these disruptions to their family life and mistreated by the firm. It did not help that our Principals were not necessarily good communicators at home!

It became apparent that we needed to do something to avoid this hostility to the firm and lack of information that could damage families and marriages and defeat our goal of a long-term group practice with shared ownership through the ESOP. Many of the spouses did not know about their family's growing ESOP account, and the estate building that was going on through principal ownership of our offices. They only saw the short-term negatives of delayed salary when our cash flow was irregular or bonuses were given back for investment in the office buildings. We were very sensitive to their plight and needed a way to directly communicate with the families. We discussed and got approval from the Principal Group to include spouses at one of the semi-annual meetings.

*Regular* **FAMILY MEETINGS** *bind the group together*

These family meetings became a regular event, held alternately at resorts or interesting major cities. The first few involved seminars and completely open question-and-answer periods specifically for the spouses. Mike, Wendy and I answered every question and you could see that the information on the ESOP and our profit-sharing programs, and on our investment program for creating principals' personal estates, came as a surprise to this audience. The company was actually doing something important for their family!

Janne led some spouse functions, and one of the most significant benefits to the spouses was the chance to talk to each other about their fears and misgivings. It was a revelation for them to find out their spouse was not singled out, as every principal was equally overworked and had the same retentions and bonus deductions for investment. We had opened a direct line of communication and made it clear that any questions they had would be answered at these meetings or anytime, and that their spouse and family were owners of the company.

But the most telling moments came when they saw what their spouses and the firm were doing, and why. We put together at each spouse meeting a special slide presentation of all the significant work of that year. Each Principal explained their work when it came on the screen. The work was beautiful and engrossing. Many of them saw for the first time what all the time and effort their spouse put in was about, as they heard each Principal describe their work with intense feeling and dedication. They began to understand it was the Principals who had control of their projects—and the extra effort the Principals decided to put in helped make a project outstanding. They saw how the group practice challenged each Principal to do their best and it was the quality of the work that meant the most to them.. It took some time, but the spouses began to see that it was that quality that would build a good reputation for each Principal and the firm. This reputation would help keep their spouse gainfully employed and would provide security for their family.
The family meetings allowed the principals' spouses to participate each year

in the professional as well as business aspects of their spouse's career. They did not feel as powerless as they had, and they began to feel a part of the group. In the ensuing meetings we encouraged principals to bring their children along, and it began to feel like a family reunion in later years as the children sat on the floor up front watching slides and later videos of their proud parents' work. A whole generation of SWA GROUP principals' children grew up together in these joyous events!

### *Recognizing Clients as* **COLLABORATORS**

A professional consulting practice does not exist without clients. They provide the projects that make up the practice. They are in one way or another involved in land use, and the physical building of places, cities and communities. SWA GROUP provides an essential ingredient in making that possible. They are architects, real estate developers, public agencies, corporations, non-profits, educational or cultural institutions, or interested landowners. Each client has its own motivation for engaging services, and it is necessary to understand those diversities. The Principals seek out clients who share their desire for excellence in both the process and realization of the final product of the services.

SWA GROUP is fiercely loyal to their clients, and for fifty-five years have built a practice that encourages working together on multiple projects where they and their clients get to know each other well and learn to work together more efficiently. Some of the clients have been passed from one generation of Principals to the next, with both organizations working on tens or even hundreds of projects together. The Principals focus from time to time on one client, but never exclusively, as there is usually more than one Principal working with most of the clients. Even so, they highly value any client even if there is only one project with them. The quality of the project is always the highest priority.

These clients are the very best in the world at what they do. For that reason, SWA GROUP has won over seven hundred awards with them, never forgetting that the great projects and the many awards are in large part due to the vision and resolve of the clients. In over fifty years of professional practice, I have always understood that as professionals we cannot achieve our goals unless our clients' goals align with ours—and we are our clients' true partners in accomplishing these goals. I particularly valued the close associations we formed with some of the world's best architects as our clients or as our collaborators. SWA GROUP has been extraordinarily fortunate in finding and continuing to find these wonderful people and organizations.

I realized from my day-to-day practice and my role in running the firm that the work we were doing was making a significant difference in the quality of people's lives around the world. But our profession's and firm's contribution, unlike that by architects and engineers, was not well understood by the public, or even to some extent by those involved in planning and developing cities and communities. I began early on to get involved with making landscape architecture and our firm's key role more visible to those involved in creating places for people, and to the general public, which was gradually awakening to the need for better design of cities and communities.

Much of this was done through projects and firm outreach activities to professional and educational institutions, but I also include below my involvements with key national and international organizations to increase the visibility of our firm and profession to the public. These beginnings have been substantially supported and enhanced by many SWA GROUP principals and in addition include writing books and articles, teaching, speaking at conferences and supporting the remarkable SWA GROUP website.

## The Urban land Institute (1976 to present)

In 1976, Peter Walker and I joined the Urban Land Institute, a non-profit educational organization dedicated to improving land use and real estate development. We had noticed that some of our best developer clients were members, and they were the ones who had the longer-term view and dedication to the quality of their work that was by no means universal in real estate development. It soon proved that the organization, with its rigorous publications, meetings and education programs, attracted a cross section of the best, most professional developers, financial institutions, educators, public officials and professional service providers to the industry. It enabled us as land planners and landscape architects to become a highly visible group within the service providers, and helped connect us to the best developers, architects, engineers and real estate economists, marketing advisors, and legal firms around the country.

Primarily covering North America in the middle twentieth century, ULI has become a global force for good development around the world in the twenty-first century. I made a significant time commitment to ULI, participating in the semi-annual national meetings, where I made presentations and appeared on panel discussions. I became a full member and served on several of the highly interactive and instructive product councils, such as the Recreational Development Council as a vice chair, Sustainable Development Council as a founder and vice chair, and the Community Development and International Councils. I participated in a number of weeklong Panel Advisory Service panels around the country as well, and chaired a number of Transit Oriented Development panels for the San Francisco District Council. I also wrote many articles for Urban Land, the ULI's bi-monthly magazine, and authored a book and coauthored a chapter on Sustainable Land Planning in the first "green" ULI publication.

All in all, the exposure for SWA GROUP to the ULI has resulted in many new clients, good friends and projects, not to mention a much better understanding of the whole development process for our firm. We now have four full members and solid support from the firm to continue our involvement

Opposite Page Bottom Left An article in Urban Land Magazine about my experience in planning for major developer in large portions of the City of Boca Raton, Florida. Bottom Right The Urban Land Institute Panel Advisory Service study that I participated in for improving this historic deteriorated section of the City of Chicago.

Above An article in the Urban Land Magazine about sustainable site and land planning that I authored with Patrick Curran.

Material appears
in English and Japanese

# PROCESS
# :Architecture

## 103

第103号　1992年5月1日発行
毎月1日1回発行
昭和59年11月15日
第3種郵便物認可

Landscape Design and Planning at
## The SWA Group

*SWAグループ：ランドスケープとプランニング*

in both the professional development and client relationship aspects at the Institute. Elizabeth Shreeve has also taken on a leadership role in the ULI Sustainable Development and District Councils, as has Sean O'Malley in the Southern California District Council.

## Process Magazine (1992)

In 1991, while working in Japan, I was introduced to Murotani Bunji, publisher of Process Architecture, a series of monographs on design firms around the world. He had heard we were working in Japan on a number of projects and asked if we would be interested in his publishing such a monograph on SWA GROUP. I had seen previous editions of his publications and knew they were comprehensive and of a high quality.

We were just entering the Japanese market and his publications were always in English and Japanese, so I thought it would help us in reaching out to the robust activity that then characterized Japan. Also we had never had a third party publication about SWA GROUP, so it would serve to raise the awareness of our approach and work to a broad audience, since the publication was widely distributed around the world.

Bunji-san asked me to take on the role of editor-in-charge, which meant we would supply the text and photographic content. He would then have his people produce and print the monograph in Japan. We decided to organize the monograph with a series of "articles," including an introduction by me, a retrospective about the history of SWA GROUP by Melanie Simo, a conversation of several of us with Alan Temko, architectural critic of the San Francisco Chronicle, and biographies of our Principals.

The bulk of the book was comprised of illustrated major works, divided into the categories of Planning, Communities, and Places, followed by a section on Current Works, Competitions and Professional Programs. It was a very successful snapshot of the firm, and when published in 1992 as Process Architecture 103: Landscape Design and Planning at the SWA GROUP, proved to be a popular publication for our clients and design professionals around the world. We had finally begun to spread the word about our work and about our practice of landscape architecture to a much larger audience than ever before.

## The Cultural Landscape Foundation (2002 to 2012)

In 2002 I met Charles Birnbaum at a California Preservation Conference in Sonoma County. Charles was Coordinator of the Historic Landscape Initiative and Cultural Landscapes for the National Park Service, and had recently begun a small foundation on his own, The Cultural Landscape Foundation (TCLF). He was serving as executive director during his personal time in an attempt to gain more public awareness of designed landscapes and their value to our society. I was somewhat interested in historic landscapes, but it was his focus on the work of landscape architects that seemed vitally important to me, particularly as I saw the profession growing to incorporate more important roles in building and conserving our urban and natural environments.

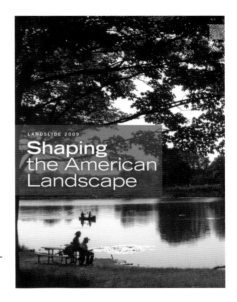

**Opposite Page** Process Magazine Number 103 about the SWA Group was the first third party publication on the firm and aided our foreign work as it was published in both Japanese and English.

**Above** This publication identifies culturally significant landscapes at risk for alteration or destruction in 2009 through the Foundation's "Landslide" program.

Charles asked me if I could join his Board and help him and them with his goal of establishing the foundation as a viable institution so he could leave the Park Service and take a full time role in pursuing its mission. I agreed and felt I could use my experience in shaping SWA GROUP as an institution to assist him and the great people on the Board he had developed for TCLF. This would also align our firm in support of the important messages the TCLF, as an educational non-profit organization, could deliver on the behalf of the profession.

The use of the term "cultural landscapes" was in some ways confusing, since it was not readily understood. As trained landscape architects, we tended to think of landscapes as natural or manmade; urban, suburban or rural; and historic or contemporary. But most people did not make those fine distinctions, making many landscapes—and the effort put into designing and building them—invisible to them. It was much easier for people to understand the work of architects or engineers, as they were finite structures made of mostly artificial materials.

To bridge this gap, the Foundation was using a Park Service designation to get people to think anew about the landscape legacy they see all around them. Landscapes are really a much more subtle mix of natural, modified natural, and designed elements. Many of the designed elements are made of both organic and artificial materials. Landscapes are less "objects" and more surrounds and complete environments. "Cultural landscapes" is a new term meant to help people understand that many of the places they treasured, such as distinct districts of cities or suburban communities, parkways and boulevards, riverways, parks, private estates or gardens, college campuses, farmlands, even industrial areas or scenic highways, were the work of landscape architects. These were no accident, rather they were manmade and expressed their time, culture and identity: they were designed as integral parts of day-to-day culture.

With hard work by the board and Charles, we were able to structure the Foundation's finances and organization to achieve Charles' goals in a few years, and he left the Park Service and took full time charge of TCLF as President, gradually building staff and Board resources. The Foundation has developed several important programs, which include Landslide, an annual list of endangered landscapes, as well as resources that aid local groups in protecting important landscape resources, whether they are parks, trees, monuments or plazas. The TCLF also works closely with magazines such as Garden Design and provides travelling exhibitions about these threatened resources.

In addition to its advocacy efforts, the Foundation publishes a book, web video, and oral history series about historically important landscape architects and designers called Pioneers of American Landscape Design. They honor stewardship of landscape resources by Mayors, private conservation organizations or private estates, and they provide "Cultural Landscapes as Classrooms" guides for teachers in public and private schools. In coordination with the American Society of Landscape Architects and other institutions, they provide conferences, lectures and seminars on related topics. Charles has become an international spokesman for the profession and cultural landscapes, and is a columnist for the Huffington Post and also writes articles in the New York Times and other national media.

Recently the Foundation created "What's Out There" a comprehensive database on their much-visited website featuring the country's most important designed landscapes, historic landscapes, and landmark landscapes, with

**Opposite Page Above** This 2008 publication celebrates designed landscapes that illustrate the Modernism movement in architecture and landscape architecture. **Middle** This publication explains the Foundation's tools to promote education about and stewardship of culturally significant landscapes. **Bottom** This publication by the Cultural Landscape Foundation provides information to the public about the significance of cultural landscapes.

276

texts by scholars, multiple photographs and drop-down menus for easy reference. In connection with this rapidly expanding database, there has been a series of regional and extremely well attended "What's Out There" meetings and tours of significant landscapes in major metropolitan areas. In 2012, the Foundation's "What's Out There" program won the Communications Award from the American Society of Landscape Architects.

Having helped launch the Foundation as a sustainable institution, I retired from active Board duty in 2012, turning my post over to Rene Bihan, Principal at SWA GROUP. Rene has received the full support of SWA GROUP in keeping this important educational venture going, and has added his energy and talents to the Foundation's continuing work.

### Establishing the SWA Group Archive at the Harvard Graduate School of Design (2005 on)

In 2005, Bill Callaway as CEO of the SWA GROUP met with Peter Walker of Peter Walker Partners about finding an appropriate place to archive the professional materials produced by both firms in one venue. Since we had overlapping project histories, it would benefit both firms to be in one place. Bill asked me if I would take on finding the best place to archive our materials. I agreed with Bill and Pete that this could provide researchers, students and writers with ready access to our project and firm materials. While we have historically not produced a large body of academic or media writing, nor publication or research on landscape architecture, we wanted to foster these pursuits as the profession gained more stature in society. We hoped joining with other professionals at a highly capable facility might "up the ante" for our discourse on the profession.

With a representative of Walker's office, I reviewed about six archives that housed Landscape Architectural materials. I visited Archives at the University of Pennsylvania, The University of California at Berkeley and the Harvard Special Collections Library. In the end, Harvard was the obvious choice, due not only to the important role they played in our history and the fact that SWA employees have long been both students and teachers at the school, but also for their unique technical abilities and direct connection to the overall University Library System that would assure long-term capabilities.

We made our first gift in 2008, which consisted of SWA GROUP materials from 1957 to 1990, including drawings and microfilm records of drawings, work files, slides and other photographs. In 2012 I made a second gift consisting of my personal project files, reports and drawings, firm brochures and promotional materials, and semi annual newsletters of current projects ranging from the 1960's to 2011. SWA GROUP and Peter Walker Partners both intend to continue archiving materials at the Special Collections Library and to thus support research and education in what is becoming a vital profession in the 21st Century.

### Authoring *Master Planned Communities, Lessons from the Developments of Chuck Cobb,* Urban Land Institute (2011)

Chuck Cobb, a great friend and developer, has been responsible for many outstanding Master Planned Communities at Kaiser Aetna, Arvida, Disney Development and now Cobb Partners. Chuck and I had a discussion in late 2009 about our work together on these communities spanning over forty years. Were these works, as some academics said, early pioneers of Smart Growth? What kind of places had they become?

Since there was no organized record of our work, we came up with the idea for a book that would revisit twenty of these built-out Cobb developments, the majority of which were planned and designed by myself and SWA GROUP. We set off to profile these projects and to see how successful they were in becoming smart and sustainable communities.

I spent the next year-and-a-half organizing the book, doing research, visiting the communities, talking to people there, and drawing upon interviews not only with Chuck but also with six of his key people in the "Cobb Web," his unique organizational structure for developing of the communities. Working closely with my longtime colleague at SWA and renowned landscape photographer Tom Fox, we planned out two hundred sensational new photographs to show these vibrant communities directly to the reader.

We found that each of these communities, built from the late 1960's onward, still managed to accomplish most if not all of the "Ten Principles" adopted by the Smart Growth Network twenty to thirty years later in 1996. We saw how our use of strategic public/private planning in the Master Planned Communities served as prototypes for the future development of cities, with private sector participation helping to provide infrastructure and add amenities.

Protecting and enhancing the local history and heritage of places like Coral Gables and Boca Raton in Florida not only greatly increased the appeal of these communities, but also created more profitable development opportunities. The communities acted as robust economic engines, creating almost a quarter-million permanent jobs that continue to support their economic sustainability today. Large employment and commercial sectors made the Master Planned Communities more attractive for homebuyers, and in turn the range of residential products made the communities more attractive to employers. It was a win/win situation.

We provided community-wide landscape concepts and complete landscape development of the public streets, spaces, neighborhoods and gathering places to create a unified sense of place early on and set the tone of the communities. Adding to this sense of place, the clubs, resort activities and community associations that were provided began a vibrant social activity that continues on today. Quality educational and health facilities in all the communities placed an emphasis on physical activities such as hiking, walking or bicycling to increase fitness and wellness and the overall desirability of living in these communities. All the communities also had major open spaces and natural environments that were protected and sustained for nearly a half century by community associations and enthusiastic residents, in most cases permanently incorporating and even increasing their extent by ordinance or covenant.

**Opposite Page** My book "Master Planned Communities, Lessons from the Developments of Chuck Cobb" published by the Urban Land Institute in 2011.

There were just two areas where our efforts were not fully successful: housing affordability and multimodal transportation. This was mainly due to local and national policies and market preferences that favored lower densities and automobile access, the prevailing opinion at the time the communities were developed. Fortunately, in a number of the cities some of these policies and preferences have moved toward Smart Growth, though others continue on today. With their balanced mix of land uses, jobs, variety of housing types, commercial, educational and recreational facilities, open space and parks all in close proximity—and ample infrastructure and the means to maintain it—the Master Planned Communities are readily adaptable to changes in housing and transportation policy should it come along. Indeed, they have already adapted in many ways.

From what we learned by looking back and doing the book, I would conclude that Master Planned Communities are still the best and most sustainable way to shape and control any new greenfield development—which by most projections will be comprise one half of America's future urban growth— though they can also play a role in larger infill or redevelopment growth. The National Association of Real Estate Editors must have agreed, as in 2012 the book received NAREE's highest honor for a book published in 2011, the Gold Award.

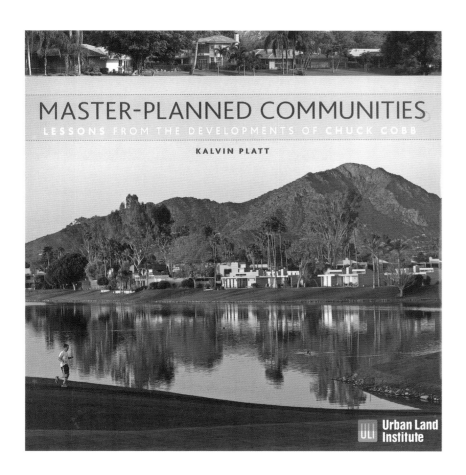

This book traces a personal journey of over 55 years searching for better ways to plan, design and build cities, communities and places. My early experience in cities and my education led me to join an exemplary landscape architectural practice as the best place to do my life's work. My architectural and city planning background fit well into the firm's concept of a seamless transition from planning to design in the building of the landscape structure of cities and places, working in real collaboration with architects and engineers. By establishing close working relationships with the landscape design and field construction principals, I was constantly amazed with their sensitivity and creativity as we translated our plans into inspiring built places for people.

This exposure to such a vital and talented group of landscape architectural professionals helped me understand the potential dynamics and advantages of a group practice for the complex work of building cities, and in teaming to do the work with citizens, clients, architects, engineers, environmental scientists and economists. So as I became the first president of SWA GROUP as it emerged from Sasaki, Walker Associates in 1974, I set out with the original principals to shape the new firm to accentuate these diverse skills in designing the urban landscape of cities and places for people.

Under new leadership the firm has broadened and strengthened these skills significantly coming into the 21st century with the best physical planning and landscape design professionals recruited from 15 countries. Having over 200 people in 7 offices in the U.S. and China, SWA GROUP in 2013 is one of the largest in the landscape architectural field and has an increasing impact on designing the public realm and landscape infrastructure in major cities, sustainably planning suburbs that are true communities, and creating and crafting places that inspire people in existing or new habitations.

In the 21st century, according to the United Nations, the world will experience the greatest growth in people living in cities and urban places ever seen. Currently 50% of the world lives in urban places but by 2050 more than 67% of the people in the world will have to be accommodated in urban places. For perspective, during SWA GROUP's 40 year history from 1974 to 2014 the world grew by an amazing two billion people in urban places, but in the next 40 years that growth will be a larger 2.75 billion people. Even in the U.S. the growth in the next 40 years will be a slightly larger than the past 40 years, 103 million new people in urban places. And in China the next 40 years will see a somewhat less but still huge growth of 340 million, with a recent plan to resettle 250 million people in the next 12 years! India and Africa will also see enormous growth in urban places. All of this is happening with climate change, sea level rise and energy issues compounding the challenge

In this epilogue, I put together my thoughts with those of some powerful observers and visionaries in the field of city design about better ways to plan, design and build cities and places during these challenging times. Not currently active on projects in the firm my comments below come from my long experience and observations of current work by the landscape profession and the seven SWA GROUP offices. This is how I see landscape architecture and SWA GROUP fitting into one of the most critically important enterprises of this century.

**Opposite Page** A perspective sketch of the redevelopment of the Hangzhou Hubin District in Zhejiang, China showing the new lakefront promenade and pedestrian connections extending back into the revitalized district of Hangzhou.

**Above** The promenade replaces a roadway that was relocated in a tunnel, opening the City of Hangzhou to West lake, a World Cultural Site. **Middle** The Hangzhou promenade is a linear park and plazas with multiple uses.

*SWA 50/50: Landscape Architecture can have a* **SOCIAL IMPACT**

First I want to start with a very humble but significant example of why I think landscape architects will continue to have an important role in social sustainability in the 21st century. This follows a long tradition begun by Olmstead when he clearly stated that urban parks and gathering places play an indispensable social and even political role in a democracy. This example is very much of the current times.

2007 was the 50th anniversary of the founding of Sasaki, Walker Associates, the precursor to the SWA GROUP. The principals decided the celebration should be called 50/50 to indicate they were not just commemorating a past but making a statement about a future. They would do this by going beyond a firmwide party to a significant participatory event. After considering many options, they decided that the entire company—all 190 employees in the five offices at that time—would come to San Francisco. There, as a group the employees would build with their own hands a socially significant community landscape project in one day. This would involve an intense several months by all the offices cooperating on the selection of the project, working with the community client, designing the overall plan, working out the details of building it, getting the materials and tools to the site, and showing up to complete the installation in one day.

The project selected was the Bayview Opera House, an 1888 structure that sits in the middle of a poor minority community in the Bayview-Hunters Point section of San Francisco. Rene Bihan, the Managing Principal of the San Francisco office, spearheaded the selection by working with the City Arts Commission and finding that this beautiful old structure had never been used as an opera house! Rather, it had become a community center, but over the years it had been neglected and needed some attention and improvements. We were going to get that attention by doing a landscape installation that would be recognized by the community, the media and the Mayor!

In an amazing process by all the SWA GROUP people in all of the offices, this was planned, designed and coordinated with the community and city in just a few short months. On construction day, everyone showed up at 8 am, arriving on the Third Street Light Rail that had recently been built next to the Opera House. With generous donations of materials and tools by local landscape providers and contractors the installation was successfully completed by 5pm with no casualties and great fun. The community was left with a complete landscape that included trees and shrubs, an information kiosk, and an outdoor theater with seating and artwork. Who would think this many landscape architects could master nail guns as well as they could plant shrubs? The effort paid off in droves for the community. After the work was done, the Mayor showed up and joined in a great feast, which was also attended by many locals and attracted significant media attention. The people expressed a deeply emotional appreciation of the attention this activity brought to this neglected but highly valued part of their community.

Significantly shortly after that work was done, the Opera House was scheduled for a new paint job that brought out its historic merits, and a section of road next to the Opera House was closed for the construction of a new park that connected the Opera House to an adjacent school. The Opera House was given the Best of Bay Area Award by the San Francisco Guardian newspaper and the Beautification Award from San Francisco Beautiful,

Illustrated in this chapter are SWA Group's Global Award of Excellence projects and a portfolio of other recent work that demonstrate design leadership into the 21st Century.

**Opposite Page Above** Walking from internal Hangzhou toward the promenade and West Lake. **Bottom** Light towers lead the way at night from the waterfront to the interior of the Hangzhou Hubin District.

further enhancing its potential to attract more community or even city wide events, something very important to the community. In 2011 it was listed on the National Register of Historic Places.

For me the best part was getting everyone to work together on something that used their skills for primarily a social purpose, thereby following the great tradition set by Frederick Law Olmstead for landscape architects. It showed that this group practice of landscape architects was ready for the challenges of this new century, working with and getting direct feedback from the people in bettering their lives. They could see for themselves the difference that could be made for a community by creatively working together.

*Landscape* **INFRASTRUCTURE** *can solve environmental problems by integrating natural and cultural systems in cities and urban areas*

SWA GROUP President Gerdo Aquino and his Managing Principal partner at the Los Angeles office, Ying Yu Hung, authored an award-winning book in 2010 called Landscape Infrastructure. The book uses a variety of case studies of the design of these critical networks that can integrate natural and cultural systems into multi purpose infrastructure corridors in cities and urban places. The examples show the firm working as the leader or as a part of multidisciplinary teams addressing critical issues ranging from pedestrian and transit movement throughout high density urban places to enhancing water quality and conservation, integrating hydrological patterns and ecologies into city design The importance of their book is that it looks to current work and future proposals and shows how SWA GROUP is using a wide variety of new ideas about landscape infrastructure in highly urban, suburban and rural areas around the world appropriate to the needs of rapid urbanization and mounting environmental challenges..

One of the projects in their book is the Gubei Pedestrian Promenade in western Shanghai, which was coincidentally designed by Aquino and Hung. In the December 2012 Landscape Architecture cover article on the promenade, the author Mary Padua states, "SWA has demonstrated how sustainable infrastructure in crowded Chinese cities might look...a superior kind of urban street that draws upon Shanghai Western as well as Chinese traditions and adds elements of ecological sustainability...an enviable example for designers around the world to follow." This amazing project directly addresses a range of the key issues as China struggles to become an urban nation.

The book and its case studies are one important step in setting out standards for the integration of the design of human settlements within the emerging broader views of landscape in a century where the very survival of the planet is at stake. Rather than the older view of landscape as a way to mitigate the difficulties of building practice, lessen the impacts of invasive infrastructure elements, or to heal fractured public space and natural systems, this newer view sees landscape as a logical starting point and purpose to incorporate natural systems into the planning from the beginning. It thereby allows for better siting and orientation of buildings and the design of multipurpose infrastructure systems, public and private spaces to make them vital, usable and sustainable, inspiring lasting support and care therefore improving the quality of life for the public.

**Above** An ampitheater on the Gubei Promenade holds community wide events for this Shanghai district. **Middle** Retail uses at the Gubei Promenade in Shanghai add vitality and convenience for the residents. **Bottom** The Gubei Promenade offers families outdoor activities to complement their dense apartment living.

**Opposite Page** The Gubei Pedestrian Promenade in Shanghai is flanked by a dense district of 20 story residential towers with commercial, and community uses and parks at ground level.

**A GROUP PRACTICE** *allows for meaningful discourse that can bring better solutions*

The Landscape Infrastructure book contains a perceptive essay by Charles Waldheim, Chair of the Department of Landscape Architecture at Harvard and a prime advocate for Landscape Urbanism which contends that landscape architecture has in fact replaced architecture and urban design as the primary discipline that establishes the framework for contemporary city-making. Waldheim speculates on where he thinks SWA GROUP is heading by saying:

"Aquino and Hung formed a studio of SWA in downtown Los Angeles in October, 2004. Given SWA's historic footprint in California, and the proximity of the Laguna Beach office, one would read the formation of this new studio as motivated by something other than simple market share; the formation of the LA studio has at once reinvigorated SWA's commitment to studio culture and reinforced the autonomy of its principals. It is possible to view the recent work of the LA studio as forming a contemporary alternative to the popular perception of late SWA as a large multinational, corporate landscape architecture and planning firm....Aquino/Hung et al, as well as the supportive senior leadership of SWA, may have intended to use the LA studio as a kind of think tank. One could also imagine that they hoped to speculate on future forms of cultural production to reposition SWA GROUP's work as relevant to design and planning professions increasingly focused on design leadership."

Waldheim correctly understands SWA GROUP's culture of continuing to reinvent themselves and the role of design. I believe Gerdo and Ying Yu are following that culture of discovery by connecting back to academia through teaching at the University of Southern California and Harvard, as has been done by Principals of every generation. This kind of search for better ways to do things involves all the professionals and goes on in different ways in each of SWA GROUP's design studios. This is reinforced by the large number of SWA GROUP professionals that have advanced degrees not only in landscape architecture but in planning, urban design and environmental studies.

For almost the last 30 years a "Projects" publication of all current work in progress has been prepared for each semi-annual Principals Meeting. It is used for discussion there and for reference in each design studio. In this way the principals in each studio bring their latest work into a learning and critical process in all the studios. "IDEASWA" magazine, a publication Gerdo has fostered over last few years, has thoughtful contributions from all the studios attempting to find better ways to think about how to plan, design and build urban landscapes in more sustainable ways. Recently, an initiative to evaluate projects "post occupancy" has begun to add more focus on how people use these places over time, and the SWAP website has had increasing use for sharing information and insights.

A group practice can build high quality projects and foster meaningful discourse at the same time. It is a patient and constant search. It is worth repeating a remarkable quote I used earlier in the book from composer Philip Glass: "When I talk to young composers, I tell them, I know you're all worried about finding your voice. Actually you're going to find your voice. By the time you're thirty you'll find it. But that's not the problem. The problem is getting rid of it. You have to find an engine for change. And that's what collaborative work does. Whatever we do together will make us different".

**Opposite Page Above** Looking down from the building at the entry gardens of the Burj Khalifa tower. **Middle Left** The tower garden with native and drought resistant planting mitigates the harsh climate at the Burj Khalifa in Dubai. **Bottom Left** The Burj Khalifa tower park fountains provide a pleasant nighttime environment for people. **Bottom Right** The world's tallest building, the Burj Khalifa in Dubai is set in a 28 acre park.

**Above** The entry gardens and plazas provide a human scale to the spectacular Burj Khalifa in Dubai.

*Landscape Architecture, Planning and Urban Design now have* **WORLD WIDE** *significance and increasing relevance to economic, social and environmental sustainability*

In 1999, at the cusp of the twenty-first century, World Architectural Review magazine wrote, "SWA GROUP has a particularly strong world wide reputation with respect to high image projects that set a standard for design and environmental excellence." The accuracy of this statement can be found partially in the 700 awards received over the years by professional landscape architectural, architectural, urban planning, development and governmental entities throughout the world. But until recently there were no relevant awards that were given on a worldwide basis.

This changed in 2005, when the Urban Land Institute (ULI), a US-based nonprofit educational institute whose guiding principle is that the achievement of excellence in land use practice should be recognized, created a new category the ULI Global Award of Excellence. The ULI has for over 35 years given their Awards of Excellence to the sponsors of projects in the Americas, Europe, and Asia Pacific, and SWA GROUP and other projects with landscape architects making significant contributions have received a number of these regional awards. This new global award takes the winners in each geographic category and further judges them to designate the best projects in the world in a given year.

This was in recognition that this great American institution has itself become global. The ULI Global Awards carry the significance that the winners not only display great planning, design and building skills but they meet the requirements of economic, social and environmental sustainability and achieve management and operational success in meeting these goals. This is critical for the 21st century where hundreds of millions will be settled in cities and urban places. In doing so the most successful prime mover has been public-private partnerships working within real estate and financial markets and assisted by supportive public policy and infrastructure subsidies. This is critical in making the award winning projects serve as good models for better future growth. It also features the use of planning and landscape design to add value in an economic and social sense as well as in place making and environmental terms. Since the ULI began this global award, there have been other world wide awards developed but I think the comprehensive and broad sustainability aspects of the ULI approach make them particularly relevant to the 21st century.

One of the first three ULI Global Awards of Excellence awarded in 2005 was won by the Hangzhou Hubin Waterfront Redevelopment in China, a project where SWA GROUP led by Principal Scott Slaney provided key Planning and Landscape Services. This was an Area Master Plan and Landscape Design for Hangzhou's large waterfront, which reconnected this important city to the sacred and famous West Lake by removing the roadway that separated the city from the lake and replacing it with a waterfront promenade, linear park and civic gathering place. The plan also connected these enhanced facilities back into the heart of the city. This was a clear statement by the ULI on the importance of the role of coordinated planning and landscape architecture in global city design, economic and social development and building places.

Subsequently, SWA GROUP and its clients have won three more Global Awards for Excellence. One in 2008 was for Beijing Finance Street, a large

**Above** The mall at the Center follows a recreated City Creek and commemorates its historic role in the founding of Salt lake City.

**Opposite Page Above** City Creek Center is the complete redevelopment of 4 large blocks in downtown Salt Lake City into a pedestrian oriented mixed use center. **Bottom Left** A light rail station, pedestrian overpass and parking garages make City Creek Center very accessible to multi modes of transport. **Bottom Right** With its boulders, plantings and fish, the recreated City Creek is an attraction for shoppers, workers and residents of the mixed use center.

mixed use redevelopment area in central Beijing. Working closely with SOM architects, Principals Bill Callaway, Rene Bihan, Hui-Li Lee, Jim Lee and Ye-Luo provided urban design and landscape design and development. The project includes hotel, convention, office, retail and residential areas around an active green city park that is larger in size than Tiananmen Square. A second, in 2010 was for the California Academy of Sciences in San Francisco, where Principals John Loomis, Larry Reed and Bill Callaway led the effort to set this redeveloped institution within the landscape of Golden Gate Park and includes a unique green roof that blends in with the park and is used as a scientific resource with native plant habitats and as an exhibition for educational purposes. The third in 2013 was for West Village, the largest zero net energy community in the U.S. at the University of California, Davis, led by Principals John Wong, Elizabeth Shreeve and Cinda Gilliland. This was an intensive effort of planning and designing a sustainable landscape structure for student and faculty housing, academic and support facilities in a bike centric, energy generating and conserving village.

Also to be considered is that in 2006 SWA GROUP's Luohu Station a multilevel, major transportation hub in Shenzhen, China, and Victoria Gardens, a new town center in California were runners up for the Global Awards. Foundry Square, covered in chapter 7 of this book was a runner up in 2010, and City Creek, a revitalization of downtown Salt Lake City was a runner up in 2013. The fact that SWA GROUP projects have won four Global Awards of Excellence and had four runners up in six of the nine years of the Global Awards of Excellence program's existence clearly supports World Architecture Review's statement on world wide reputation in design and environmental excellence. It convincingly supports the firm's recent characterization of itself as a "World Leader in Landscape Architecture, Planning and Urban Design".

I would add that all these award winning projects represent the evolution of SWA GROUP's seamless design process using physical master planning, urban design and landscape design elements that when taken together are a proven and potent way to resolve the complexities of these 21st century places for people. I have included photographs of these award winning projects as well as some others I find as notable examples of better design of places in cities. Another source is the 2013 Monograph "Landscapes for People, SWA Works" that covers many of these projects in more detail and includes others that demonstrate unique solutions to pressing issues around the globe ranging from a street to an entire city.

*The* **SPACES IN BETWEEN** *–an unique Landscape Architectural contribution to designing the public realm to make better cities, communities and places for people*

Landscape architects are expanding their scope globally in shaping the private and public realms of cities. These are the places and the natural systems that support these habitations where people live a good part of their lives and seek both the solace of nature and the excitement of community. Planning, urban design and landscape development of the public/private realm is the key to that work. It links architecture, infrastructure and natural systems, and when designed and built with sensitivity and intelligence makes the difference between livable great places for people and the appalling habitations

**Opposite Page Above** The California Academy of Sciences in Golden Gate Park is a major attraction for its multiple levels of exhibits. **Middle Left** Set in Golden Gate Park the California Academy of Sciences has a trellis with solar panels, a green roof and other sustainable energy elements. **Bottom Left** The green roof of the California Academy of Sciences in the foreground blends in with Golden Gate Park in San Francisco. **Bottom Right** The native plantings on the green roof of the California Academy of Sciences in San Francisco are used as a popular visitor exhibit and a scientific research laboratory.

**Above** The redevelopment of a major portion of central Beijing into Beijing Finance Street has a major park larger than Tienamen Square as the overall organizing element. **Middle Right** The Beijing Finance Street park is a gathering place for all ages. **Middle Left** The Beijing Finance Street park attracts families with children from its residential towers and throughout central Beijing. **Bottom Left** The major retail street along the park attracts shoppers, workers, residents and tourists.

**Above** The zero net energy West Village at the University of California at Davis uses bicycle ways as the major transportation mode. **Middle Left** University of California, Davis students arrive at the dormitories by walking or biking. **Middle Right** The West Village at the University of California at Davis is the largest zero net energy community in the U.S. and was awarded a 2013 Urban Land Institute Global Award of Excellence. **Bottom Right** The West Village center at University of California, Davis at night with efficient LED lighting.

293

that millions of people suffer amidst the rapid urban growth that characterizes these times.

This landscape architectural approach to designing cities and places includes the classic great parks, riverways, waterfronts and open spaces that have distinguished great urban places in the past, but in the second half of the 20th Century the importance of the treatment of other urban spaces was reemphasized. I looked back first to Hideo Sasaki who in 1956 observed, "In the more densely built up section of the urban environment, the spaces between buildings are often of more significance than the buildings themselves. Heretofore considered negative spaces, they are now seen as positive design elements". This was significantly reinforced in1973, around the time Sasaki Walker Associates was beginning its transformation to the SWA GROUP, when Nathaniel Owings, one of the founders of the great architectural firm Skidmore, Owings and Merrill (SOM) wrote a visionary book, The Spaces in Between.

Owings uses the Weyerhaeuser Headquarters Peter Walker at SWA GROUP designed with Chuck Bassett of his firm as an example of creating "something new under the sun... a skyscraper set on its side with a series of horizontal terraces, each surface converted into a park... facing outward toward a man made lake reflecting color, light and motion for the people working there." He ends by stating:

"Nonarchitecture open spaces will be the objective, and the buildings will simply frame them. We can use the oldest of all forms, yet one which is considered new today: we can reintroduce into our crowded cities the open space—the plaza—where man can dance, celebrate and experience the joy of living in the spaces in between."

Bringing these prescient ideas to current times is a recent take on city building written by Michael Kimmelman, architecture critic of the New York Times in his July, 2013 article "The Plan to Swallow Midtown." It is a critique of the city's plans for reshaping midtown Manhattan by focusing on buildings not what is around them and thereby lacking place making as its prime goal. He summarizes the City's failed effort by stating "But its plan for East Midtown fails to recognize a fundamental paradigm shift. The focus in designing cities has now turned from buildings to the spaces between those buildings-sidewalks, plazas, parks-whose disposition requires planning". His point of view was reinforced when the city withdrew this plan for the midtown district. And I would add that it is exactly this kind of planning that landscape architects and particularly, SWA GROUP have evolved over four decades of practice, and this approach to landscape urbanism is increasingly being noted by visionary public agencies.

**WORKING TOGETHER** *in meeting the challenges of the 21st Century*

Looking back at my journey as an architect, naval civil engineer, city planner and landscape architect, I have gained a deep appreciation of the contributions of all these design professions. I am pleased that during my time at the SWA GROUP, I have seen the return and ascendance of the landscape architectural profession to join architects and engineers in true leadership roles in the physical design of cities and urban places. The unique combinations of natural and cultural systems characteristic of landscape design have made the total process all the more effective and meaningful as our impact upon the earth becomes more challenging. Throughout my long term career I have

**Above** A grid of 500 geothermal wells under Guthrie Green supplies energy for the surrounding district redevelopment and fun for kids.

**Opposite Page Above** Viewing a performance from the Pavilion at Guthrie Green in downtown Tulsa **Bottom** Guthrie Green is designed for daytime and night time use in downtown Tulsa.

seen our best work and the best results for people and the environment come out of true collaboration and mutual respect between all these design disciplines. The great joy I have experienced working within a group of great landscape designers and planners was made even more satisfying by working with some of the best architects, engineers, economic and environmental consultants in the world as we jointly created for our amazing and supportive clients the projects that are displayed throughout this book.

This is why I believe that working with visionary architects, engineers, entrepreneurs, companies, public agencies and others that share these values, landscape architectural firms like the SWA GROUP are actively taking on leadership roles in meeting the global challenges that this new century brings. They are providing the appropriately balanced physical master planning, site planning and landscape designs for building better ways for people to live in dignity, health and joy during the largest surge toward building cities the world has ever seen. At the same time, they are addressing the sustainability of these settlements, the protection or enhancement of the quality of their land, air and water resources and the reduction of their carbon footprints.

Within the landscape architects contribution to this complex process the best ideas, the big ideas in the creating of communities and responsible human places requires a seamless continuum of social, economic and environmentally responsible planning, beautiful and inspired urban and landscape design, resulting in carefully crafted urban landscapes for people. This can only come from a deep understanding of the connections and relationships of people to these urban places and to the natural environment.

For someone who as a young child found out that the tree was there before the city, this has been and continues to be an amazing journey. I hope that my journey will bring some perspective and encouragement to the passionate professionals that direct or participate in the work of SWA GROUP and to all those in the landscape architectural, architectural, city planning, engineering, building, development and stewardship professions who continue into the 21st century designing places for people and the environment.

**Above** An illustration of the central business district, transit center and wetland restoration for the new city of Dongtan, Korea outside Seoul. **Bottom** A sketch of the multi modal transit center that forms a subsidiary hub to Seoul in the new city of Dongtan, Korea.

**Opposite Page Above** The redevelopment of the Buffalo Bayou in central Houston combines flood control and waterborne recreation with a new linear park for downtown. **Bottom Left** The Buffalo Bayou promenade hosts events and varied community use for greater Houston. **Bottom Right** The Buffalo Bayou Promenade has a 1.2 mile segment of a bicycle and pedestrian trail that connects downtown with greater Houston.

# ABOUT KALVIN PLATT

Over three decades, Mr. Platt was the first President, CEO and then Chairman of the SWA GROUP, an international Landscape Architectural design and planning firm that emerged in 1974 from Sasaki, Walker Associates. He was instrumental in shaping this award winning firm into a multi office, employee owned, global group that has earned a reputation as a "World Leader in Landscape Architecture, Planning and Urban Design". Today he continues as a member of the Board of Directors and as a Consulting Principal. His over 55 years of experience as a planner, architect, urban designer and landscape architect begins with early work creating the first Comprehensive Plan for the Metropolitan Miami-Dade County Government in Florida, a design driven Downtown Zoning Plan for San Francisco, to city plans for Santa Ana, California and Downtown Richmond, California.

During his 47 years with the SWA GROUP his experience expanded to the planning, designing and building exemplary cities, communities and places for people and the environment. His work in California includes the 30,000-acre Central Irvine Ranch Plan and the 1700 acre Village of Woodbridge for the Irvine Company, winner of the 1994 ULI Award for Excellence; the 44,000 person, job balanced Mountain House New Town, the 290,000 acre Tejon Ranch Vision Plan that created a mix of planned development with three quarters of the ranch preserved as rural and major open space and conservation areas; urban waterfront plans for the cities of Long Beach and San Diego; the Monterey Downtown Custom House Center; and. planning the 100,000-acre Golden Gate National Recreation area for the National Park Service.

His international planning work ranges from the 100,000 person Alphaville Lagoa Dos Ingleses New Town in Brazil with major employment, education and recreation facilities; planned communities in the Philippines and China; to teaching a three year Landscape Design work/study course in Tokyo and working on the Karuizawa Resort and Tokyo University for Foreign Studies. He wrote the book, "Master Planned Communities, Lessons from the Developments of Chuck Cobb" published by the Urban Land Institute in 2011, which covered more than 30 years working with Cobb and the Arvida Corporation in Florida at the City of Boca Raton, the Sawgrass Resort, the Cocoplum community in Coral Gables, Walt Disney World, the Longboat Key Resort, the Town of Weston and the University of Miami. The book won the Gold Award for best book of 2011 from the National Association of Real Estate Editors.

Kalvin Platt is a Fellow of the American Institute of Architects (FAIA) in Urban Design, and a member of the American Society of Landscape Architects, American Planning Association, Urban Land Institute and former board member of The Cultural Landscape Foundation. He holds a degree in Architecture from the University of Florida and a Masters Degree in City Planning from the Harvard Graduate School of Design where he later taught the Development Studio and Professional Practice course. At the Urban Land Institute he was a founding member of the Sustainable Development Council, Vice Chairman of the Recreation and Community Development Councils and authored articles on 'Sustainable Land Planning', City Greenways' and 'Lessons from Boca Raton'.

**Opposite Page Above** The Ningbo Eco-Corridor transforms a 3.3 km brownfield into a living filter to restore the ecosystem by combining water management and treatment with park uses as it traverses the city of Ningbo in China. **Bottom** An illustration of the Ningbo Eco- Corridor environmental restoration and park uses in Ningbo, China with a wind farm to create renewable energy.

# LIST OF ILLUSTRATIONS

All of the photography in the book except those listed below are owned by the SWA GROUP and taken by the SWA GROUP photographers Tom Fox, lead photographer and Director of Media Services, and Gerry Campbell, Dixie Carillo, Tom Lamb, Lina Schnaas, Jonnu Singleton, Trevor Tallman, Bill Tatham and David Thompson.

The author, Kalvin Platt's photographs are on pages 16, 24, 25, 26, 28 and 30.

PAGE 14 ◆ Up Above Central Park, Michael S.Yamashita, National Geographic Society, 1950's

PAGE 15 ◆ The Big Three, Army Air Forces, U.S. National Archives, 1937

PAGE 20-21 ◆ Frank Lloyd Wright sketch from Frank Lloyd Wright at the University of Florida, a monograph by Ken Treister

PAGE 32, 34 ◆ Preliminary Plan, Metropolitan Dade County Planning Department, Metropolitan Dade County, Florida

PAGES 12, 38, 39, 40 ◆ Downtown Richmond, a Plan for Redevelopment Action, Redevelopment Agency of the City of Richmond, California

PAGE 42 ◆ Santa Ana, California General Plan Program, City of Santa Ana, California

PAGES 45, 46, 48 ◆ San Francisco Downtown Zoning Study, City and County of San Francisco, California

PAGE 66 ◆ Prince Hotels

PAGES 272-273 ◆ Urban Land Institute

PAGE 274 ◆ Process Magazine

PAGES 275, 277 ◆ The Cultural Landscape Foundation

CASE STUDY INDEX

Metropolitan Dade County Plan ◆ PAGE 33
Downtown Richmond Plan ◆ PAGE 37
Santa Ana General Plan ◆ PAGE 41
San Francisco Downtown Zoning ◆ PAGE 44
Future Urban Transportation Systems ◆ PAGE 62
The Kohala Coast Resort ◆ PAGE 65
Oakland City Center ◆ PAGE 68
Central Ranch/Village of Woodbridge ◆ PAGE 71
Villages of Arvida ◆ PAGE 75
Sun Valley/Elkhorn Village ◆ PAGE 84
Monterey Conference Center ◆ PAGE 89
Golden Gate Recreation Area ◆ PAGE 102
Long Beach Shoreline ◆ PAGE 107
San Diego Embarcadero ◆ PAGE 111
Griffith Park Master Plan ◆ PAGE 115
Lakewood Hills ◆ PAGE 118
Lantern Bay ◆ PAGE 121
Alameda Marina Village ◆ PAGE 124

Development Studio Case Studies ◆ PAGE 140
University of Miami Master Plan ◆ PAGE 144
Walt Disney World Resort ◆ PAGE 150
Kezar Corner, Golden Gate Park ◆ PAGE 158
Greenway Communities ◆ PAGE 161
Mountain House New Town ◆ PAGE 165
Marin City USA ◆ PAGE 172
Landscape Design Training, Tokyo ◆ PAGE 189
Tejon Ranch Vision Plan ◆ PAGE 194
Heron Bay, San Leandro ◆ PAGE 200
Alphaville Lagoa dos Ingleses Town ◆ PAGE 204
Beijing Wellbond International Golf ◆ PAGE 209
Foundry Square, San Francisco ◆ PAGE 218
Courthouse Square Competition ◆ PAGE 220

Consulting on Coastal Properties
    Sonoma County ◆ PAGE 222
    Mendocino county ◆ PAGE 225